Second Edition

Microfinance Management

Pradeep Kumar Mishra
CMA (IMA, NJ), Fellow (IRMA, Anand)

Associate Professor
School of Rural Management
XIM University, Bhubaneswar

Australia • Brazil • Canada • India • Mexico • Singapore • United Kingdom • United States

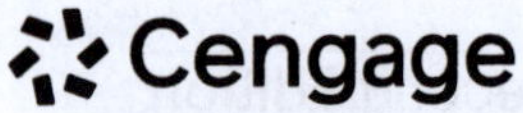

Microfinance Management, 2nd Edition

Pradeep Kumar Mishra

Cover Image © Getty Images

For product information and technology assistance, contact us at **asia.infoindia@cengage.com**

For permission to use material from this text or product, submit all requests online at **www.cengage.com/permissions**

ISBN-13: 978-93-6660-785-6
ISBN-10: 93-6660-785-3

Cengage Learning India Pvt. Ltd.
T-303, 3rd Floor
DAV Complex, Plot 3
Mayur Vihar Phase 1
Delhi 110091

Cengage is a leading provider of customized learning solutions with employees residing in nearly 40 different countries and sales in more than 125 countries around the world. Find your local representative at: **www.cengage.com.**

Cengage is committed to creating inclusive and diverse products, including perspectives that represent the diversity of people across all backgrounds, identities, opinions, and experiences. If you have any feedback related to this, please contact us at **support.cengage.com.**

To learn more about Cengage products, platforms and services, visit **www.cengage.co.in.**

Printed by:
VA Global Ground Floor,
Plot No. 41, Pocket J, Sector-2,
Bawana, DSIDC, Delhi-110039

Printed in India
Print Number: 01 Print Year: 2025

Preface to the Second Edition

Microfinance has grown into a distinct and impactful industry. It has developed into a large employer, a great platform for policy interventions, and a tool for poverty alleviation and financial inclusion. It has also been a subject of debate and discussion across the world. The enormous growth of microfinance as a field of practice and as a body of knowledge has made it a challenging task to comprehend this subject. This textbook is an attempt to explain the concepts and practices of microfinance. Considering the needs of postgraduate students in the field of management, economics, development studies, and social sciences, this book explains the topic through theories, cases, and exercises.

When the first edition of *Microfinance Management* was published in 2019, the sector was already undergoing significant transformation. However, in the years since, microfinance has proven to be even more dynamic than anticipated, shaped by rapid regulatory shifts, market developments, and unexpected crises.

This second edition comes in response to the enormous changes that have taken place in the intervening years. Most notably, the Reserve Bank of India (RBI) has introduced several new guidelines aimed at redefining the operational framework for microfinance institutions (MFIs) and other regulated entities operating in the space of microfinance. These regulatory reforms have altered borrower classification, interest rate caps, risk assessment, and institutional responsibilities—fundamentally changing how MFIs engage with low-income clients. In parallel, the sector has faced multiple crises, including socio-political disruptions, regional over-indebtedness, and the far-reaching impact of the COVID-19 pandemic. These events have tested the resilience of MFIs and forced them to adapt in unprecedented ways.

This edition has been revised and updated to reflect these developments. It aims to provide students, practitioners, and policymakers with a comprehensive understanding of both the foundational principles of microfinance and the evolving landscape in which it operates. Where the first edition laid the groundwork, this edition expands upon it—offering a timely and critical perspective on managing microfinance in a volatile environment.

I hope this edition serves as a useful guide in navigating the complexities of a sector that remains essential to financial inclusion, poverty alleviation, and inclusive development.

Pradeep Kumar Mishra

June 2025

Preface to the First Edition

The field of microfinance has gone through enormous changes in the last two decades. Starting as fringe operations of various development schemes, the field developed as an independent activity. Today, it has transformed into a full-fledged industry and is considered a specialised wing of financial services. As these transformations were supported by numerous documentations, a plethora of literature is available in public domain.

For someone who wants to learn about microfinance, these documents provide an extensive challenge. Similarly, for a teacher or trainer who wants to deliver this subject to the participants, it becomes a challenge to decide on what to cover and what to leave. This issue germinated the idea of this textbook to solve this problem.

The aim of this book is to meet the needs of university students (post-graduate) who study microfinance as a subject, either as an independent course or as a part of any course curriculum. The book has been divided into five parts that cover theoretical aspects (Part I), operational aspects (Part II), monitoring and evaluation (Part III), regulatory provisions (Part IV), and strategic issues of microfinance (Part V), which would be relevant for Business Administration, Economics, Rural Management, Development Studies, and related programmes. In particular, the students of business schools and economics would find it directly relevant. It would also be a useful resource for newly joining managers and officers in banks and microfinance institutions, who want to get a basic orientation about microfinance.

Key Features of the Book

- In-depth explanation of topics in an easy-to-understand language
- Written in the context of challenges thrown by the recent emergence of small finance banks
- Important aspects of microfinance—fundamentals, operations, evaluation, policy, and strategic issues—are covered
- Box inserts and closing cases in chapters for better understanding of concepts and to encourage critical thinking
- Chapter-end exercises (review question, application-based questions, and multiple-choice questions) to test conceptual learning
- Comprehensive cases at the end of the book illustrating various organisations in microfinance industry and the issues faced by them are included

To understand this book, one does not need a strong background in accounting or mathematics. The book contains theories, exercises and cases for better understanding of the concepts. Cases, at the end of the book, can be used as examples as well as a platform for decisions. There are some quantitative aspects, for which one needs to understand basic financial statements and arithmetic. For management students, all these parts are necessary, while the students of social sciences may like to focus on the theoretical, policy-related and strategic issues. However, with a bit of reading, one can easily understand the quantitative aspects of financial statements.

This is a modest attempt to bind a vast body of knowledge into a small book. I have tried to capture the basic tenets of all the important aspects of microfinance industry. I understand that in making this book, there may be some shortcomings. I would be happy to receive the readers' feedback and improve it in future.

Pradeep Kumar Mishra
2019

Acknowledgements

Creation of a book is an enormous task and cannot be completed singlehandedly. While writing this book, I received support and guidance from several people and would like to take this opportunity to acknowledge them.

At the outset, I thank the MBA-Rural Management students of Xavier University Bhubaneswar, whom I taught for the last four years. I also thank Professor Prabal Kumar Sen, from whom I learned the basics of institutional finance, and Professor S. S. Singh, my senior colleague at Xavier University, for encouraging me to take up this task.

I would like to acknowledge some of my friends and colleagues from whom I learnt the fundamentals of microfinance, not in any classroom but through interactions and discussions. Dr. Sankar Datta, former Dean of The Livelihood School (BASIX), is one such persons from whom I learnt the intricate relations between poverty and microfinance. Mr. Srinu Babu, Mr. Hitendra Singh, Mr. Sanjay Jena, Mr. Ashutosh Kumar, Mr. Ram Krishna Atre, Mr. Yeshwanth and Mr. Swamisharan Varma were some others who helped me with the complexity of MFI and SHG related operations. I am grateful to Mr. Aniket Thakur who provided me with inputs for preparing cases. I discussed the implications of the policy aspects of microfinance with Mr. G. Subba Reddy, whose inputs played a crucial role in shaping this book. Professor Sibajan Mishra's comments on the financials were quite helpful. I would also like to thank Professor Satyendra Nath Mishra, who went through the first draft and suggested changes.

A large part of my understanding of microfinance is centred on my knowledge about organisations, such as BASIX, MYRADA, Annapurna Microfinance, SKS Microfinance (now known as BIFL), Microsave, and Ujjivan. These organisations have shared their documents extensively in the public domain. I'm grateful to them for sharing such information, as it made giving real-time examples to readers easier.

This book would not have been completed without the encouragement and support of my family members. I thank my wife, Rajashree, and my children, Anwesh and Shreenihita, for standing by me during those critical days.

Last but not the least, I would like to thank the team of Cengage India for providing me with an opportunity to publish this book. Their continuous support and assistance helped me bring this book to life.

Pradeep Kumar Mishra

Brief Contents

Detailed Contents

About the Author

Pradeep Kumar Mishra, *PhD*, is Associate Professor at the School of Rural Management, XIM University, Bhubaneswar. He received his doctorate in Rural Management from the Institute of Rural Management, Anand, and has more than 25 years of experience in government, industry, and academics. Dr. Mishra has published numerous articles in several international peer-reviewed journals.

PART I
Foundations of Microfinance

1. Introduction to Microfinance
2. Basic Concepts of Microfinance

CHAPTER

1

Introduction to Microfinance

Chapter Outline

Learning Objectives

After reading this chapter, you will be able to:

- provide an overview of the microfinance sector.
- describe the evolution of microfinance as a practice.
- map the different models of delivering microfinance products and services.
- provide a roadmap for studying this book.

1.1 Introduction

Nobel laurate Prof. Robert Shiller says that microfinance is one of the few initiatives of the financial sector towards making a good society. Banking services typically served relatively well-off, and the creditworthiness of poor was always questioned. According to Prof. Shiller, this issue was addressed by microfinance, which resulted in democratisation of banking services (Shiller, 2012). In the aftermath of the global financial crisis of 2008 when the financial institutions came under severe criticism for the unscrupulous elements and unsavoury records, it was a saving grace for people associate with finance. For microfinance as a field of practice and study, such a remark was definitely a kind of accolade.

Globally, microfinance industry (in March 2025) has a gross loan portfolio (GLP) of USD[1] 225 billion[2] (Research and Markets, 2025). In 2023, the GLP of USD 195 billion and covered about 142 million low-income clients. The industry recorded a growth of 10.1 per cent in terms of loan portfolio and 8.4 per cent in terms of number of clients (Akhtar, 2024).

In India, the industry has a visible presence. The comparable figures for India in 2025 are USD 80 billion of loan portfolio. As on March 2025, commercial microfinance industry has a gross loan portfolio of INR 408,049 crores (about USD 48 billion) having 8.01 crore unique clients (MFIN, 2025). The self-help group (SHG) have about 278,077 crores of loan outstanding. Together the sector (both commercial and non-profit) has a combined loan outstanding of about 686,126 crores (about USD 32 billion) (NRLM, 2025). These figures say a lot about the importance of the microfinance sector[3].

---

1 As on 31 March 2025, the value of US dollar is about 85 Indian Rupees

2 One billion = 100 crore (1000 million). One million = 10 lakh. One lakh = 100 thousand. In India lakhs and crores are often used, while internationally 'million' and 'billion' are more common. In this book the latter has been used unless specifically mentioned.

3 The term 'microfinance sector' and 'microfinance industry' are often used synonymously. However, in this book the term 'sector' refers to the entire microfinance services including commercial and government funded /non-profit operations, while the terms 'industry' is limited only to commercial operations.

In the last five decades, microfinance sector has grown from scratches to a huge and impactful industry. With goals like poverty alleviation and financial inclusion, in many places, it has evolved into mass movements. The importance of this industry generates out of the phenomenal impact it makes on poor people's lives. It is also a major point of policy decisions. Regulatory bodies have taken keen interest in dealing with microfinance-related issues.

From a managerial point of view, microfinance has emerged as a huge field of operations. The field is dynamic and in the last 15 years, since 2010 so to say, it has been evolving significantly with the new technologies, new policy environment and global uncertainties. The role of a manager in microfinance has been changing fast. With the change in regulations, technology and demand in the market, managers face several unprecedented challenges. In this book, such challenges have been identified.

1.2 Defining Microfinance

The microfinance gateway portal defines microfinance as follows:

> "*Microfinance is the provision of financial services to low-income people. It refers to a movement that envisions a world where low-income households have permanent access to high-quality and affordable financial services to finance income-producing activities, build assets, stabilise consumption, and protect against risks. Initially the term was closely associated with microcredit—very small loans to unsalaried borrowers with little or no collateral—but the term has since evolved to include a range of financial products, such as savings, insurance, payments, and remittances.*"
> (*Microfinancegateway*, www).

Ledgerwood defines microfinance as

> "*.... the provision of financial services to low-income clients, including the self-employed. Financial services generally include savings and credit; however, some microfinance organisations also provide insurance and payment services. In addition to financial intermediation, many MFIs provide social intermediation services such as group formation, development of self confidence, and training in financial literacy and management capabilities among members of a group. Thus, the definition of microfinance often includes both financial intermediation and social intermediation. Microfinance is not simply banking; it is a development tool.*" (*Ledgerwood*, 1999: 1)

Thus, microfinance has the following features

- *Small amounts of finance* This is the fundamental characteristic of microfinance. Microfinance clients require small amounts of money for meeting their financial needs.
- *Provided to low-income households* Microfinance targets the low-income households. Without having this characteristic, the primary goal of microfinance gets defeated.
- *Doorstep services* Generally, bank branches are found in well-populated places, and people living in remote villages find it difficult to access the financial services. Microfinance business is based on reversing the flow of financial delivery – rather than the client seeking the service at bank branches, the MFIs provide the service at doorstep of clients.
- *Without collateral* The major bottleneck of bankers in dealing with poor clients is that the latter cannot provide collateral that guarantees the recovery in the event of non-payment. Microfinance tries to make alternative strategies like putting peer pressure to ensure recovery.
- *Simple procedure* Banks have a lot of procedures to follow before they finance anybody. For small amounts of finances, these procedures may not be necessary, and it also adds to the transaction cost and delays the process. Microfinance systems have developed simple procedures that that eases the process of service delivery.

One myth associated with microfinance is that it is equivalent to microcredit. It is true that the microfinance sector has evolved beginning with microcredit, but microfinance refers to the complete package of financial services: savings, insurance, credit, remittance, pension, and all kinds of related services.

1.3 Evolution of Microfinance

Popular literature in microfinance traces the roots of microfinance to Grameen Bank and Muhammad Yunus, but there have been other initiatives too. In 1970s there were three major initiatives: SEWA Bank in India, Accion International in Latin America, and Grameen Bank in Bangladesh.

SEWA Bank In 1972, Ms. Ela Bhatt established the Self-employed Women's Association (SEWA). Started as a trade union, SEWA turned out to be a movement for empowering women workers involved in informal sector, mainly involving vendors, wage labourers, and home-based workers. As the banks of that time were not comfortable with opening accounts of informal sector workers, SEWA started its own cooperative bank, namely Shri Mahila Sewa Sahakari Bank (popularly known as SEWA Bank). (SEWA, n.d.). Starting with a moderate 4,000 members each contributing INR 10 of share capital (SEWA, n.d), today, the bank has 134, 230 members and INR 2.07 billion of share capital, and INR 2.15 billion of advances, and profit of INR 25.72 million as during 2023-24 (SEWA, 2024). SEWA, today, has several businesses including an insurance service providing agency named VimoSEWA.

Accion International Joseph Blachford founded ACCION International in 1961 in Venezuela and in 1973 turned it into a microcredit; it today operates across several countries in South America, North America and Africa (Roy, 2018). Blachford was a Berkeley law student. In 1970s, the organisation started issuing small loans to small entrepreneurs in Recife, Brazil, expanding to 14 countries in 1980s. Accion was the co-founder of Bankosol, Bolivia. In recent times, it has gone into seed funding, fintech, and inclusive recovery programmes (Accion, n.d.)

Grameen Bank It was Mohammad Yunus, a US-educated professor in Bangladesh, turned to micro-credit, and experimented the idea of lending to poor. This came out to be a feasible idea, and it was slowly expanded. The idea was simple; lend small amount to groups which would through peer pressure ensure recovery of the loans and the clients would be happy to get relatively cheaper loans. This venture became Grameen Bank in 1983. This marked the beginning of what is today known as microfinance. The year 2005 was declared as International Year of Microcredit by the Economic and Social Council of the United Nations. In 2006, Grameen Bank and its founder Mohammad Yunus were awarded the Nobel Prize for peace for their efforts on poverty alleviation.

Other than the above a few important initiatives must be noted in international context:

- John Hatch formed the idea of village banking in 1982 and established FINCA bank in 1985 that operates in Latin America (FINCA, www).
- Bank Rakyat Indonesia (BRI) used to have a government-directed subsidised programme for farmers. When the country went for a deregulated regime, BRI went for a microfinance model that is known as 'unit' or small sub-branches at village level that took deposit from and provided loans to poor people (Armendariz and Morduch, 2010). The BIMAS programme[4] of Government of Indonesia (started in 1970) which was primarily an agriculture subsidy programme later evolved into microbanking division of BRI in 1983 (Seibel, 2005).

In India, the term microfinance became popular in the 1990s, but a few events are important before we discuss it. In the pre-independence era, the need for agricultural finance was recognised but the focus still

4 BIMAS programme is an agricultural diversification scheme which had a microfinance component

was on cooperatives. In 1949, when India had already become a free country, it was already accepted that commercial banks were not interested to fulfil the credit needs of rural areas (Fisher and Sriram, 2002). In India, the nationalisation of bank in 1969 was a major landmark, it was followed by the establishment of regional rural banks in 1975. Despite these interventions, institutional finance could not approach the needs of the poor and thus microfinance carved out a niche for itself. These events are to be kept in background as they cannot be brought under the description of microfinance.

The Integrated Rural Development Project (IRDP) starting in 1980 was a subsidised individual loan scheme of Government of India. Irrespective of all criticisms levelled at it for its corruption and defaults, this remains as an important landmark in microfinance in India. Learning from the observations that individuals default loans, but they behave differently in groups because of peer pressure, the Mysore Resettlement and Development Agency (MYRADA), a Karnataka based non-governmental organisation (NGO), started a group-loaning experiment. MYRADA's experiment of affinity groups (which we today know as Self-Help Group or SHG) started in the year 1985 (Fernandez, 2006). Based on this experience, the SHG-Bank Linkage Programme of the National Bank for Agriculture and Rural Development (NABARD) was launched in 1992. By March 2024, there are 14.42 million SHGs involving 178 million households and a loan outstanding of INR 2.569 trillion (NABARD, 2024).

In 1993, Rashtriya Mahila Kosh (RMK) was established that looked forward to micro-credit operations through NGOs. RMK is an autonomous body under the Ministry of Women and Child Development of Government of India. It operates as a single window facilitator for financial services, through SHGs, and implemented with the help of NGOs (RMK, www).

Professional Assistance for Development Action (PRADAN), an NGO established in 1983, also followed the SHG approach as part of its development interventions. While working on this strategy, some of its promoters observed that there is a dearth of availability of loans for the poor and because of that poor people had been paying huge amount of interest. This provided an opportunity that poor can be served profitably. It was a win-win situation for both – the service provider as well as the clients. Thus in 1996, Vijay Mahajan established a commercial venture called BASIX. The commercial microfinance in India thus got started in a decade many other entities joined this league. By 2005, it was clear that microfinance was going to be the next big thing in the development and financial sectors.

Meanwhile, internationally, Grameen Bank and a few other commercial initiatives had already flourished. The Microcredit Summit of 1997 was a major event that popularised the concept of microfinance. The United Nations observed the year 2005 as the International Year of Microcredit. In 2006, Muhammad Yunus and Grameen Bank received Nobel Peace Prize. During 2006 to 2009 a number of investors including private equity players started investing in microfinance in India. While this pumped in funds in the sector, it also brought in the pressure of commercial investors to deliver more and more return.

Parallel to this, in 1999, the IRDP was revised and the Swarnajayanti Gram Swarojgar Yojana (SGSY) was launched. The programme was designed based on the learning from IRDP, where it was observed that it succeeded in places where there was sufficient infrastructure and institutional support (Dash, 2019). The point of difference here was the SHG approach and group lending. The programme continued for about a decade. The National Rural Livelihood Mission (NRLM) is a modified and expanded version of SGSY, that covers almost the entire country.

Some of the NGOs also had taken microfinance activities and they wanted to convert into commercial operations. The Small Industries Development Bank of India (SIDBI) supported many NGOs in this process. Some of such NGOs were Share Microfinance, Spandana Spoorty, SKS Microfinance, and Bandhan. This provided boost to the field of commercial microfinance activities (Roy, 2018). This led to rapid growth of the sector. Attracted by such growth many private equity funds started pumping money into microfinance business.

In 2010, SKS Microfinance, found that it was relatively easier to deal with the demands of public investors rather than bending to the private equity funds, and listed itself in the stock exchange. The initial public offer

(IPO) was a great success. However, by this time, the commercial microfinance sector had already attracted criticism from some of its stakeholders for its exploitative practices. In October 2010, the Government of Andhra Pradesh, promulgated an ordinance which squeezed the microfinance institutions, and they found it difficult to recover the amount lent. This not only affected the microfinance operations in the state but also had a ripple effect on other parts of India too.

It took three to four years before the microfinance industry could show some resilience. By 2015-16, the sector was almost revived, although some of the older players were yet to rise. But a new set of institutions had emerged to take the baton ahead. The policy regime also changed to support the cause of smaller banks. In 2015, Small Finance Banks and Payment Banks were provided licenses. One of the two organisations that got bank license was Bandhan, which was a microfinance institution. However, the commercial microfinance sector was negatively affected by the demonetisation that took place in November 2016. The pandemic (Covid-19) also took a large toll on the industry. Such effects have been considered as temporary.

In 2014-15, the Government of India brought out a number of schemes including the Pradhan Mantri Jan Dhan Yojana (PMJDY), which was also a landmark in the direction of attaining financial inclusion, which is the goal of microfinance. Later the differentiated banks like small finance banks and payments banks were initiated that changed the entire range of financial inclusion platform in India.

In the non-commercial segment of microfinance sector, the NABARD's SHG Bank Linkage programme (SBLP) continued and has almost reached to the level of saturation. In 2011, the National Rural Livelihood Mission (NRLM) with a lot of revisions of SGSY was launched and nowadays is an important programme of Government of India.

Microfinance sector has seen significant progress. Table 1.1. provides an overview of the present status of the sector:

Table 1.1 Microfinance sector in India at a glance (progress as on 31.03.2024)

SHG-Bank Linkage*	
Total Number of SHGs	14.42 million
Total Savings with banks (in INR billion)	650.89
Number of households covered	178 million
Number of SHGs having outstanding loans	5.48 million
Amount of loans outstanding of SHGs (INR billion)	2596.63
Commercial Microfinance**	
Number of clients (unique borrowers)	79 million
Number of loan accounts	139 million
Gross loan portfolio (in INR billion)	1,502.82
Gross loan portfolio of banks to microfinance sector (in INR billion)	1,264.37
Gross loan portfolio of Small Finance Banks to microfinance sector (in INR billion)	626.86
Gross loan portfolio of NBFCs to microfinance sector (in INR billion)	436.75
Total outstanding loans – commercial	₹ 3830.80 billion
Total outstanding loan – commercial and SHG Bank linkage	₹ 6427.43 billion

* *NABARD* (2024); ** *MFIN* (2024)

1.4 Models of Microfinance

Microfinance is not a narrowly defined operation, and it can be delivered through various channels. Broadly speaking there are two kinds of models – SHG-Bank linkage model which is generally facilitated by a third party (say NGO), and the microfinance institution (MFI) model which runs on commercial basis. However, if we look into closely, there are several variations of these models. The recent addition to the important models is the Business Correspondent Model.

The traditional government schemes and cooperative banking are the two older models in which microfinance was delivered. The Integrated Rural Development Programme (IRDP)[5] implemented in India during the 1980s was the greatest example of microfinance, although at that time the term was not used. As part of IRDP a few initiatives such as the Development of Women and Children in Rural Areas (DWACRA)[6] and Training of Rural Youth for Self-Employment (TRYSEM)[7] were taken, which can also be categorised as some of the specific early efforts of microfinance.

Similarly, cooperative banks like SEWA were the first generation of self-reliant initiatives that lent the poor. The rural networks of cooperative banks which had a three-tier structure starting with primary agricultural cooperative society (PACS) at village level, District Central Cooperative Bank at district level, and state level cooperative bank at state level was another example. Although cooperative banks did not always cover the rural poor, they had good amount of disbursement to relatively less well-off.

Other that the above, across the world several other models are also followed which has some similarity with the models to be discussed. People associated with microfinance should be aware of the following:

- *Rotating Saving and Credit Associations (ROSCA)* These are associations of people, where individual members save and rotate the credit in a phase-wise manner (Armandariz and Morduch, 2010). Suppose there are a group of 20 people who form a ROSCA. They will save, Rs. 1000, each for 20 months. Thus, at the end of the 20 months, everybody's savings will be Rs. 20,000 each. But the group, as a whole, will have Rs. 20,000 at the end of the first month. This can be delivered to a member. In the second month, another person is given Rs. 20,000 and so on. On completion of 20 months every member has already received Rs. 20,000 each. Generally, the order of receipt is fixed but sometimes there are instances of bidding for a particular order (for example, a member may want to get the money in the first month and is willing to bid for a higher interest rate). The chit fund practice in India is similar in nature, where the collection goes to the highest bidder.
- *Solidarity Groups* This consists of five to eight microentrepreneurs who organise themselves into a group and they receive credit and other technical assistance (Otero, 1986)
- *Village Unit Bank* This was followed by Bank Rakyat Indonesia (BRI). These are a kind of sub-branches of a bank branch.

In India there are three models of microfinance: SHG-Bank Linkage, Microfinance Institutions, and Business Correspondence as detailed follows:

SHG-Bank Linkage Model The launching SHG-Bank Linkage Programme (SBLP) was the breakthrough in the field of microfinance. There are several models of SHG-Bank Linkages, but the core binding institution is the SHG. Under this programme, SHGs are promoted by a facilitating agency (popularly known as Self-Help Promoting Institutions or SHPI), this can be an NGO, or government agency. The SHGs are formed and strengthened by the SHPIs. Funding to the SHPIs for promotion comes generally from a donor or government, however, sometimes banks themselves also act as SHPIs and fund it themselves. Once the SHGs become capable enough, they are linked to banks for further loaning. The loans are utilised by the

5 IRDP was launched on pilot basis in 1978-79. In 1980, it was extended to the whole country. Its objective was to bring the below poverty line households out of the trap of poverty.

6 The objective of DWACRA promote women's groups that could undertake income generation activities. The programme was launched as a sub-component of IRDP in the year 1982-83.

7 TRYSEM started in the year 1979 with an objective of skill building and providing employment assistance to rural youth. This programme was an integral part of IRDP.

SHGs for their livelihood enhancement. NABARD and the present day NRLM programme follow such kind of model.

A slight variant of this model is the **on-lending** programme. Here the SHPI takes loan from a funding agency or a bank and starts lending it further to the SHPI. The role of SHG promotion still continues. But the major difference from the SBLP model is the active involvement in credit delivery. In SBLP the SHPI plays the role of a catalyst (See Box 1.1).

Box 1.1 On-lending or Facilitation?

Hiralalji Sharma is the head of a Rajasthan based NGO. Established in the early 1990s the organisation has been operating in two districts of the state Its area of interventions include natural resource management and women empowerment. Besides other interventions, the organisation had formed about 50 SHGs and these SHGs were involved in regular savings and credit activities, and they constituted the basis of the community organisation works undertaken by the NGO. Most of the SHGs had been linked to banks and loans for agricultural and other income generating purpose had been taken.

In the late 1990s the Rashtriya Mahila Kosh floated a scheme as part of which NGOs could be involved in onlending activities. This meant the NGOs would take loan from RMK at low interest rate and would further extend loans to SHGs adding a mark-up. Many NGOs who were engaged in SHG Bank Linkage Programmes took this as an opportunity. When the organisation was approached for getting involved in this programme, Mr. Sharma was not very enthusiastic. Being true to the nature of voluntary sector's member, he said that it was not the job of NGOs to be directly involved in lending and recovery. That job should be left to the banks and financial institutes. He believed that the role of NGOs should be limited to facilitation activities.

(*based on interaction with the author*)

There have been several instances where the SHGs form federations of their own and the federation takes the role of the facilitating agency. This is another model of SHG-bank linkage programme. Technically this is same as the SHPI. Chapter 3 provides more details of SHG model.

Microfinance Institution Model The other important model is steered by the microfinance institutions. Microfinance institutions (MFIs) are generally commercial organisations (this may be noted that there are some not-for-profit MFIs too), and in India these are at present recognised as NBFC-MFIs. The MFIs generate their own resources through equity or debt, and they lend it to SHGs, Joint Liability Groups (JLGs), or Grameen Groups.

In the case of SHG-linkage, generally the MFIs lend to an existing SHG already formed earlier. For the SHG, the MFI is another source of loan. Here the SHPI do not have any link with the MFI.

The JLGs are a set of five members who come together in order to take loan from an MFI. In case any member is not able to make the payment due, the other four members of the JLGs are liable to make the payment. Such groups are widely used by MFIs.

Grameen Groups (groups following Grameen Bank approach) are also five-member groups, but they operate in a different manner. In a village many such groups are formed, and the meetings are held for all groups together. The village becomes a unit, although the groups operate at the ground level. This helps in building peer pressure, and it also helps in reducing the cost of the MFI. This model was started by Grameen Bank; hence it is known as Grameen Group. In India, MFIs like Cashpor and Share Microfinance have used the model extensively.

It is clear that the SHGs are independent institutions, while JLGs and Grameen Groups are for the purpose of providing financial services. Irrespective of whether lending is done by the MFIs or not SHGs are likely to continue, this cannot be true for other groups. Further, SHGs are flexible in nature, while other kinds of groups are rigidly tied with the concerned MFI. On the other hand, formation and strengthening of SHGs is a time taking process, other groups can be formed quickly. One may lead to conclude that the cost of SHG lending would be higher, but experience shows that this higher cost is rendered for short term only. In long run lending to SHGs is more cost effective (Harper, 2003).

The major difference between JLGs and Grameen Groups are that the formers are independent groups, while the Grameen Groups are sub-units of the whole village. Further, Grameen Groups do not practice joint-liability clause, and operate primarily based on peer pressure.

It may be noted that the SHG model has been more widely practiced in India, while the Grameen model was more popular in Bangladesh. Harper (2003) says that there could be several factors behind this:

- In the democratic culture of India, institutions like SHGs found an acceptable space
- Grameen Groups are relatively more costly to monitor and manage, in Bangladesh this flourished because of cross-subsidisation. This may be noted that the per-head development aid that Bangladesh received was about five to six times higher than that India received.
- Higher population density in Bangladesh (more than two times that of India) made a loan officer coordinating with larger number of groups.

Business Correspondent Model In India, the Business Correspondent (BC) model has been taking off. The BCs are nothing but intermediaries like individuals, NGOs, MFIs, post offices, registered as BC, operate on behalf of a bank to extend the financial services. The role of BC includes identification of clients, collection of applications, disbursal of loan, collection of deposits, collection of third-party products, and delivery of payment and remittance instruments (RBI, 2006). In this model, the BCs operate in the normal course of business of banks and the only difference from a bank's direct operation is that this is conducted outside the premises of the bank's branches (RBI, 2006: para 3.3). The banks pay a commission (which ordinarily ranges from 0.25 per cent to 0.50 per cent of transaction amount) to the BCs towards such services. Today there are a number of BCs, including large companies like Sub-K Impact Solutions Ltd (promoted by BASIX) that serves about seven million customers.

More details of BC model are given in Chapter 2.

1.5 Benefits and Limitations of Microfinance

As given in the definition, the basic purpose of microfinance is to meet the financial services of poor people. This is where the first and foremost benefit goes to. Had there been no microfinance, either the poor will remain unserved, or they will be served with a higher cost and sometimes such services could be exploitative too. The second benefit of microfinance is that the poor get services at a relatively lower cost. Finally, microfinance have helped people in increasing their income and asset ownership.

From the lenders point of view microfinance has always provided a higher recovery than other financial institutions. The greatest advantage however is that unlike the traditional subsidy-based programmes which makes a large burden to the public exchequer, commercial microfinance is market based. Even the government promoted microfinance programmes have a major component of market-based interventions.

Like the benefits, there are many limitations too. The cost of microfinance has invariably been higher than alternative formal channels like banks. The cost being higher, in order to maintain sustainability, MFIs need a considerable scale. They also operate under adverse conditions such as strong competition from banks, adverse policy framework, and confusion between developmental and financial objectives. Further, MFIs have often been alleged to be following coercive practices for recovery. These issues will be described in further details in subsequent chapters.

1.6 Challenges of Studying Microfinance

The field of microfinance operates in contradicting spaces. One, while the MFIs have to make a profit out of serving the poor, which is a difficult task. In a society, where charging interest has often been equated with exploitation, there is often a thin-line difference between being usurious and earning an acceptable profit.

Hence the manager of microfinance is often subjected to criticism for his/her decisions. If the decision leans towards higher profits, he/she is criticised for profiteering, while if compromises on profit, he is considered as moving towards an unsustainable model.

A major problem the managers of microfinance sector face is that the cost of lending is higher than competitors. This happens because MFIs cannot accept deposit, hence funds have to come from either equity or debt. Being a financial agency, equity cannot always cover the funds requirement. Debt has a fixed cost which is much higher than that of deposits.

Changing policy regime puts a lot of difficulties for MFIs' managers. Restrictions on fixing interest rate, restrictions on recovery mechanism, norms of capital adequacy, and political decisions like loan waiver brings in troubles for managers.

Finally, the financial sector in general and microfinance sector in particular have been going through a lot of changes. Changes in technology, demands of clients, and the evolution of business models in microfinance are a few things that has transformed the task of managers completely.

The above problems bring in two-pronged challenges for managers. Not only the field itself is dynamic, but the associated dimensions are changing fast. Hence, the manager has to change his/her strategy frequently. This has negative implications on standardizing the processes, in the absence of proper understanding of a dynamic phenomenon, one has to update the knowledge continuously. This results in additional costs for training and orienting the microfinance professionals.

1.7 About this Book

While the subject of microfinance is full of topics that are dynamic and complex, for the readers it throws a few more challenges. Microfinance is primarily a set of financial services. Hence, the reader should have a knowledge of financial aspects such as financial instruments, financial institutions, regulation, and financial markets. At the same time, there are institutional and social aspects such as SHG management and poverty alleviation. The latter is not emphasised by people like bankers who are trained in financial aspects. On the other hand, people from NGOs who have good understanding of social and institutional aspects, do not appreciate financial aspects. A student or practitioner of microfinance must make a balance between the social and financial aspects. But there are a few texts which make such reasonable balance. As a result, most books either deal with financials, or with the social aspects. This book tries to fulfil this gap.

This book will be useful for advanced students like those studying post-graduate studies including MBA, Ph.D., MA/MSc. Economics, and Public Policy and related studies. This book can also serve the purpose of new appointees to MFIs and banks who would like to understand the fundaments of microfinance services.

This book has been presented in five parts. The first part, including two chapters, covers the foundations of microfinance that include the context of Indian microfinance, theories and concepts related to microfinance such as transaction cost, group based approach. It also describes the microfinance models such as SHG model, JLG model, Banking correspondence etc.

The second part has four chapters, and it focuses on microfinance operations. It starts with operations of SHGs and then goes into the products and services, how these are delivered and ends with the process of product development.

The third part has three chapters, and it covers how microfinance programmes and operations are monitored and evaluated. It starts with how grading is done and what principles are followed to develop strong SHGs. The next chapter discusses how commercial microfinance are evaluated with financial ratios. This part of the book ends with how social performance management is assessed.

The fourth part of the book focuses on the regulatory environment. It discusses RBI guidelines on SHGs and NBFC-MFIs and provides the details of guidelines related to small finance banks and payment banks. Another chapter discusses various policy issues and debates including self-regulatory organisations, interest rate, and other relevant matters.

The fifth and the last part of the book starts with a critical analysis of microfinance crisis of Andhra Pradesh. The next chapter looks into governance issues in MFIs – particularly the issue of control, funding, and promoters' interest. The subsequent chapter discusses the issue of how changing technologies are shaping the field of microfinance. Another chapter tries to find the difficulties associated with transformation of MFIs. The penultimate chapter discusses the issue of funding in microfinance. The last chapter discusses how microfinance is set to be shaped in future.

Summary

- Microfinance includes provision of all kinds of financial services to the poor and vulnerable sections of society.
- The basic features of microfinance are small amounts, low-income households, door-step services, collateral-free, and simple procedures
- Grameen Bank (Bangladesh), Accion International and FINCA (Latin America) and Bank Rakyat Indonesia are some of the pioneers of microfinance internationally. In India, SEWA, MYRADA, PRADAN, BASIX, NABARD, SIDBI played a key role in the initial stage in building the stage of microfinance industry.
- The important models of microfinance are: SHG-Bank Linkage model, Microfinance Institution model, and Business Correspondence model.
- Microfinance have proved to be a win-win situation for the financers and customers. However, it has its own challenges too. One important problem is the contradiction between social objectives and financial sustainability; in this process an organisation may get drifted away from its mission.

Exercises

A. Multiple-choice Questions

1. Which of the following is TRUE about microfinance?
   (a) Microfinance started in Bangladesh
   (b) Microfinance means microcredit
   (c) Microfinance can be a profit-based business
   (d) Cost of microfinance is lower than other channels of financing
2. SHG Bank Linkage programme was started by
   (a) MYRADA (b) NABARD
   (c) SGSY (d) RBI
3. ROSCAs are groups that
   (a) Rotate the disbursal of total savings every month to a member
   (b) Rotate the interest rate on savings of members
   (c) Rotate the leadership of institutions
   (d) All of the above
4. SHGs are popular in India because of
   (a) Democratic environment
   (b) Poverty
   (c) High funding by donors
   (d) None of the above
5. JLGs differ from SHGs in terms of
   (a) Number of members in a group
   (b) Being specifically associated MFIs
   (c) Liability of other members of group
   (d) All of the above
6. Grameen Group model is followed in
   (a) Bangladesh
   (b) India
   (c) Several countries including Bangladesh and India
   (d) None of the above
7. Through the BC Model the client receives
   (a) Pure banking services
   (b) MFI services
   (c) NGO services
   (d) All of the above
8. Microfinance institutions lend to
   (a) SHGs (b) JLGs
   (c) Individuals (d) All of the above
9. Which of the following is the first commercial microfinance institution in India?
   (a) Grameen Bank (b) BASIX
   (c) PRADAN (d) SEWA
10. NGOs borrow money and lend it to SHGs: this is _______ model.
    (a) MFI (b) Onlending
    (c) SBLP (d) BC

B. Review Questions

1. Is microfinance same as microcredit? Explain.
2. What are the salient features of microfinance?
3. What microfinance models were followed in India before the onset of SHG Bank Linkage programme?
4. What are the different models of microfinance followed in India?
5. Distinguish among SHGs, JLGs and Grameen Groups.
6. What are the five major events in the history of microfinance in India:
7. Many NGOs have taken up the role of microfinance. Do you think such roles gel properly with the character of NGOs? Critically analyse.
8. What are the challenges in microfinance?

C. Application-based Questions

Government has brought in various initiatives of financial inclusion. One such initiative is the PMJDY, by which everybody can have a bank account. The mission of opening bank account has been almost successful. After that the small finance banks and payments banks were also licensed. This means that the one can get the basic deposit and payment services at every post office or the retail stores of some companies like Vodafone-Idea. Mobile payments like PayTM have also been very popular. Given this, some policy makers argue that microfinance is not required anymore.

In this context you have been invited to a forum, where there is a debate on 'Is microfinance relevant today?' You are part of a discussion panel; you have been asked to prepare a speech of 12-15 minutes followed by question-and-answer session.

Further Readings

- Prof. Robert Shiller's book *Finance and Good Society* is an enjoyable reading, which is not exactly on microfinance, but it deliberates on various dimensions of financial markets and institutions. It would provide a context in which microfinance is relevant in today's world.
- *The New Microfinance Handbook: A Financial Market System Perspectives*, edited by Ledgerwood provides a good guide on various aspects of microfinance. Chapter 1 and Chapter 7 of this book are useful for an introductory reading.
- Thomas and Fisher's book titled *Beyond Micro-Credit: Putting Development Back into Micro-Finance* (Chapter 2) provides a chronological account of how the financial system of India has grown. This reading will provide the context in which microfinance has grown in India. This book goes into some fundamental debates like microfinance vs. livelihoods.
- Md. Yunus' book *Bankers to the Poor* is a biographical account of the development of microfinance, particularly in the context of Bangladesh. It also provides the details of how Grameen Bank developed as an institution. This is a useful reading for understanding the nuances of commercial microfinance.

CHAPTER

2

Basic Concepts of Microfinance

Chapter Outline

Learning Objectives

After reading this chapter, you will be able to:

- provide an idea of various perspectives from which microfinance is studied.
- provide an overview of poverty and its linkages with microfinance.
- provide a discussion of market failure and its related concepts.
- discuss how market failure is addressed through microfinance.

2.1 Perspectives of and Approaches to Microfinance

Generally, microfinance is conceptualised in two perspectives, development perspective and market perspective.

The developmental perspective is related to institution building and it generally concerns with promotion of self-help groups (SHGs). Such interventions are generally funded by government or funding agencies. This includes grant-based programmes, such as SHG-Bank Linkage Programmes. As part of this, the Self Help Promoting Insitution (SHPI) plays a very important role, the cost of the SHPI's operations has to come from grants. It takes a heavy toll on treasury, as majority of such programmes are funded by the government. This places a limit on the scaling up of the programmes.

The market perspective, on the other hand, does not depend on grants. It is based on the assumption that poor are creditworthy and at present, the banks do not cater to them. Hence, the poor end up depending on the informal and sometimes exploitative sources of funds and invariably end up paying a far higher interest rate than that the banks charge. Ordinarily a bank in India charges 1.0 per cent to 1.5 per cent interest rate per month, while the informal lenders charge 5 per cent to 10 per cent interest per month. Here, the market-based models provide a win-win situation, they do not have to depend on the limitations of grants and the poor would also gain by way of getting finance at lower costs. Community is considered as a client rather than as a beneficiary.

Both the perspectives have their own pros and cons (see Table 2.1). While models based on development perspectives have the limitations of being tied up to the grants and cannot go for large-scale expansions, the models based on market perspectives do not have that problem. But the market-based models are based on competitive framework and can often be exploited by the market forces. It may lose the sympathetic views of the developmental perspective as observed in the Andhra Pradesh microfinance crisis in 2010 (discussed in detail later in Chapter 12).

There have been some efforts to develop hybrid models, where some part of the cost is provided as grant, while the core component of finance is provided as loan. However, such models have not yet become very successful.

Table 2.1 Development vs. Market Oriented Model of Microfinance

Features	Development Perspective	Market Perspective
Source of funds	Grants	Equity or debt
Financers	Donors, Government, CSR funds	Investors
Community is treated as	Beneficiaries	Clients
Focus of intervention	Institution building	Efficient financial services
Long-term goal	Empowerment of community	Financial inclusion

While deciding the products, two approaches have been followed in microfinance, minimalist approach and integrated approach. When commercial microfinance started, it was assumed that the poor people did not have access to credit and hence micro-credit was thought to be the panacea for all problems. As a result, initially microfinance was almost synonymous with micro-credit. This was the **minimalist approach** to microfinance. Over a period of time, however, it was observed that micro-credit was not able to serve the purpose:

- There were risks associated in enterprise development
- Clients often lacked technical expertise. For example, a client taking dairy loan need not be an expert on dairying, he/she needed technical inputs like veterinary services.
- While many would be good in production, they could not deal with marketing aspects.

Thus, in the subsequent phase, microfinance started being associated with other services, such as institution building, business developments, agriculture and veterinary services and so on. This kind of approach is called as **integrated approach** to microfinance.

Given this backdrop, a question arises here, Is there a theory of microfinance? The more focussed question is, Is there a separate theory of microfinance that is not there in the field of economics and finance? It is hard to say that a theory would be specific only to microfinance. However, microfinance as a field would not emerge if it did not have its specific theories and concepts. Here we will discuss concepts and theories that are applicable in the field of microfinance. This will deliberate on poverty, market failure, risk, group lending and cash-flow financing.

2.2 Poverty

Poverty can be understood from various angles, and it would not be wrong to say that it can equally be misunderstood too. If we go through the scholarly efforts or even the policy makers' efforts to define poverty, we can find that there is hardly any consensus on what poverty is, and in turn, there are differences in understanding about who a poor person is. Let's first look at the various typologies. According to Drewnowsky (1977), there are three kinds of poverty:

1. **Absolute Poverty** Absolute poverty is defined in terms of a particular measure, for example, poverty line which is nothing but a level of income (say, USD 1.25 per day, at present one US dollar is equal to about ₹70). If a person's income is less than this level, he/she is below poverty line, and thus is a poor. This is absolute poverty. It can also be defined in terms of nutrition. If a person is able to get adequate level of nutrition in a day, we consider that person is not poor. If he/she is not able to get that specific amount of nutrition, he/she is poor.
2. **Relative Poverty** The problem with the concept of absolute poverty is that such definitions do not consider the variations required in terms of income and nutrition from place to place. A factory worker, a whiter collar worker, a farmer and a housewife would require different levels of nutrition. The nutrition need would also differ depending upon the age, geographical location (plane area, hilly

area) and various other factors. Similarly, the level of income approach may not capture the needs of the people. In the 1980s, even in urban areas of India, telephone connection was a sign of being well-off, while in rural areas, even the rich did not have such facility. Today almost everybody can afford a cell phone connection. From a luxury, telephone communication has receded to be a necessary item. Poverty is easily understood if we compare a person with others in the society. Such an approach is referred to as relative poverty.

3. **Subjective Poverty** Subjective poverty is judgemental. One may perceive that he/she may be poor. Similarly, others may have their own opinion about that person's poverty status. Such perceptions are built intuitively and a number of factors, such as experience, surroundings, ideology and information determine such perception.

It is one thing to classify poverty, but to measure poverty is a different ball game. Measurement of poverty is based on certain theoretical approaches. Sen (1981) classifies various approaches in the following terms:

1. **Income Approach/Headcount Ratio Approach** This is the basis of measurement of poverty line. The problem with this approach is that it does not take into account the distribution of income. According to Drewnowsky (1977), it does not measure the depth of poverty (here depth of poverty means degree of poverty like extremely poor, moderately poor, etc).
2. **Biological Approach** This relates to measurement of nutritional requirement.
3. **Inequality Approach** This is the foundation of understanding of the idea of relative poverty. Inequality primarily refers to the skewed distribution of income in a society. Policy makers generally use the tool of income transfer from the high-income groups to the low-income groups to curb the problem of poverty.
4. **Deprivation Approach** Sen calls it a relative deprivation approach where a particular group of people are deprived of certain conditions, such as employment opportunity and income.

The above-mentioned is only a basic classification; subsequently, scholars have enriched the discussion on poverty. Today we have a much broader understanding of poverty. Streeten (1981) brought out the idea of **Basic needs approach** in which not only material deprivation, but deprivation from non-material aspects was also recognised. Amartya Sen's further work led to the idea of **Capability approach** in which poverty is conceptualised in terms of deprivation from attaining capabilities to earn the commodities required for meeting basic needs. Sen considered this as as an entitlement failure.

The concept of vulnerability is also related to poverty. This, unlike the previous understanding, is a dynamic concept. What it means is that just by having sufficient income, it is not necessary that one can distance himself/herself from poverty. Vulnerability is drawn from shocks, trends and seasonality. A very well established income source can be damaged seriously by shocks like natural disasters (flood, earthquake, drought), changing trends can bring down the level of income from an established source (e.g., a weaver may find that people are no longer buying his produces), and prices may fluctuate drastically across seasons to affect the incomes of producers. All these negatively affect the livelihoods of people and it may turn them into poor. A related concept is that of five capitals, physical capital (road, building), natural capital (forest, water), financial capital (saving, credit), human capital (skill, labour), and social capital (social relationships) are key to the sustainable livelihoods of people. People may have access and control over these capitals, if not, they are not likely to have sustainable livelihoods. For further discussion on sustainable livelihoods, see Chamber and Conway (1992) and Department for International Development (DFID) (1999).

2.3 Causes of Poverty

The above discussion shows the multidimensional conceptualisation of poverty. This also means that poverty is caused by several factors. The following provides a summary of the different causes of poverty:

- **Lack of Resource Base** For any kind of regular income, there is a need of a resource base such as land, labour, capital, or a combination of any two or more of them. A farmer needs a piece of land for cultivation and from that resource base he/she earns some income. A factory worker or an agricultural worker engages in factory or farm (respectively) to earn some wage. An entrepreneur invests capital for running a business and earns some profit. This resource base is fundamental to any kind of earning. If a person does not have access and control over such resources, it is likely that he/she would not be able to earn. Fragmentation of land has reduced the landholdings and now the farmers do not have sufficient land to earn enough income to run their families. Similarly, government makes land acquisition for construction of roads, rails and farmers lose their land. Many times, government land is used for construction of factories, but before such construction livestock owners used that land for grazing their animals. After the land is used for commercial purpose, farmers' source of grass is gone. Similarly, demand for various skill set has been changing and sometimes workers do not find it easy to acquire new skills. Capital is not always available to anybody who wants.

- **Poor Technology** Technology is a great enabler of higher production. Application of hybrid seeds have resulted in higher production of agricultural crops. Use of mechanised implements have cut down the cost of cultivation, thus leading to higher level of income. If such technology is not available or if the farmer is not able to afford such technologies, he/she is likely to get a low income.
- **Lack of Access to Market** One may have access to resources and technology, but without access to market, higher rate of production would be meaningless. If the producer does not have access to market where the produces can be unloaded it leads to a situation of high supply and low demand. This will lead to fall in prices. Ultimately, the producer loses the investment. When the operations of Amul Dairy started, the availability of market in Bombay (now Mumbai) was a great enabler. Without such access to market, possibly dairy cooperatives in Gujarat would not have been successful. Lack of employment opportunity is also a kind of shortage of market access to the labour market.
- **Structural Inequality** Sometimes social structure of a society is responsible for poverty. Many times, we can see that in villages, some dominant castes control the public resources. Others do not get the benefit of such resources. Women are deprived of holding property rights in many places. This leads to poverty.
- **Lack of Social Security** Not everyone in a society has the ability to earn. Children and old age people have to depend on the earning members of family. Differently abled people, even if they are in the earning age, would often not find suitable jobs. Widow and orphans often find themselves as destitutes. This occurs because of lack of a robust social security system. Earlier, due to the joint family system, there was at least some social security. Now with the working youth migrating to distant places, old people are left to their own. Such destitution brings in the vagaries of poverty.
- **Business Cycles** Business cycles refer to recessions and booms. For some years, the economy may see high growth, which is followed by low growth rate, i.e. recession. During recession, profits of companies go down. In order to stay in business, these companies go for downsizing. As a result, many people lose jobs. Unless they have enough savings, and if the government does not provide unemployment allowances, people fall into the trap of poverty.

2.4 Microfinance and Poverty

By definition, microfinance caters to the financial needs of low-income groups. Hence it is expected that microfinance would help in eradication of poverty. But it is not clear how microfinance causes such poverty alleviation.

Poor do not find it easy to get financial services. In particular, they do not get loans. Banks do not find them creditworthy because the poor do not have much asset and they cannot provide any collateral. Poor people in rural areas also have the difficulty reaching out to the banks, which are located in distant locations. A visit to bank often results in loss of wage and cost of transport for that day. Microfinance not only provides door-step delivery, but is also collateral free. It increases access to finance. In a way, it solves the problem of 'lack of access to capital'. With access to finance, poor people also have a better reach to technology and skills. Thus, their productive capacity is increased.

The problem of credit-worthiness is solved by microfinance by the method of group lending where because of peer pressure, the moral hazard of non-repayment comes down significantly. As discussed in a separate section in this chapter (section 2.7), group lending also helps in decreasing transaction costs and adverse selection. Thus, there is a better profitability for the microfinance agency or the bank. This further helps in increasing access to finance.

Institutional arrangement like SHGs often brings in affinity among the group members. Not only a social capital is built but their bargaining power also increases. Their social position also improves and thus they have more decision-making power. Overall, it can be said that microfinance leads to more empowerment of members. Thus, the problem of structural inequality is addressed.

Thus, microfinance can help in curbing poverty. However, there are some limitations of microfinance also. Microfinance alone may not be very effective, unless accompanied by technical and institutional support. Further, the poorest of the poor may not benefit much from the microfinance interventions.

Microfinance is generally associated with reducing poverty. Hence, it is important that an understanding of poverty is developed. Poverty is a multi-dimensional concept (Chambers, 2006), the three most discussed dimensions are as follows:

- **Low Income** Poor people have the common characteristic; i.e. low income.
- **Material Deprivation** This was highlighted by the World Development Report, 1990. The idea behind this conceptualisation is that people do not have access to materials needed for meeting basic needs. The subsequent World Bank reports, however, added that deprivation need not only be limited to material components, issues like health and education can be added to it as well.
- **Capability Deprivation** Amartya Sen's capability approach explains that human development is caused by capability of people, when the latter are deprived of capability to live a dignified life, poverty arises (for more details, see Sen, 1999).

It can be observed that microfinance can address capability related concerns, i.e., it provides financial inclusion and thus provide easy access to finance, particularly for capital. Microfinance operations are often packaged with technical and institutional support. The problems like low income and material deprivation can generate out of this.

2.5 Market Failure

The basic economic theory says that when supply is low, the demand rises, and thus prices. Thus, the existing suppliers start making a profit. This is where many more suppliers intervene to take a pie of the windfall gain, and the market become flooded with goods or services, and as a result prices decline. This results in suppliers withdrawing and supply decreasing. This cycle continues and that is how a market operates. This should happen in the credit market too, as poor people require money. Ideally, banks should run after them to lend, But they do not. This is a classic case of market failure.

Why does it happen? There are two related concepts, **information asymmetry** and **transaction cost**. Banks do not have the information of where the market demand lies. Or it is possible that the client did not know that the bank provides loans, hence he/she did not approach the banks. There are also issues like the client did not meet the criteria of the bank, which is a different matter and will be discussed later. When we talk about market failure, information asymmetry plays an important role.

2.5.1 Transaction Cost

The other factor that leads to market failure in credit market is that the transaction costs of dealing with poor is too high to be viable for banks. A bank has to bear a certain fixed cost to operate even a small branch. Let's say that it is ₹20 million. In order to be viable, the bank needs to earn more than this amount. Suppose the bank lends at an average interest rate of 10 per cent per annum; in that case, at least the average loan outstanding should be ₹200 million. Then there are provisions of bad loans too. In order to have a reasonable profit, the bank should sell at least ₹250 million of loan for the entire year.

What strategy will be suitable for the bank manager? Should he/she provide credit to several clients who need small loans, or a few clients who need large loan? If the first strategy is followed, say each client on an average is given ₹10,000, then the manager needs 25,000 transactions to fulfil the target. In a year of 250 working days, it means 100 loans every day. For a small branch, where there are only a few hands to work, this is a big deal. But if an industrialist seeks ₹250 million in loan, the job of the manager becomes easy. The cost of 25,000 transactions would be much higher than the cost of a single transaction. Thus, transaction cost is the other reason why bankers do not want to fund poor.

Information asymmetry has far reaching implications. It has two direct outcomes leading to **adverse selection** and **moral hazard**.

2.5.2 Adverse Selection

In a market, the sellers and buyers do not have proper information about the demand, supply and the real value of a product or service. This information asymmetry leads to distortion of prices. George Akerlof's work on market for lemons provides relevant ideas for this problem. In a market for used cars, the buyer would always like to buy a good used car (peach), but the owners of good peach are not likely to sell. This leaves the market flooded with bad quality used cars (lemon) and the buyer has no mechanism to find out the quality of car (Akerlof, 1970). In a market for financial products the banker does not have complete knowledge of the quality of the borrower's project and the extent of actual risk factors. It is possible that the good quality borrowers will easily get finance from low-cost sources, and the majority of risky borrowers will approach the open market. The banker here is likely to lend to a risky borrower, thus ending up in adverse selection of clients.

2.5.3 Moral Hazard

Risk can arise after the banker finances the project or even at later stage. The term moral hazard is used in various contexts. In the context of insurance, moral hazard arises when a person whose vehicle is insured, he/she do not drive carefully because the insurer would bear the cost of damage. In the context of a loan, the banker expects that the borrower will work in a wholehearted manner.

2.5.4 Ex-ante Moral Hazard

Suppose 'A' is a dairy farmer who takes loan for buying a cow, which he will repay from the proceeds of milk produced. The idea here is that the farmer would work sufficiently to earn enough money and would repay the money. But if the farmer becomes lax, and does not earn that much money to cover the operational cost, then he is not likely to pay back. This is called ex-ante moral hazard.

In the case of a dairy farmer, at least, the banker can resort to seize the cow and sell it in the open market. This does not guarantee that the banker would realise the loan plus interest amount, but at least there is some kind of collateral, from which the banker can recover a part. But in the case of microfinance, most of the loans are not collateral based. Say, a vegetable vendor takes loan for working capital. If the borrower fails, the bank has nothing to recover. Armendariz and Morduch (2010) call this as 'limited liability. (This concept is more known for its application in a limited liability joint stock company, where in the event of shutting down of the company, the shareholder is liable only to the extent of his/her equity holding). Here it means that if the borrower fails in his/her venture, the lender cannot recover the amount because there is no collateral attached to the loan. In the case of the vegetable vendor, if his/her business fails, the lender will be in this situation. When the banker lends to the vegetable vendor, he/she has no idea whether this venture will succeed or not. Further, there is no way to understand whether the borrower will make enough effort to make this succeed.

2.5.5 Ex-post Moral Hazard

The other kind of moral hazard is ex-post moral hazard. This is more a kind of enforcement problem that the lender faces. In this case, the borrower already makes money from the project but does not make the payment. If the borrower runs away with the profit, it also creates ex-post moral hazard.

2.6 Risky Borrowers

It is impossible to avoid risks in lending, and hence there would always be risky borrowers. Thus, a lender must take this into account in pricing the loans. If all of the borrowers are safe, the lender can simply charge the cost of capital to break-even. However, for risky borrowers, interest rate has to be adjusted upwards.

2.6.1 Impact of Risky Borrowers on Interest Rate

In any of the above circumstances, the banker loses money. How would the banker maintain the business in such events? Suppose a portion of borrower is risky, while the other portion of borrowers is safe. The banker has to charge the amount lost from the risky borrowers to the safe borrowers. Eventually, this will push the interest rate higher. This may force the safe borrowers out of the loan market (Armendariz and Morduch, 2010).

In any banking business, the banker knows that some borrowers are safe while some are risky. If the banker knows specifically that a particular borrower is safe, he/she can lend the borrower at an interest rate of 'k', where k = cost of capital, including the principal. Suppose in an event, the total cost of capital and expenses in lending is 10% of principal. In order to break even, the bank will charge

$$k = \text{Principal } (100) + \text{interest } (10) = 110$$

Suppose the banker knows that the borrower is risky and there is a probability of p of successful repayment. Considering p = 90%, the banker will charge for breaking even:

110/90% = 122.22, or in other words an interest rate of 22.22%.

The problem arises when the banker is not able to segregate safe borrowers from risky borrowers. But the banker knows that a certain portion 'q' is safe borrowers, which means that:

Proportion of safe borrowers = q

Proportion of risky borrowers = 1-q

Suppose q = 50%, then breakeven cost say, 'R_b'

$\Rightarrow$ $[q + (1 - q)\, p)] \times R_b = k$

$\Rightarrow$ $R_b = k / [q + (1 - q)\, p)]$

$\Rightarrow$ $R_b - k = [k / \{q + (1 - q)\, p)\}] - k$

$\Rightarrow$ $R_b - k = k \times [1/ \{q + (1 - q)\, p)\}] - 1$

$\Rightarrow$ $R_b - k = k \times [\{1 - q - (1 - q)\, p\}] / \{q + (1 - q)p)\}$

$\Rightarrow$ $R_b - k = k \times [\{(1 - q)\,(1 - p)\}]/ \{q + (1 - q)\, p)\}$

$\Rightarrow$ Say, $R_b - k = A$

$\Rightarrow$ Or $R_b = k + A$

Or, in other words,

$$A = \frac{k(1-q)(1-p)}{q+(1-q)p}$$

In the event of p = 50% and k = 1.1 (i.e. cost of capital is 10%), the banker must charge 46.67% interest from all borrowers in order to break even. This is a huge rate of interest and the safe borrowers are likely to exit from the market which eventually will further increase the interest rate. For elaborate discussion on this issue, please see Armendariz and Morduch (2010).

2.7 Group Lending

Another concept associated with microfinance is that of group lending. As mentioned in Chatper 1, there are three kinds of groups, joint liability groups (JLG), Grameen Groups and self-help groups (SHGs). At this stage, it is important to understand the need of group lending.

When the Integrated Rural Development Programme (IRDP) in India failed, some NGOs like Mysore Resettlement and Development Agency (MYRADA) tried out the SHG model that worked on peer pressure. Similarly, the MFIs banked upon the joint liability system of the groups. Group lending, since then, has become a standard and widely used practice. The advantages of group lending are:

- Because of peer pressure, repayment rate becomes high
- This brings down the transaction cost in several ways. First, there are bulk transactions through the group and second, the monitoring cost comes down because the group monitors the process
- The group also has a good understanding of the locality and hence, it helps avoiding the risk factors like adverse selection and moral hazard

The group-based lending works because of peer pressure for incentives and disincentives. If group pays regularly, it will receive larger loans which can help in increasing the income of the members substantially. In case the group does not repay, borrowers are not provided further loans. There are a few disadvantages of group lending also. Group formation, particularly that of SHGs, is a time-consuming process and adds to the transaction cost.

2.8 Cash Flow Based Financing

Generally, banks follow asset-based financing in which the asset which is built up in the project remains as a collateral with the bank. For example, if the bank lends a person to set up a shop, the shop itself remains as a collateral. In order to avoid risks, the banks do not provide 100 per cent of the value of the shop as loan. The financing is shared with the owner and bank in say 20:80 or 25:75 ratio. In development finance, the banks or financial institutions follow the cash flow financing approach. Under this approach, the free cash component of the future cash flow is projected and based on that the loan amount is calculated. Generally, this remains as unsecured loan (Von Pischke, 1991). But it is possible that the bank may ask for other assets as collateral. This cash flow financing approach is the basis for microfinance as the poor do not have sufficient assets to provide as collateral.

For example, a producer company is in the business of aggregating the products collected from farmers and it sells vegetables. For procurement from farmers, it would require working capital. Suppose every day, the total collection from farmers is ₹50,000, and the payment cycle is 30 day, accordingly it would require ₹1.5 million. But being a simple trading organization, it may not have the assets, other than a small warehouse or a transport vehicle. Even these assets are generally taken on rent. Virtually, it does not have any asset to put on collateral. Based on this asset size, any financer would stay away from giving loans to this company. But even with a 10% margin, its monthly income would be ₹0.15 million, i.e. ₹1.8 million in a year. The financer can easily recover its working capital interest on its loan. But if the bank refuses, the producer company would have no option but to seek loans from private sources of funds. Thus, cash-flow based financing is a win-win situation, benefiting both the lender and the borrowers. The lender makes easy interest earning, while the borrower has access to cheaper funds.

2.9 Financial Inclusion in India: An Overview

Financial inclusion refers to the process of ensuring access to appropriate financial products and services—such as savings, credit, insurance, and remittances—at affordable costs and in a fair, transparent manner to all individuals and businesses, particularly the vulnerable and underserved sections of society (RBI, 2021). Financial inclusion has also been understood in very specific terms:

> '*In India, the primary goal of financial inclusion has been to free the poor from the clutches of the usurious moneylenders by integrating them into the formal financial system and providing them with an affordable way of transacting in in a money economy*' (Gupta, 2024: 13).

The need for financial inclusion as a conscious policy measure arises because despite the several innovative banking and other initiatives a large chunk of population remains excluded from the traditional financial services (Dash, 2019). It is considered essential for inclusive growth, poverty alleviation, and reducing socio-economic inequalities. To address the systemic issues limiting financial inclusion, RBI constituted the Committee on Comprehensive Financial Services for Small Businesses and Low-Income Households, chaired by Dr. Nachiket Mor, in 2013. The committee proposed a vision where every adult Indian should be able to access a full range of financial services through a universal electronic bank account by January 2016. It advocated for differentiated banking models (such as Payments Banks and Wholesale Banks), expansion of Business Correspondents (BCs), and use of Aadhaar-based KYC to promote inclusion (RBI, 2014a). The committee also introduced the concept of a "Financial Inclusion Index" based on access, usage, and quality dimensions.

2.9.1 Financial Inclusion Measures and Index

The Reserve Bank of India launched the Financial Inclusion Index (FI-Index) in 2021 to comprehensively capture the extent of financial inclusion across the country. The FI-Index is a composite measure ranging from 0 to 100, with higher scores indicating deeper financial inclusion. It is based on three broad parameters:

1. Access – number of bank branches, ATMs, Business Correspondents, etc.
2. Usage – number and volume of transactions in savings, credit, insurance, etc.
3. Quality – financial literacy, consumer protection, and grievance redressal mechanisms.

As per RBI data (2023), India's FI-Index stood at 60.1, showing steady improvement due to initiatives like Jan Dhan Yojana, Aadhaar-based Direct Benefit Transfers (DBTs), and mobile-based banking services. The following policy measures were taken to ensure financial inclusion:

- **Pradhan Mantri Jan Dhan Yojana (PMJDY)** Launched in 2014, this flagship programme led to the opening of over 550 million zero-balance accounts with Rupay debit cards and insurance coverage (source: https://pmjdy.gov.in)
- **Digital Infrastructure** The JAM (Jan Dhan–Aadhaar–Mobile) trinity has enabled direct and transparent transfer of subsidies, significantly reducing leakages.
- **Payments Banks and Small Finance Banks** Following the Nachiket Mor Committee recommendations, RBI licensed new Payments Banks (e.g., India Post Payments Bank) to serve unbanked and underbanked populations, and small finance banks (e.g. AU, Ujjivan, and Utkarsh)
- Microfinance Institutions (MFIs) and Self-Help Group–Bank Linkage Programme (SHG-BLP) have played a critical role in providing access to credit, especially in rural India and among women.

2.9.2 Inclusion Measures and Index-Based Monitoring

To assess and monitor the depth and breadth of financial inclusion, multiple indicators and indices are used:

1. RBI's Financial Inclusion Index (FII):

   Launched in 2021, this composite index captures three dimensions:

   - Access: Number of banking outlets, ATMs, and branches
   - Usage: Credit and savings penetration, remittances
   - Quality: Grievance redressal, financial literacy, and service delivery

   The index ranges from 0 (complete exclusion) to 100 (full inclusion). India's FII score stood at 60.1 in FY2022, showing gradual improvement.

2. CRISIL Inclusix:

   Developed by CRISIL, this index covers:

   - Branch Penetration
   - Deposit Penetration
   - Credit Penetration

   It offers granular insights across states and districts, showing regional disparities.

3. Global Findex (World Bank):
   - Tracks financial inclusion indicators globally. According to the 2021 report, 78% of Indian adults had a bank account, up from 53% in 2014—largely due to the Pradhan Mantri Jan Dhan Yojana (PMJDY).

The Global Findex Database, launched in 2011 by the World Bank with funding from the Bill & Melinda Gates Foundation, provides comparable data on how adults in over 140 countries save, borrow, make payments, and manage financial risk. It is updated every three years (2011, 2014, 2017, and 2021 are the most recent editions). The 2021 report, in particular, tracks progress on bank account ownership, mobile money usage, digital payments, gender gaps in access to finance, and financial resilience during Covid-19. According to the 2021 Global Findex, India's situation of financial inclusion has improved substantially (World Bank, 2022).

Case Study 2.1 Determining the Interest Rate

XYZ Foundation runs an SHG-based on-lending programme in a backward district. Earlier, the organisation used to receive grants from donors and government to run this programme. But in the recent past, there has been no grants. Hence, it has decided to run the programme as a commercial venture. However, being a not-for-profit agency, it has decided that efforts would be made to cover the costs. Any surplus, if arises, will go to reserves for meeting unforeseen expenditure. On-lending seemed to be way out.

As part of this arrangement, the organisation borrows funds from a government body at 6.0 per cent per annum interest rate and the lender allows the organiation to carry out on-lending to SHGs at 12.5 per cent interest rate. Operating costs of the organisation at present is 4.5 per cent of loan portfolio. Recently, the government made some changes in the provisions of the scheme and issued a new set of guidelines. According to these, from now on, the on-lending can only be done for enterprising activities. Recognising that enterprises
XYZ Foundation runs an SHG-based on-lending programme in a backward district. Earlier, the organisation used to receive grants from donors and government to run this programme. But in the recent past, there has been no grants. Hence, it has decided to run the programme as a commercial venture. However, being a not-for-profit agency, it has decided that efforts would be made to cover the costs. Any surplus, if arises, will go to reserves for meeting unforeseen expenditure. On-lending seemed to be way out.

As part of this arrangement, the organisation borrows funds from a government body at 6.0 per cent per annum interest rate and the lender allows the organiation to carry out on-lending to SHGs at 12.5 per cent interest rate. Operating costs of the organisation at present is 4.5 per cent of loan portfolio. Recently, the government made some changes in the provisions of the scheme and issued a new set of guidelines. According to these, from now on, the on-lending can only be done for enterprising activities. Recognising that enterprises have risks of failure, it has added a provision that interest rate could be charged up to 15 per cent annum. For every SHG, there is a provision of ₹5.0 lakh, and there are 800 SHGs in the field. As per the recent grading, it has been identified that about 600 of them are eligible for taking loans.

The SHGs do not default ordinarily. Minor default, though rare, is observed for a temporary period of 3-4 months. An estimate says that in any case, no more than one per cent of payment would need to be written off. However, the recent provision of loans for enterprising activity changed the situation. People in the area deal with dairying, collection and selling of non-timber forest products and goat rearing. In such businesses, on an average, there is going to be a risk of 10 per cent of people failing in their commercial ventures. The foundation expects from these unsuccessful ventures, a loss of about 50 per cent of repayment. It also knows that the demand of enterprise loans (expected to be paid in three years) are as follows:

200 groups: ₹500,000   150 groups: ₹400,000   100 groups: ₹300,000

100 groups: ₹200,000   50 groups: ₹100,000

The manager of the organisation discussed the risks with the director of the funding agency (government body). The head of the organisation said that he was open to making minor revisions (maximum one per cent) in the interest rates for on-lending. He also suggested that insurance could also be thought of. But the insurance companies charge 5.0 per cent of loan amount as premium every year.

It is expected that with the increase of scale, the operating cost may decrease to 4.0 per cent. A detailed presentation on the risks, costs associated and options needs to be prepared for the Director of the funding agency.

Discussion Questions

1. Should you take up the enterprise funding project?
2. What interest rate should the foundation charge in order to break even, assuming that it has a mandate to generate 2.0 per cent of loan amount as reserve funds?

Summary

- Microfinance can be studied from developmental perspective or market-oriented perspective. In the developmental perspective, the grant-based models are followed, while in the market-oriented perspective, revenue-based models are followed.
- Microfinance helps in reducing poverty by way of enhancing access to finance, building robust institutions and encouraging enterprises.
- Microfinance sector is affected by lack of information about the clients. Also due to the transaction-intensive nature of the business, costs increase. This leads to the situation of market failure.
- As the banker is not able to differentiate between risky and safe borrowers, s/he has to charge a higher interest rate to all the borrowers.
- Group lending neutralises some of the impact of information asymmetry and transaction cost.
- Cash-flow based financing is an alternative to the collateral-based financing.

Exercises

A. Multiple-choice Questions

1. Market failure is caused by
   (a) Information asymmetry
   (b) Transaction cost
   (c) Adverse selection
   (d) All of the above
2. Adverse selection is caused because of
   (a) Information asymmetry
   (b) Transaction cost
   (c) Both (a) and (b)
   (d) None of the above
3. Because of adverse section
   (a) Interest rate decreases
   (b) Interest rate is not affected
   (c) Interest rate increases
   (d) Cannot be determined
4. Ex-post moral hazard is a problem of
   (a) Selection of appropriate borrower
   (b) Monitoring the success of the project
   (c) Enforcing the repayment
   (d) All of the above
5. Group lending helps in
   (a) Decreasing transaction cost
   (b) Avoiding adverse selection
   (c) Increasing repayment rate
   (d) All of the above
6. Group lending succeeds because of
   (a) Low transaction cost
   (b) Peer pressure
   (c) Decrease in moral hazard
   (d) All of the above
7. Capability approach was propounded by
   (a) Vijay Mahajan
   (b) Amartya Sen
   (c) Muhammad Yunus
   (d) None of the above
8. Interest rate is higher in microfinance because of
   (a) High default rate
   (b) High amount of frauds
   (c) High transaction cost
   (d) All of the above

9. The problem of risky borrowers is compounded by
   (a) Information asymmetry
   (b) Information overload
   (c) Information technology
   (d) None of the above

10. Microfinance can not solve the problem of
    (a) Lack of access to market
    (b) Lack of capital
    (c) Business cycle
    (d) None of the above

B. Review Questions

1. Poor are creditworthy but they lack capital. Comment.
2. How does microfinance help in reducing poverty?
3. Explain adverse selection and moral hazard. How does it affect the banker's business?
4. Microfinance borrowers have a limited liability! Comment.
5. What are the advantages and disadvantages of group lending?
6. Microfinance organisations have no other option than charging a relatively high interest rate as compared to banks. Do you agree with this statement? Justify.

C. Application-based Questions

1. You are planning to start an enterprise and for this you require `15 million. You approached a bank that agreed to lend you, however, it would charge a higher interest rate to offset the risk in the proposed enterprise. Generally, the bank charges 12% per annum interest from safe/no risk borrowers. According to the bank manager's estimate your enterprise has 50% risk of success. How much interest he/she should charge having the same margin that the bank earns from a safe borrower/venture?
2. Suppose in an area 80% of borrowers are safe, the rest 20% have a risk factor of 75% in successfully making repayment. What is the interest rate that the banker should charge in order to break even? Assume that the cost of capital is 8% and operating cost is 4% per annum.
3. A bank started lending in a new area and you, the bank manager, do not have any idea of who is safe and who is risky borrower. But a sample survey showed that 10% are risky borrowers. It was also found that about 30% of the business enterprises for which you are planning to fund have the risk of failure. What amount of interest rate would you charge to break even if your cost of capital and operating cost together comes to 10% of the capital invested?
4. Suppose you work for a bank that provides business loans. You have the past record that 40% of your clients are risky and the rest repay the loans regularly. But you do not know which particular client is safe or risky. You know that the risky clients have a chance of 80% of success in their business. Assuming your cost of capital is 10% per annum, what percent of interest should you charge in order to break even?
5. You work for an MFI that provides business loans. Past experience shows that 25% of your clients are risky and the rest repay the loans regularly. You have no idea on which particular clients are safe or risky. All you know is that the risky clients have a chance of 80% of success in their business. Assuming your cost of capital is 10% per annum and your MFI has an operating expense ratio of 5%, what rate of interest should you charge for break-even?

Further Readings

- *The Economics of Microfinance* by Armendariz and Morduch provides a theoretical account of various issues like risky borrowers, group lending and some other issues. To get a broader idea about the issues discussed in the chapter, the reader may go through this book.
- *Financing at the Frontier* by Von Pischke is a foundational discussion on the background of microfinance models. It is a must read, particularly for the students interested in advanced learning.
- On the issue of poverty, there is a need to develop a perspective in order to link it with microfinance. Amartya Sen's works, particularly those related to capability approach, would be useful for developing a greater understanding.
- The sustainable livelihood framework (also called DFID framework) provides a theoretical explanation of how vulnerability, poverty and livelihoods are related. This would provide the reason behind microfinance (Chamber and Conway, 1992; D FID,1999).

PART II
Microfinance Operations

CHAPTER

3

Self-Help Groups: Institution Building Operations

Chapter Outline

Learning Objectives

After reading this chapter, you will be able to:

- discuss the process of SHG formation and management.
- provide an overview of the rules and regulations of SHG management.
- provide an idea of the organisation structure of SHG based programmes.

3.1 Introduction

The Integrated Rural development Programme (IRDP) saw high levels of defaulters and that was a matter of concern for the government and the banks. But alongside, there was an experiment going on that tried to solve the problem of non-repayment. An NGO in India, known as Mysore Resettlement and Development Agency (MYRADA), brought in the concept of affinity groups, later known as self-help groups (SHGs), in which poor women were organised into groups and these groups not only undertook savings and credit activities but also became an instrument for women empowerment. In particular, it was observed that because of peer pressure, the loan defaulter rate came down almost to zero level. In the 1980s, some other NGOs like Professional Assistance for Development Action (PRADAN) also followed this model. Support was provided by NABARD; In 1992, the programme got a boost when National Bank for Agriculture and Rural Development (NABARD) launched the SHG-Bank Linkage Programme (SBLP).

Many NGOs with support from NABARD or other funding agencies took up SHG promotion programmes. By the end of 1990s, government also recognised the need of SHGs and the Swarnajayanti Gram Swarozgar Yojana (SGSY) programme, a revamped version of IRDP, also pushed the SHG based model. The National Rural Livelihood Mission (NRLM), which is being implemented now, is primarily an SHG-based programme. It may be noted that as a part of SBLP (supported by NABARD), about 8.7 million SHGs have been formed (details in chapter 1), which makes it about 105 million members, thus covering about 400-500 million population. On any count, this must of one of the most widespread and scaled up models of development.

3.2 What is an SHG?

An SHG is a group of 10 to 20 members from the same locality and having some degree of homogeneity. The basic requirement is that there must of some kind of affinity, be it in terms of caste, socio-economic status and/or occupation. The characteristic of affinity is invariably highlighted by MYRADA, the pioneer in SHGs.

The basis of the self-help groups exists prior to any intervention. The members are linked by a common bond like caste, sub-caste, blood, community, place of origin or activity. The intervenors, whether from the NGO, bank or government must have the experience to identify these natural groups which are commonly called the affinity groups. Even when the group members are engaged in a similar traditional activity, like basket weaving, the basis of the group's affinity is a common caste or origin. (Fernandez, 1995:1)

Although the number 10 to 20 is the generally accepted rule for an SHG, there are exceptions too, and under some circumstances, groups having less than 10 members have also been recognised as SHGs.

Homogeneity is an important characteristic of the group. Members must be from the same socio-economic background, otherwise there may be chances of power play. It is observed that they are from the same hamlet/village, this helps them meet each other regularly with ease. Also, they can be from the same social category, such as caste, and they may be from the same occupation also (such as all of them are farmers). Many government programmes often look forward to common interest groups as found in the World Bank supported District Poverty Initiative Project (DPIP) and hence there is a tendency among the facilitators to form groups having the same occupational interest. However, this need not be the essential characteristic of the group, it is possible that in a village, the members may have different occupational interest but have affinity towards other members.

3.3 Purpose and Functions of an SHG

The purpose of an SHG is to make collective effort for the development of its members. The ultimate goal of an SHG is to empower its members.

That said, SHGs undertake some concrete activities:

- Meeting at regular frequency (say weekly or monthly)
- Thrift and credit activities
- Promoting enterprising activities directly or indirectly
- Raising voice in the interest of members

It is, however, not necessary that the group is involved in enterprising activity. Many SHGs are involved in non-financial activities like health and education and contribute immensely to the cause of women empowerment.

3.4 SHG Management Process

SHG formation and management is a time-consuming process. It takes about three years to have a complete cycle of SHG formation to make it an independent institution. There are four stages in the process of SHG management.

The first stage of SHG management is **SHG formation**. As a part of this, the facilitator has to visit the concerned area to understand the need of development and the need of organising people (particularly women) in the area. The most important point to be observed here is to identify whether a particular village comprises poor community. Once the poor community is identified, then the next agenda should be to organise them into groups. For this, meetings can be conducted in which the importance of SHGs, need of women empowerment and the process of formation should be discussed. In these meetings, the facilitator also can identify potential groups. Further meetings can be done in these small groups. Once a potential group is identified, the facilitator should discuss the roles and responsibilities, functions and procedure of SHG formation. Once the members agree to form a group, the following should be done:

- A resolution by group members that they have agreed to form the group. All the members should sign in the resolution.

- Decision should be made on how much monthly savings the members would be undertaking.
- Election of office bearers, i.e. president, secretary and treasurer. These office bearers would also act as the signatory of bank account of the SHG.
- Opening of bank account in a nearby bank.
- Formulation of the basic rules and regulations for running of the group.

All these activities may take quite some time, may be three to six months. During this period, the SHG meetings should be conducted regularly. Frequency of meetings should be decided by the SHG (like weekly, monthly) depending on the convenience of its members.

The second stage of SHG promotion involves, **strengthening of the internal processes** of the SHG. In this stage, the amount collected from the members in the form of savings are subjected to lending to the group members. This process is called internal loaning/lending (sometimes it is called simply as 'interloaning'). This process goes on for about six to nine months. During this process, the group members get into the habit of regular thrift and credit. The facilitators should also take care that during this process, the office bearers are trained to keep the records in order. Also, the members should get some exposure and training on how to run the group in an effective manner. Other than the saving and credit activities, members should be encouraged to discuss issues of their general interests. They also should be trained to make decisions in a democratically appropriate manner.

The third stage of SHG promotion involves **enterprise promotion and bank linkage**. While many would consider this as the most important phase, this is only the superstructure of the institution building process. The foundation laid in the previous stages are equally important because without a solid foundation, the institution is likely to crumble down. It is understood that before the third stage starts, the SHG is already into a solid footing and is ready for grading by an external agency, such as bank. In this stage, the SHG members are trained and positioned to undertake enterprising activities for which they would require bank finance. The raising of funds through bank financing is known as bank linkage. Once the bank linkage is done, the SHG is provided hand holding support by the facilitating agency for developing an effective enterprise. Once the enterprise runs effectively, the members would be able to pay back the bank loan and may see additional loans for further expansion of the enterprise. This stage tests the strength of the institution and also the viability of the enterprise. This stage takes about 12-18 months.

The fourth and the last stage of SHG promotion is the **withdrawal** of the facilitating agency. By this time, the SHG has already operated for about two years and is habituated with saving, credit, external loans, and repayment activities. It is at this point of time that the facilitators start withdrawing from their constant interventions and encourage the SHGs to take independent decisions. This can be done in a phased manner. Another way of withdrawal is to federate the SHGs and train the SHG federations' leaders to manage the operations themselves. The issue of SHG federations will be discussed in a separate section. The withdrawal stage generally takes about 6-12 months.

In a nutshell, the four stages of SHG promotion can be presented, as shown in Table 3.1.

Table 3.1 Stages of SHG Promotion

Stage	Activities	Duration
1. Formation	Initial meetings, identification of members, resolution, election of office bearers, bank account opening	3 – 6 months
2. Strengthening of internal processes	Internal lending, training of office bearers, training of members, strengthening of record keeping	6 – 9 months
3. Enterprise promotion and bank linkage	Identification of enterprise, developing proposal, bank loan application and fund raising, hand holding for running enterprise, repayment of loans	12 – 18 months
4. Withdrawal	Federation building, facilitating independent decisions, handover charges.	6 – 12 months

Box 3.1 Community Resource Person (CRP)

The CRP model of programme delivery in SHG promotion has been a time-tested practice. Initially, full-time employee of SHPIs were appointed for facilitating the process of SHG formation and management. Often such employees were external people, and they did not understand the complexity of rural society. When a sizeable number of SHGs had been formed in the initial decades, some of the SHG members and leaders got an exposure of the SHG management process. Such people were called community resource persons (CRPs), and many SHPIs including state-sponsored programmes took the services of these CRPs. CRPs were more acceptable at local level and were cost effective also.

Ordinarily, it takes about 36 months for a complete cycle of SHG promotion activity. However, sometimes it can be completed in 24-30 months and under some circumstances, it can take longer than three years. There is no way of making short-cut in the process of SHG promotion, because it is not about fulfiling target, rather the goal is to build sound institutions which takes time.

3.5 Records Maintained by SHGs

An SHG undertakes saving and credit activities regularly. As it deals with money, it is required that it maintains appropriate records. However, SHGs generally comprise poor women who are illiterate, otherwise also may not be proficient in reading and writing. It is necessary that records are maintained, but there should not be too much of them. In view of this, some simple records are generally maintained by SHGs.

1. Proceedings register/Minutes register
2. Attendance register
3. Cash book
4. Savings register
5. Loan register
6. Ledger
7. Bank passbook
8. Individual passbooks

Other than this, documents like membership register, cheque book, stock register and visitors book also may be maintained depending on the requirement.

3.6 Rules and Regulations of an SHG

When an SHG is promoted, it is desired that the group members would obey some rules and regulations. It is often seen that the facilitators, in a hurry, provide a set of rules to the SHGs. This is not a good practice. The SHG members should formulate the rules for themselves. It is the role of the facilitator to guide them through the discussion on formulating rules. Rules are formulated on the following points.

1. *Membership* This includes rules on eligibility criteria. Whether men or women could be members, what should be the age (generally, people aged 18-60 are taken), locality (from the village, hamlet and so on), membership fee, procedure for new members, termination of membership, withdrawal of membership, etc.
2. *Savings* The group must decide the amount of contribution the members make every month.
3. *Frequency and location of meeting* Whether the group would meet on any specific day of the month/week, and the location where they would meet is decided.
4. *Quorum* When there is a meeting, what should be the minimum number of members to be present in order to have a valid decision?

5. *Loan* Criteria for approval of loan (for example, preference to medical emergencies)
6. *Interest rate* Rate of interest that the group should charge for loans is decided
7. *Penalty* Penalty for defaulters and absentees is also decided.
8. *Election, term and role of office bearers* The role of president, secretary and treasurer are defined. Further, how they would be elected and their term should also be clearly laid out. Continuous terms are generally not encouraged that may help in creating power centres.
9. *Distribution of profit/surplus* Mechanism of distribution of profit and surplus should be defined.
10. *Dissolution of the group* Under which circumstances, the group would be dissolved.

3.7 What is a Good SHG?

A good SHG is one that meets the quality of a robust institution. An institution is treated as robust if the rules and regulations (or norms) are adhered to by its members. This is the fundamental characteristic that is assessed when looking into the strength of an institution. There are several tools and techniques of understanding whether an SHG is an effective one or not. Generally grading is undertaken to understand this. The NRLM follows something called as *panchsutra* (five principles), i.e. regular meeting, regular saving, regular repayment, inter-loaning and proper maintenance of records. This is not exactly equal to grading, but can be understood as a set of guiding principles. MYRADA and NABARD follow grading methods to see whether an SHG is fit for bank linkage or not. Later in this book (chapter 7), grading has been discussed.

In a way, the good and not so good SHG can definitely be understood by using some grading technique. But in the process of standardising the SHG promotion, it should not be forgotten that these are primarily institutions, and they cannot always be relegated to standard measures. It always helps to use a measurement, but the fundamental point is that SHGs are institutions, which are an end in itself. They cannot always be treated as instruments.

3.8 Advantages and Disadvantages of SHGs

Self-help groups provide several benefits, such as economy of scale, collective learning, democratic culture and capacity building (Fernandez, 1995):

- They provide economy of scale. The SHGs are channels of routing financial services and the financial institutions have to only deal with one body, i.e. the SHG. The SHG, in turn, is responsible for dealing with individual members. This significantly decreases the cost of delivering the financial services.
- Collective learning takes place in the environment of an SHG. The members meet regularly and discuss their problems and issues. They learn from each other and such learning cannot be done in a formal set up.
- In SHGs, decision making takes place by way of democratic processes and this culture of democracy is imbibed in the members.
- As a part of the SHG promotion, the SHPI undertakes a lot of training and exposure programmes that enhances the capacity of the members.

Overall, it becomes a platform for empowerment of members (which can be equated with empowerment of women, as most of the SHGs are women groups).

However, the SHGs have some weaknesses too. It is time taking to form and promote a strong SHG. It takes about three years on an average to promote one SHG. This also has its cost and a significant amount of resources is required to build SHGs. In the livelihood programmes based on the SHG model, the major complaint of people is that institution building takes too much of time.

There are some process related problems of SHG promotion. On a lot of occasions, the SHPIs are given target of formation of SHGs. In the target-oriented projects, many of the processes like identification of members having affinity is compromised. Internal lending starts too early and bank linkage is made before the groups become strong enough to manage funds. As a result, when the SHPIs withdraw, a significant proportion of the groups become ineffective. There is also a lot of variation in the quality of SHGs promoted by good NGOs and government agencies, who would generally go with target orientation.

Another problem with SHGs is that they remain sound on paper but do not maintain the spirit of an affinity group. This is difficult to diagnose for outsiders too. Sometimes, an influential member controls the group while the other members remain for namesake. This situation is ordinarily found in government run SHG programmes. Another problem that is found in recent times is that the SHGs have been looked up as a political vote bank and politicians often use them for distribution of freebies particularly on the eve of elections.

Despite the above problems, SHGs have been time-tested institutions. The greatest thing about them is the aspect of women empowerment. They have actually been effective in making financial delivery successful. Further, SHGs today are the foundation of implementing a large number of development programmes.

3.9 Cost of an SHG Programme

Running an SHG programme has its own protocols. While it is important to understand the processes and phases of SHG promotion, the major question lies on who would promote such programme. Generally, it is done by an SHPI. The SHPI can be a bank, a government or a non-government organisation. Banks would generally not have a separate structure for promoting SHGs, hence their link with SHGs is limited to providing loans. But the government agencies and NGOs put a committed structure to promote SHGs. In this section, we will discuss the organisation structure of such SHG promotion projects.

A small-scale SHG programme comprising 50-100 SHGs would not require a separate organisation structure. But when the numbers increase, there have to be sufficient functionaries who would run the operations. At the ground level, there is generally a functionary of the level of field executive or project associate or some other designation. The official is the frontline executive of the SHPI and his/her roles are:

- Conducting meetings at village level
- Identify SHG members and discuss with them the possibility of forming SHGs
- Formation of SHGs
- Collection of documents and opening of bank accounts
- Helping the group in forming the rules and regulations
- Helping the group in conducting regular meetings
- Follow up of decisions taken in meetings
- Liaison between the SHPI and the SHG

Depending on the need and stage of the project, one frontline executive can deal with 15 to 30 SHGs.

The next level of executive can be at a cluster level (generally called a cluster coordinator). A cluster generally includes four to five villages or *Panchayats,* depending on the distance at which they are located and the number of SHGs. The role of the cluster coordinator is to monitor the activities undertaken by the frontline activities and also to feed regular reports to the SHPI.

At the next level, which can be at block or district level, there are specialists. There must be experts who have solid understanding of enterprise development, management information system and gender issues. At this level, a project manager or coordinator may also be required. In programmes having focus on enterprise development, it is useful to have technical experts on the issues of agriculture, livestock, handicrafts, etc., depending on the local requirement.

All these require substantial resources. Let us assume that an NGO is running an SHG programme over two to three districts which might have some three thousand SHGs. For this, it would require the human resources shown in Table 3.2.

Table 3.2 Cost of SHG Promotion Project

Designation	No. of employees	Salary per month/person	Total amount in ₹
Field executive	100	10,000	1,000,000
Cluster coordinator	20	15,000	300,000
Experts	5	30,000	150,000
Coordinator	1	50,000	50,000
		Sub-total	**1,500,000**
Support staff*	2	15,000	30,000
Travel cost (assume 10% of salary)			150,000
Office rent		25,000	20,000
Utilities		10,000	10,000
Administration (assume 10% of total)			170,000
		Total	**1,880,000**

For 36 months, the budget would be something around ₹67.50 million, which brings the average cost of an SHG to about ₹22,500. Some adjustments can be made here. It can be accepted that the SHGs would require intensive hand holding for about 18 months after which, during the withdrawal phase, the type of interventions would change and hence the cost can be reduced. Assuming that the need of field executives would come down by half, the total budget for the three years would be ₹57.8 million, and the average cost of an SHG would come down approximately to ₹19,250. This is still a significant amount. This is an indicative budget and it can differ from place to place, and the requirement of functionaries and the local salary structure may be different.

Cost structure of an SHG project can be reduced in another way. It has been tried out in various places, where the existing experienced SHG office bearers, who have facilitation skills, can be involved in SHG promotion. This not only helps in reducing cost of SHG promotion, but also brings in the learning of past SHGs into the new ones. The NRLM projects often use the concept of Community Resource Persons (CRP) for this purpose.

3.10 Performance of SHGs

There are about 14.42 million SHGs, and about 83.52% of them are women SHGs. In all, 7.74 million have savings accounts.

Table 3.3 Performance of SHGs as on March 2024

No. of SHGs as	14.42 million
No. of all-women SHGs	12.04 million
SHGs having credit linked	7.74 million
Outstanding loan	₹ 2596 billion
Average savings per SHg	₹ 45,132
Average credit per SHG	₹ 381,758
NPA	2.05%

Source: Srinivasan, 2024

There is no fixed savings on SHG savings, and every 5-7 years they distribute the interest income. On an estimate well-functioning SHGs receive about 15% interest rate. However, given the subsidized interest rate provided to the SHGs, particularly in southern states, SHGs prefer taking bank loans rather than from their savings (Srinivasan, 2024).

As of now, the growth in the number of SHGs have come down as almost all eligible women have been covered under the SHGs. In fact, about 5-6% dropout rate has been observed (Srinivasan, 2024).

3.11 Federation of SHGs

The idea of federations is nothing new and it has been effectively used in the context of SHG management. It has been observed that in the context of dairy cooperatives, federations have been formed. The Gujarat Cooperative Milk Marketing Federation (GCMMF) is a cooperative federation, popularly known as Amul. Using the same principles here, SHGs have also been federated.

Federations have been used for several purposes:

- The SHPI cannot continue in the project forever. However, SHGs still would require support from time to time. Under this condition, the federation can takeover the role of the SHPI.
- Being a federation of cooperative nature, it can also undertake lending and other financing activities.
- It provides a platform for SHGs for raising their issues at higher level.
- It enhances the bargaining power of SHGs.
- It helps in promoting and providing a platform for local leadership.

An SHG federation, if properly managed, can be a sustainable institution without depending on external grants or support organisations. It can charge a service fee to the member SHGs, and it can also provide the financial services at a mark-up (for example, it can take loans at 10% and charge, say, 15% interest from the members). It can become the channel of service delivery for other financial products like insurance. It can also provide institutional services, such as technical support (like veterinary services) and capacity building.

It has been seen that federated SHGs perform better than non-federated SHGs on several counts, such as attendance in meetings, amount of savings, internal lending, amount of credit sanctioned and the percentage of group members benefitting from the credit activities. In terms of frequency of meetings and interest rate, there was not much difference. But maintenance of record and rotation of leadership was better in non-federated SHGs (Kumar, 2016).

There is also some criticism regarding federating. According to Harper (2003), it just adds another layer of middlemen. Federations should be formed only when they are necessary, and can serve only as a temporary measure. He pointed out that SHG federations can be exploited for political purpose. This is not a far-fetched criticism, as we have seen the way cooperatives have been used for political purposes. The phenomenon of channelling freebees like interest rate subvention to SHGs and distribution of mobile phones to SHG members confirm Harper's criticism.

Case Study 3.1 Enterprising SHGs

In 1999, Mr. Rajvir Singh, Project Director at District Rural Development Agency of a Western Indian district, was planning on how to implement the SHG-based programme in the district. He got to know that Community Development Organisation (CDO), an NGO working in the district, has a good SHG programme and decided to send a group of officers on exposure tour to the SHGs of CDO.

CDO, established by Mr. Dhiraj Sharma, has been operating in the district since early 1980s. Dhiraj Ji had worked with a pioneering voluntary organisation in Rajasthan (also famous in India as well as internationally) for more than 10 years with the stalwarts of civil society, and had a sound understanding of various approaches and methods of development. Initially, CDO started with educational interventions, particularly adult education and literacy campaign and also started some primary education programmes. In doing this, the organisation found that the lack of funds was one of the impediments of promoting education in the area. People were exploited by moneylenders. Women had no role in decision making nor had any control over their income and alcoholic use among the males was very high.

In this context, Mr. Sharma was suggested by some that formation and management of women's groups in the area would be a useful intervention. With support from a funding agency, CDO formed about 25 groups in a few panchayats. The women's groups (named Self Help Groups – or SHG) comprised 15-20 members, who lived in proximity so that they could meet regularly. For the first six months, each member contributed savings of ₹20 to ₹25 per month. At the end of six months, each group had savings of around ₹2000 - ₹2500. Then the group members thought that it would be useful if the amount was lent to needy members. Two members took a loan of ₹500 each at an interest rate of 1.5 per cent per month and paid back the same in five instalments. This internal lending went on for about another six months.

After this, the organisation provided a loan of ₹10,000 to each group at an interest of 8.0 per cent per annum. The SHGs lent the same at 18 per cent rate of interest to the members. By 1995, the groups had savings of about ₹10,000 to ₹12,000 each. The income from interest, about ₹800 to ₹1000 per annum, was distributed equally among all the members. All these transactions were recorded in account books and registers. The secretary of the SHG or any literate member maintained the records under supervision of the community organiser of CDO. A few training programmes were also conducted in the CDO training campus from time to time.

The members used the loan amount primarily for agriculture and for buying goats. They believed that access to loans in time was quite helpful loans were sanctioned in monthly meetings with consensus. For meeting emergencies, the secretary of the group had ₹500 which was given out for medical treatment in the event of death or any tragedy in a family.

In about 10 years, the SHG programme of CDO expanded and reached to 250 SHGs. Ten full-time Community Organisers were working in the programme. The SHGs had a well-organised system for record maintenance and CDO had a good Management Information System (MIS) that had up-to-date information of the amount of savings and loans of each member, defaulters, purpose of loan, etc.

In the year 1999, when the government sponsored SGSY programme started, the district administration wanted the groups to be linked with the programme. A team of officials went to the field and observed the groups' operations. They reported that the groups were managed meticulously, but were not involved in any income generation activities. Any such activity was only undertaken by individuals and the groups only provided financial support.

When the officials interacted with groups, the members were quite vocal. A member told that earlier they were not able to hold any savings, and all savings were with the male member. "Now that the money is deposited with SHGs, our control over savings is higher", said another. For agriculture operations, loans were sanctioned to the women member, not the men. This also provided an upper hand to the women. The procedures and mechanism of the SHG management were well-established. Hence, they would not even depend on CDO, unless some problem came up.

The problem with the SGSY officials was that they were looking for a group-based activity. Ideally, occupational groups (like SHGs of members having dairying as occupation) were more suitable for group-based enterprises. Such groups were hard to find in CDO's area of operations.

Mr. Sharma said that the groups should be viewed as institutions leading to women empowerment. Earlier, they could not even speak to outsiders. After becoming a part of SHGs, they could make presentations of their achievement. Their voice in household decisions, sometimes even in community level decisions had also increased. This was a great achievement, he added.

However, Mr. Singh, Project Director of DRDA who had to run the SGSY programme, was not happy. He confided to the officials, "These are not ideal groups. Ultimately, what is the purpose of SHGs if they are not involved in enterprising activities?"

Discussion Questions

1. Do you agree with Mr. Singh that the above groups are not ideal?
2. What should Mr. Singh do in order to promote SHGs in the districts?
3. Can there be good SHGs without enterprising activities?
4. What are pros and cons of group-based enterprises?

Summary

- An SHG is an informal body of 10-20 members, who meet regularly and are involved in saving and credit. They are also engaged in enterprising activity and operate as an affinity group.
- SHG promotion is undertaken by a self help promotion institution (SHPI) and the process goes through four stages, formation, strengthening of internal process, enterprise development and bank linkage, and withdrawal.
- SHGs need to maintain simple procedures, and hence, the basic minimum documents, such as cash book, proceedings register, passbook, and ledger should be maintained at this level.
- The rules and regulations of an SHG should be formulated by its members rather than by the SHPI or facilitators. The rules should be formed on various aspects, such as membership, interest rate, criteria for loan sanction, penalty, election of office bearers and dissolution.
- SHGs help in bringing down the transaction costs, increasing access to finance and empowering the women, but is also a time taking process.
- Cost of an SHG programme can be brought down if it is implemented in phases. Federations of SHGs can also help in sustaining the SHG's activities.

Exercises

A. Multiple-choice Questions

1. SHG members must have
   (a) Same occupation
   (b) Same caste
   (c) Affinity among one another
   (d) None of the above
2. It ordinarily takes about ________ months to form an SHG.
   (a) 3 – 6
   (b) 6 – 9
   (c) 12 – 18
   (d) 24 – 36
3. SHGs generally have ________ members.
   (a) 10 – 20
   (b) 15 – 20
   (c) 5 – 10
   (d) 10 – 15
4. SHGs are ________ entities.
   (a) Registered
   (b) Unregistered
   (c) Cannot be determined
   (d) None of the above
5. Which of the following activity is not a part of SHG promotion?
   (a) Identification of SHG members
   (b) Opening of bank account of the SHG
   (c) Registration of SHG
   (d) Capacity building of SHG
6. Which of the following indicates that an SHG has a good banking habit?
   (a) Operative bank account
   (b) Robust internal lending
   (c) All female members
   (d) None of the above
7. Internal lending in an SHG means
   (a) SHG lends only to its members
   (b) SHG lends to non-members too
   (c) SHG lends to its members out of their savings
   (d) SHG lends to its members out of bank loan
8. Office bearers of an SHG include the following
   (a) President, secretary, treasurer
   (b) President, accountant, cashier
   (c) President, secretary, accountant
   (d) Secretary, vice-president, cashier
9. It ordinarily takes ________ months to complete one cycle of SHG programme.
   (a) 3 – 6 (b) 6 – 9
   (c) 12 – 18 (d) – 24 – 36
10. Interest rate charged by an SHG from its members should be
   (a) Zero per cent
   (b) Same as bank interest rate
   (c) As fixed by RBI
   (d) As fixed by the SHG members

11. Leadership in an SHG should be
    (a) Selected by the SHPI
    (b) Rotated regularly
    (c) Appointed by the government
    (d) None of the above

12. SHG federations help in
    (a) Continuing the activities of SHPI
    (b) Providing a platform for raising the SHG's issues
    (c) Enhancing the bargaining power of SHGs
    (d) All of the above

B. Review Questions

1. Describe the stages of SHG promotion.
2. Now that the stages of SHG promotion have been standardised, do you think that they can be promoted in a short duration, say one year? Justify.
3. What are the records maintained by an SHG? What if these records are not maintained?
4. What rules and regulations are followed by SHGs?
5. Do you think SHGs are the panacea of all problems faced by poor people, particularly women? Explain.
6. Prepare a critique of SHG model of microfinance.
7. Critically analyse the need of federating SHGs.
8. Are SHGs better than JLGs/Grameen Groups? Justify your view.
9. SHG model has its own limits. It is necessary but not a sufficient condition for women's empowerment. Comment.
10. In the process of scaling up of SHG programmes, what kind of problems does the facilitating agency face?
11. An SHG must be linked to an enterprise-related activity. Do you agree? Justify.

C. Application-based Questions

1. You are the SHG Coordinator in a government-funded project. A community organiser reported that a particular SHG in her field area was not operating properly. You visited the village and met the secretary. She said that some of the members of the SHG visited the nearby town daily for wage labour. Hence they are not in a position to attend the meeting that takes place every Saturday. They are demanding that the meeting should be held only once in a month. However, they are not able to fix any suitable date. The secretary has asked you to fix a date the meeting would be held on every month. She said that nobody would be able to disobey the order of the coordinator. What would you do?
2. You are a senior officer in a state government that received a huge grant from an international funding agency for livelihood promotion project. The project was proposed to be implemented with SHG-based approach. The Rural Development Minister has asked you implement the project quickly. "The election will be held after 15 months We have 12 months to spend the money", he said. What will you do?

Further Readings

- Alosys P. Fernandez's papers written as a part of Rural Management Systems Series are very useful readings for the purpose of understanding the concept of SHG and affinity groups.
  - 22: Self help groups - The Concept
  - Paper 55: Is microfinance leading to a macro mess?
  - Paper 69: A) The Self Help Affinity Group movement and the SHG-Bank Linkage Program; B) Conceptual and structural difference between SHGs formed between 1984-2000 and after 2000.
- The Centre for Microfinance, Jaipur has published a series of books on SHG processes in Hindi. The book *Adhar: Swayam Sahayata Samuh Gathan va Pravandhan Prakriyayen* would be useful for understanding the SHG management step-by-step.
- A Handbook of SHG-Bank Linkage by Deen Dayal Upadyay Antyodaya Yojana – National Rural Livelihoods Mission (DAY-NRLM) published in 2017 is the detailed guidelines for formation and development of SHGs in the NRLM programme. This provides step-by-step process for the SHG management. This will be useful in comparing how SHG programmes have been standardised.

CHAPTER

4

Microfinance Products and Services

Chapter Outline

Learning Objectives

After reading this chapter, you will be able to:

- provide an overview of various financial products in microfinance.
- discuss the non-financial products used in microfinance.
- introduce the relevant government initiatives for financial inclusion.

4.1 Introduction

Microfinance reaches the poor through its products and services which are delivered by the Self Help Group Promoting Institutions (SHPIs) and Microfinance Institutions (MFIs). Generally, there are two kinds of services:

- **Financial Services** This includes savings, credit, insurance, pension and remittance. In recent times, micro leasing has also come up as an important service in microfinance.
- **Non-Financial Services** This includes institution building, technical support and business development services.

In this chapter, each of these products will be discussed. Some of these products are offered in the context of pure banking also, which is context free, hence we will also discuss about how these products are contextual to the microfinance arena.

4.2 Savings

The fable of the grasshopper and the ant tells us that savings is important, as we cannot be productive every day. There are lean days on which weather may not favour, or say one may be sick enough to work, or say one is out of job due to recession. In other words, savings helps people in getting out of their vulnerable positions. For the poor, savings is very important, as they do not have enough social security measures.

Savings helps poor in two ways, in balancing the cash-flow fluctuations and in restraining them from spending excessively during the good days. Another important characteristic of savings is its certainty (IIBF, 2009). Ready money, as people say, is the most reliable thing.

In the context of microfinance, savings can be voluntary or compulsory. Compulsory savings includes monthly deposits made by SHG members. If not received in time, penalty is levied. Sometimes the borrower is asked to deposit some amount as a fixed deposit which cannot be withdrawn in order to obtain a loan. Voluntary savings includes all kinds of savings bank account deposits, fixed deposits and recurring deposits made by the people. It may be noted here that in India, MFIs are not allowed to take deposits, however, SHGs and federations of SHGs can take deposits. Small finance banks and payments banks also can collect savings. Cooperatives, being member-based organisations, can also take all kinds of deposits from members.

One problem for the poor is that their propensity to save is relatively low, hence the amount of savings is very little. While it is still important, it may not be sufficient to make enough for a large capital investment or add up a large amount for an event like daughter's marriage. It is under such circumstances that people are forced to take loans.

There are many kinds of savings products:

- **Savings Bank** Savings bank account can be opened in any bank (including payments banks) and one can withdraw from this at any time. Hence it is also known as demand deposits. This bears very small amount of interest like 3.5 to 4.0 per cent per annum. In exceptional cases, some banks have offered slightly higher rate of interest also.
- **Fixed Deposits (FD)** This provides that a customer can deposit an amount in a bank for a fixed period of time, which will bear interest. The duration of fixed deposits ordinarily ranges from 3 months to 5 years, however, banks also have the facility to make a fixed deposit for a week. Interest rate keeps on changing based on the market situation, however, it generally ranges from 6 to 8 per cent per annum. Withdrawal before the maturity of the deposit is ordinarily not allowed. One can still withdraw such a fixed deposit by paying some penalty.
- **Recurring Deposits (RD)** Under this arrangement, one has to keep on depositing some amount (say ₹100 or ₹1000) every month for a specific period (like 3 years or 5 years). After the specified period is over, the customer can withdraw the amount plus an interest which is around the same as that of fixed deposits.

***Illustration 1*:** 'A' has a fixed deposit of ₹10,000 at an interest rate of 8 per cent in a bank for a period of 5 years. How much will she receive on its maturity?

***Answer*:** Principal (P) = ₹10,000, Interest rate (r) = 0.08, Period = 5 years, Total sum to be received = $10{,}000 \times (1.08)^5$ = ₹14,693

***Note*:** Future value of a sum = $P(1 + r)^n$, where P = one time payment (principal), r = rate of interest, and n = number of periods.

***Illustration 2*:** 'B' has subscribed to a recurring deposit scheme as a part of which she deposits ₹500 every month. This goes on for 5 years and she receives an interest rate of 9 per cent per annum. How much will she receive at the end of 5 years?

***Answer*:** This can be calculated using the formula of future value of annuity. Here value of annuity = ₹500, number of months = 12 × 5 = 60 months, interest rate = 0.0075 per period. Future value of annuity (a) = $500 \times \{(1.0075)^{60}-1\}/0.0075$ = ₹37,712

***Note*:** Future value of annuity = $P\left\{\frac{(1+r)^n - 1}{r}\right\}$, where P = periodic payment, r = rate of interest, and n = number of periods.

In the context of microfinance, there are several kinds of savings products, such as:

- **Festival Savings** This is targeted at the upcoming festivals like Dussehra, Deepavali and others as applicable for the specific locality. As these festivals are annual in occurrence, generally the tenure is one year or less. The customer cashes upon it before the festival.
- **Savings for Marriage** The most popular of this is the savings for daughter's marriage. Traditionally, people saved in terms of gold, silver and other valuables.

A very important product, that is floated by Government of India is the Pradhan Mantri Jan Dhan Yojana (PMJDY). Technically, it is less of a savings product and more a tool for financial inclusion, but it needs a special mention here. The PMJDY account can be a basis for multiple services that the banks provide.

Box 4.1 Pradhan Mantri Jan Dhan Yojana

One of the problems in financial inclusion was that a large segment of people did not have bank accounts. A large number of factors such as illiteracy, lack of awareness, lack of access to banks, and know your customer (KYC) norms. There was a provision of no-frills accounts earlier, as part of which KYC norms were relaxed but the scheme did not help in universalising the banking access.

To address these problems, in 2014, the Government of India launched the scheme 'Pradhan Mantri Jan Dhan Yojana' (PMJDY). The aim of the scheme was to open bank accounts of every eligible Indians. The following benefits are provided under PMJDY:

a. One basic savings bank account is opened for unbanked person.
b. There is no requirement to maintain any minimum balance in PMJDY accounts.
c. Interest is earned on the deposit in PMJDY accounts.
d. Rupay Debit card is provided to PMJDY account holder.
e. Accident Insurance Cover of ₹1 lakh (enhanced to ₹2 lakh to new PMJDY accounts opened after 28.8.2018) is available with RuPay card issued to the PMJDY account holders. (one lakh = one hundred thousand)
f. An overdraft (OD) facility up to ₹10,000 to eligible account holders is available.
g. PMJDY accounts are eligible for Direct Benefit Transfer (DBT), Pradhan Mantri Jeevan Jyoti Bima Yojana (PMJJBY), Pradhan Mantri Suraksha Bima Yojana (PMSBY), Atal Pension Yojana (APY), Micro Units Development & Refinance Agency Bank (MUDRA) scheme. (source: https://pmjdy.gov.in/scheme accessed on 28 May 2025, point a to g, reflected *verbatim*)

As on May 2025, more than 550 million PMJDY accounts have been opened having a savings of ₹2597 billion in these accounts (https://pmjdy.gov.in/ as on 28.5.25) . This programme is a great initiative in universalising banking access to the financially excluded population, and it has helped in direct benefit transfer of government schemes including pensions and subsidies.

The Kalanjiam of Dhan Foundation have savings products like that for the occasions of festivals, purchase of jewellery, marriage, pilgrimage, education and housing.[1]

4.3 Microcredit

Microcredit is the most prolific service that is offered as a part of microfinance. For quite some time people interchangeably used the terms microcredit and microfinance. Even today, microcredit is the primary function of majority of the MFIs. There are various types of loans depending on various purposes. In general, the loans by MFIs are classified as productive loans and consumption loans. However, this classification is narrow and does cover important aspects, such as loans taken for housing, which is not exactly a productive or consumption loan, rather is an investment. Even loans for durables do not fit well into the category of consumption loan.

1. Reserve Bank of India (RBI), vide its Press Release dated 26.08.2014, has further clarified that those persons who do not have any of the 'officially valid documents' can open "Small Accounts" with banks. A "Small Account" can be opened on the basis of a self-attested photograph and putting his/her signatures or thumb print in the presence of officials of the bank. Such accounts have limitations regarding the aggregate credits (not more than ₹1 lakh in a year), aggregate withdrawals (nor more than ₹10,000 in a month) and balance in the accounts (not more than ₹50,000 at any point of time). These accounts would be valid normally for a period of twelve months. Thereafter, such accounts would be allowed to continue further for a period of twelve more months if the account holder provides a document showing that he/she has applied for any of the officially valid document within 12 months of opening the small account. (***Source:*** https://pmjdy.gov.in/scheme retrieved on 31 March 2019).

Rutherford and Arora's (2009) need-based classification is more comprehensive. According to this classification, there are four kinds of needs, investment needs, consumption needs, life-cycle needs and emergency needs. A slightly modified classification is presented here:

- **Loans for investment purpose** include income generation activities (IGA) or housing. The IGA loans are purely productive loans, while housing is an investment that does not provide income (unless the house is rented, and it is well known that the rents ordinarily do not generate sufficient cash flows to pay back the loan). Enterprise or IGA loans are expected to generate a stream of income. It can be for the purchase of fixed assets or for working capital. The examples of IGA loans are agriculture loans, dairy loans, poultry loans, business loans, etc. If the loan is for the purpose of buying a cow, constructing shed, land improvement, buying agricultural implements, or construction or purchase of a shop, it would be in the nature of fixed asset loan. If it is for purchase of raw material (seed, fodder and raw material for business), then it would be in the form of working capital loans. Working capital loans are short-term in nature, generally over a period of one season or one trading cycle.
- **Loans for consumption purpose** include loans for day-to-day expenditure. This is generally taken for purchase of food, clothes, education and regular medicines. People take such loans during festivals also. Logically, these kinds of loans, unlike the IGA loans, do not provide any return, hence MFIs should avoid lending for consumption but it would be impractical to do so. One takes consumption loan to meet the basic necessities. If basic necessities are not met, then there would be no human existence. The need of such loans arise because of seasonal fluctuation in cash flows or some unexpected expenditure which drains out the savings of that person. For example, just before the harvesting season, people may require consumption loans. If the concerned person is not granted loan by the MFI, he/she would go the local moneylender borrowing at a much higher cost. Consumption loan is not wrong, the only thing the MFI/SHGs should see is the repayment capacity. If the borrower has the need and is able to repay, nothing should stop the MFI from lending.
- **Loans for life-cycle needs** are taken for various occasions, such as child birth, marriage and death. Traditionally, these events are celebrated by inviting a large number of relatives, neighbours, and others, which cost a lot of money. Further, during marriage, particularly of the daughter, the household has to buy a lot of expensive materials, such as jewellery, furniture and clothes. Ordinarily, the savings of the family is not sufficient for this purpose. Hence loans are needed. Here also the repayment capacity is looked into before granting the loan.
- **Loans for emergency needs** These kinds of events are unexpected. This occurs if there is an accident and it requires huge expenditure for hospitalisation.[2] Further, if the earning member falls into such problems, then the family also might have difficulty in meeting costs of day to day expenditure. Unexpected death in the family and disasters like flood and earthquake that damage the property of the household are some of the examples of emergency loans.
- **Loans for Improving Quality of Life** These loans are generally categorised as consumption loans, but these are not exactly consumption oriented. These are loans for the purchase of durables like television, refrigerator, cooler, bike, cooking stove, etc., which help improving the quality of life. These also help in decreasing the hardship of people and thus lessen drudgery, particularly that of women. There has been controversy related to such kinds of loans as some believe that these are unnecessary loans and can be avoided. Spandana Spoorty in Andhra Pradesh had started this kind of loans and initially, it was considered as an innovation. However, later it was alleged that in order to increase sales, many MFIs pushed such products thereby increasing the indebtedness of poor.

Various organisations have offered products that meet the above kinds of needs. For example, for group loans Ujjivan provides a number of products, such as business loans for meeting business requirement, this loan ranges from ₹6000 to ₹50,000; family loans for children's school expense, home improvement, repayment of debts, social functions, durables, etc. ranging from ₹6000 to ₹35,000; agriculture loans toward the cost of cultivation and allied activities ranging from ₹6000 to ₹50,000; emergency loans that

2. In recent times, the Government of India has launched the Ayushman Bharat scheme as a part of which health insurance is provided. This helps in meeting the emergencies, but it is still not sufficient to cover the total cost of hospitalisation. Hence additional loans are required.

are provided within 24 hours to meet medical emergencies ranging from ₹2000 to ₹5000; education loans towards expenses of children's education ranging from ₹5000 to ₹15,000; top-up loans ranging from ₹3000 to ₹6000 for additional business requirement; and Vishwas loans as special loans to loyal customers to meet their additional needs ranging from ₹5000 to ₹15,000. Generally, the tenure of loans ranges from 12 months to 24 months. Up to ₹15,000 it is repaid in a tenure of 12 months. For individual loans, it provides higher education loan, agriculture loan, home improvement loan (both secure and unsecured), secure home loan, individual business loan, livestock loans, and secure business loans (Ujjivan, 2016).

The Kalanjiam of Dhan Foundation have products like basic needs loans, business loans, crop loans, micro enterprise loans, working capital loans, debt redemption loans, leasing loan, housing loans and loans for developmental needs.

The group loans of Annapurna Finance has several products like agriculture crops (paddy, sugarcane, vegetables, groundnut, etc.) agri-equipment loans (bullock, bullock cart, threshers, tractor, power tiller, paddy reaper, water pumpset, lift irrigation), agri-allied loans (dairy farming, poultry, goat rearing, piggery, fishery), micro enterprise loans (spice making, dry food processing, individual business, beetle shop, fruit shop, fast food stall, paddy processing unit, etc.), and handicraft and handloom loans (weaving loan, sarees, bamboo production, coir, brass work, etc.). The tenure and loan amount vary depending upon the repayment capacity and credit history (AMPL, 2017:29).

In microfinance in general and in microcredit in particular, the focus has been on standardised products. It is well known that the customised products are more appropriate for customers and also meet their needs. But customisation has a high cost. To decrease the cost of this transaction intensive microfinance business, MFIs often resort to standardised products. In microcredit, generally we have standardised loan products.

4.4 Micro Insurance

Insurance is one of the several tools of risk management. Risks can be either avoided, shared, reduced, retained or transferred. Insurance helps us in transferring the risks to another party in exchange for payment of a premium. Conceptually, microinsurance is no different from any other insurance. In fact, it is nothing but providing insurance to low-income groups. It has been considered as a separate category because this group of people have so far been left out from the insurance services. The need of such people is slightly different from regular insurance products. According to the Working Group on Microinsurance, microinsurance can be defined as:

> *Microinsurance is the protection of low-income people against specific perils in exchange for regular premium payments proportionate to the likelihood and cost of the risk involved. Low-income people can use microinsurance, where it is available, as one of several tools (specifically designed for this market in terms of premiums, terms, coverage and delivery) to manage their risks.*[3]

There are three models of insurance services, partner-agent model, master policy model and mutual benefit model. In the partner-agent model, the MFI/SHPI acts as a distributor of the insurance products. It acts as an agent and in lieu of its services, it receives a commission. In the master policy model, (which is also known as group insurance), the organisation takes a master policy and distributes its components to its members/employees/customers. Here, having a large group of subscribers, the master policy holder has the flexibility to bargain for changes in product pricing and designs. The third category, i.e. mutual benefit model, is self-reliant and membership based. Here, the members themselves share the risk with one another.

There is a range of products in microinsurance dealing with agricultural crop (weather index), life, health, property, credit life and disasters (Dror and Piesse, 2014).

The Insurance and Regulatory Authority of India (IRDA) defines microinsurance as 'a general or life insurance policy with a sum assured of ₹50,000 or less'[4]. Thus, there is a quantitative restriction in order to be termed as microinsurance. Further, it can be covered both in terms of life insurance as well as general insurance. In order to ensure that the companies do not ignore the importance of microinsurance, IRDAI

3. Working Group on Microinsurance, 2003 cited in Allianz AG, GTZ and UNDP, 2006.
4. http://www.policyholder.gov.in/economically_vulnerable.aspx retrieved on 1 April 2019.

mandated that under the social sector obligations, life insurance companies insure at least 5000, 7000, 10000, 15000, 20000 lives in first five years. Similarly, the general insurance companies at least have 7, 9, 12, 14, 16 per cent of total policies, (2%, 3%, 5% of gross premium thereafter).[5] Here social sector means an unorganised sector, informal sector, economically vulnerable or backward class and other categories of persons in both rural and urban areas.

The Government of India has introduced two insurance schemes for the poor:

- **Pradhan Mantri Suraksha Bima Yojana** This scheme provides life cover for death for people aged 18-70 years and it covers death or disability resulted from accidents and even natural calamities caused deaths excluding suicide. It provides an accidental life cover of ₹200,000/- and the premium is ₹20 per annum per member.
- **Pradhan Mantri Jeevan Jyoti Bima Yojana** This is a life insurance scheme for people aged 18–50 years and it covers death due to any reason. The premium is ₹436 per annum for a life cover of ₹200,000/-.

Box 4.2 Crop Insurance Product

A major problem in recovery of loans in rural areas is that farmers sometimes are not able to repay because of crop failure due to insufficient rainfall. When BASIX, in early 2000s, was going for agriculture loans, this problem was found. This is when it mooted the idea of weather insurance products in microfinance. Crop insurance was not new in India, but it had several problems. The government's crop insurance schemes had uniform premium across the country but the risk varied from place to place. Crop insurance was subsidised, hence did not reflect the actual pricing. Further, it was tied to bank loans rather than to the crop value. Also, it was not crop-specific, hence there was a possibility of moral hazard (World Bank, 2005). Benefits were used in some concentrated areas, for example, Gujarat alone claimed 58 per cent of benefits from the Comprehensive Crop Insurance Scheme (Raju and Chand, 2007). Crop cutting experiment, based on which the claims were settled, was expensive and time taking.

In collaboration with ICICI-Lombard, BASIX designed a weather insurance product that would be based on rainfall index. Rainfall was taken as proxy to production. This was a transparent and less expensive method. It was bundled with other products of BASIX. Product design was done by ICICI-Lombard, while BASIX undertook marketing and distribution (World Bank, 2005). It went on well initially, however, it still required a lot of research on rainfall data and uncertainty of rainfall.

Generally, an NGO, an SHG, or an MFI can be a microinsurance agent. Also microinsurance, to a large extent, has been provided by such microfinance intermediaries. This is because the microinsurance helps in insuring against the losses of their loans due to death, incapacity and losses due to natural calamities. However, there have been a few cases where specialised organisations have been engaged for microinsurance. One such organisation is the National Insurance VimoSEWA Co-operative Ltd. (see Box 4.3).

Box 4.3 National Insurance VimoSEWA Co-operative Ltd.

The National Insurance VimoSEWA Coop Ltd (henceforth termed as VimoSEWA) is a specialised agency for marketing and distribution of microinsurance products. It was established in 1992 for providing protection to SEWA Bank borrowers. It is registered under the Multi-State Cooperative Act and has 12,000 individual (women) shareholders from Bihar, Delhi, Gujarat, Madhya Pradesh and Rajasthan and some institutional members. By 2017, the organisation already had about 80 thousand members. Its premium charged is ₹ 225 per person up to ₹ 1350 per household for a year which provides benefits such as health insurance of ₹ 15000-₹ 50000, wage loss allowances of ₹ 200 per day for 15 days and life insurance and accidental death insurance of ₹ 35000 to ₹ 110,000 per person. Cashless facility is also provided for hospitialisation. Between 1992 and 2017, VimoSEWA disbursed ₹ 203 million to 94,000 claimants. The organisation distributes the products through direct marketing as well as through partnership with MFIs.

Source: Discussion with Mr. Shree Kant Kumar, CEO of VimoSEWA and data taken from unpublished documents of VimoSEWA.

5. https://www.irdai.gov.in/ADMINCMS/cms/frmGeneral_Layout.aspx?page=PageNo66&flag=1, retrieved on 1 April 2019.

4.5 Micro Pension

Pension is nothing but savings for the days when one is no longer able to work. This generally happens after retirement or old age, which is, not necessarily but often considered as synonymous. The main agenda is to meet the needs of a person when he/she no longer earns (Rutherford, 2008). Pensions can be provided in two ways, one can voluntarily save throughout one's working life for the old age and the government provides a pension to everybody. The second mechanism is called social pension or public pension which can be distributed out of current taxpayers' money or from a government scheme where the pensioners keep on depositing (Rutherford, 2008).

Micropension is the provision of pension for the poor. This is a relatively new addition to the portfolio of microfinance service providers. However, given the need of this product, it has potential to grow.

***Illustration*:** Suppose one member of the five crore (50 million) households of India each, saves ₹1000 per month to the pension account. It would mean an addition of ₹5000 crores (₹50 billion) to the pension funds every month!

The need of micropension is enormous. India has been transforming economically into a giant. However, it also has been changing on various fronts, as captured in the following words succinctly:

India is experiencing a demographic transition leading to lower fertility, increased life expectancy, and a consequent increase in the proportion of the elderly. Families are shrinking and transforming into nuclear units. Individualistic attitudes and rising aspirations with the accompanying changes in lifestyles are widening the generation gap (Qazi, *Business Line,* 3 January 2018).

In India, the concept of universal pension has not even been discussed till recently. Earlier, only the government servants (whose proportion was miniscule in the society) received pension. There have been some schemes for old age pensions as a part of which people get as little as ₹200 or ₹300 per month. Delivery of these schemes have been infested with corruption in many places. Earlier, the old age population used to depend on the younger generation, but in recent times, the social fabric has weakened and young people, generally migrate and settle in distant places leaving the old age parents to fend for themselves. In future, this (young) population would have to depend on itself! According to Rutherford (2008), in Bangladesh, women get married at younger age and thus outlive their husbands, which is the cause of anxiety. While responding about who would take care of them,

Many women felt obliged, first, to acknowledge that the matter lies in the hands of Allah. Then, they would say that their children (especially their sons) would care for them. But their faces showed they doubted this, and this sorrow often led them to express bitter feelings... They spoke of their envy of women with solid assets like land or housing (Rutherford, 2008: 243-245).

Under these circumstances, micropension has become an important product in the portfolio of the microfinance service providers. However, pensions products are long term in nature and generally, the MFI provides short term services. There are also interest rate and inflation risks, which may dampen pension products.

A few years ago, the Government of India came out with a pension scheme for working poor, as given in Box 4.4.

Box 4.4 Atal Pension Yojana

In 2015-16, the Government of India launched a scheme 'Atal Pension Yojana' for the workers in unorganised sector, who can save voluntarily for their old age. Anybody aged 18–40 years can apply for this benefit. One can pay between ₹ 1000 and ₹ 5000 per month and in lieu of that, a minimum pension would be guaranteed by the government. The government would pay a matching contribution of 50 per cent of the contribution of the person or ₹ 1000, whichever is lower. This scheme would be managed by the Pension Fund Regulatory and Development Authority through the NPS mechanism. In order to open the account, one needs Aadhar (unique identity) number and a mobile number. One problem is that this scheme does not tolerate default and penalises for late payment, and if such default continues for six months, the account is frozen after 12 months, it is deactivated and after 24 months, it is closed. On attaining 60 years, one may exit the scheme and opt for pension.

As the pension schemes are long term in nature and there is no immediate gain (even one opting for pension at the age of 40 has to wait for 20 years), clients would generally not agree to go voluntarily for such products. If the subscriber is working as a salaried person, it may be easy to get it through the employer, otherwise marketing such a product is not an easy task. Another thing is that it needs high levels of investment skills in order to stay alive in the market and assure a good return. Not many organisations have this ability.

However, MFIs can easily go into partnership with various pension providers and earn a commission. This would diversify their sources of revenue and they do not have to take the risk of fund management as well.

4.6 Remittance

Remittance is synonymous with migrants. Today, in India or abroad, it is very common for people to go elsewhere in search of a job and from there they send money to their dependents. According to a report of the World Bank, the global remittance market in 2015 stood at USD 441 billion and India was the top recipient having received USD 72.2 billion (World Bank, 2016). This shows that money transfer takes place at a great volume.

Poor have great difficulty in sending money. Many of them do not have access to banking facility, and hence they depend on money transfer agencies and middlemen so that their money reaches the destination. Traditionally, money order (a service provided by the India Post) was used popularly, but it was expensive (charged about 5% as commission) and was suitable for sending only small amounts. Migrants often carried cash when they visited their homes during festivals and other occasions, such as marriage of a relative. Carrying cash had some inherent risks Services of banks (like sending demand drafts) were not used by many, as very few had access to banks. In any case, all of these services took time and delay in receipt was very common.

In India, there have been several examples of remittance services by MFIs. Adhikar Microfinance provided such services for migrant workers from Odisha who worked in different parts of India. M-PESA in Kenya has also been a successful model (Nayak, 2015).

The need of remittance is a basic financial service. Remittance can help the MFI get several benefits. First, it can provide the service and charge a commission. Second, it can also use the same customer group to provide other services. Further, it can also think of bundling various products with remittance services. But a problem exists here, the MFI must maintain adequate cash flows at the other end (destination), otherwise it would lose people's trust.

Some other problems are associated with money transfer as a basic service. One needs to be a bank or licenced money transfer agency. If the MFI does not have any of these, then it can only be a collecting and disbursing agent on behalf of such an organisation. Another problem with remittance is that there have been several instances where people have used it for money laundering and frauds. MFIs must be careful about such practices.

4.7 Microleasing

Leasing is a financial service, as part of which one can use an (say expensive) equipment, which ordinarily one cannot afford, in lieu of a lease rental. There are two parties involved here, a lessor, who owns the equipment, and a lessee, who takes the equipment on lease for using. Thus, even if the lessee is not the owner of the equipment (or any other property), he/she can use it rightfully by paying the lease rental.

Illustration 1: A farmer leases in a tractor from a leasing company during the cultivation season. He pays ₹20,000 as a lease rental per month. The operating costs like cost of fuel, cost of driver and day-to-day maintenance are paid by the farmer (lessee). If the farmer had hired the tractor on per hour basis, he would have to pay much higher amount, and many times it might not be available in time. Buying a tractor would have led to spending of about ₹1 million, which is too much for the farmer. Leasing the tractor helps him in avoiding such a huge capital investment.

***Illustration 2*:** A carpenter needs an equipment costing ₹50,000, which he cannot afford. However, the same is available at ₹2500 per month. He can lease in it from the lessor.

How is leasing relevant to microfinance? Working capital loans are not suitable for purchase of an expensive asset and MFIs are not suitable to fund long-term loans (Nayak, 2015). Further, the borrower might not have enough collateral to have a long-term finance. As explained above, leasing is an alternative instrument of finance. Instead of taking loan to buy a tractor, (under these circumstances, he would have to shell out an EMI of about the same amount), simply form a lease agreement with the leasing company. Thus by investing a small amount periodically, the lessee is able to get the benefit of such a huge asset. Also, an MFI can fund the lease rental for every season like a variation of a working capital loan. The leased asset is not shown in the asset of the lessee, saving it from maintaining capital for meeting CRAR (Capital to Risk Assets Ratio).

Microleasing does not have the risks of unsecured loans, as there has been a specific purpose of taking the loans and there is no chance of moral hazard of using the loan for some other purpose. The chance of default is very low. In case the MFI or lessor expects the risks of default, there can be a tripartite agreement in this regard so that loss can be minimal.

Broadly, there are two kinds of leases, financial lease and operating lease. In financial lease, the equipment is taken by the lessee for the economic life of the asset. For all practical purposes, the equipment remains with the lessee. Costs including that of major maintenance are also beared by the lessee. Operating lease is like a short-term rental. Here, the rental amount is treated like an expense.

Microleasing has not been so widely practised, because of the complexity of the instrument, in the field of microfinance. Hence it has a great potential. There are some experience of microleasing by Grameen Bank in Bangladesh, SELFINA in Tanzania and ANED in Bolivia (Nayak, 2015).

4.8 Non-financial Services

Non-financial services are primarily of three types, institution building, technical services and business development services. The idea of non-financial services is a part of the concept of integrated approach of microfinance. Merely providing finance is not sufficient, and hence support services that strengthen the financing make sense.

Institution Building Institution building is a complex phenomenon. It is required from the need of collective action. Poor as an individual or a household, does not have the bargaining power nor the scale to deal with the market. In majority cases, they are landless or have a small fragment of land (which is often not more than one or two acres). If the household is engaged in making some artisanal product also, the scale is too small to be viable. However, similar products are also made by others in the neighbourhood. This situation brings in the need of collective action.

The most popular collectives formed in the context of microfinance are SHGs. There are more than eight million SHGs in India. However, there are other kinds of collective institutions too. Type of collective institution depends on the purpose:

- SHGs and federations of SHGs are generally programmatic institutions. This is of course a limited view of the SHGs (as discussed in Chapter 3), but in microfinance, this is the primary purpose for which SHGs have been formed. SHGs become the instrument of implementing the programme. They also undertake savings and credit and also go for enterprising activities.

- The second type of institutions are generally formed for the purpose of aggregation. Producers' outputs are of small size, which would not be economically viable if sold individually. Hence, if a number of producers, say 100, aggregate their produces, it would enhance their bargaining power as well as it would be economical to transport and store. These kinds of institutions are registered in the form of cooperatives or producer companies.
- The third type of institutions are formed for specific purposes, such as marketing. Marketing federations' primary aim is to create market linkages. An example of such institutions is the dairy federation in various states of India.

Institution building is a time taking process. It requires regular follow up with community and convincing them that it would be beneficial for them to get together and form a collective institution. Initially, people are sceptical of the success of such collective institutions. Hence it would be useful if some of them can be convinced to make an initiative. Once some benefits are observed, slowly others would join the collective as well. Why do people resist joining such institutions? The main reason is that in order to operate a collective, a member has to forego some of the individual rights and freedom.

In promoting these institutions, the role of MFI or SHPI is very important. Generally, a self-initiated institution is the best in long run. However, this is often not possible; hence a nudge from the facilitating agency is required.

Technical Services This is an additional support service, the need of which comes up when the clients take loans for certain enterprising activity. In general, activities like dairy, goatary, poultry require veterinary services. Similarly, agriculture related activities require support of agriculture experts. Fishery requires support of fishery experts. Such services are many times not available in the locality. To cater to such needs, the facilitating agency (MFI or SHPI) hires the desired technical experts and provides its services to people.

An example of such technical services is the poultry promotion initiative of PRADAN (Professional Assistance of Development Action) in Kesla where the organisation provides the services of a veterinary doctor who would visit the poultry farmers from time to time and ensure that the required vaccinations and medications are provided. Before a household takes up poultry, the members are provided details of training on how to raise the poultry. Similarly, in Jharkhand, apiculture projects and silk worm projects were supported technically by PRADAN. In Bihar, IGS (Indian Green Service) provided similar kind of supports for its system of rice intensification (SRI) project.

Business Development While institution building helps in bringing the people together, technical support helps in increasing the production. This is essential for increasing income of producers. However, if there is no proper market linkage, the supply of such produces may outnumber the demand and it would result in decrease in price. The ultimate purpose of improving the livelihood of the producers will get negated. Under such circumstances, it is important that the SHPI or MFI provides business development support.

Business development support requires that before promoting a particular activity, thorough market survey is done to see if there is a demand of that particular product. Once the production is over, then it is required to create market linkage. It requires three factors. One, it includes various activities, such as looking for new markets. This may include identifying places where the price is relatively high. At these places, the demand of that product would be high, hence the necessary linkages may be created there. Two, it requires that the customers of the area are made aware of the offer made by the organisation. Quality, price, and availability may be highlighted in this process. This can be done through advertisements, events and sales promotions. Three, it requires the establishment of supply chain that includes activities like identifying retailers and distributors who can make the last mile delivery. In this regard, tie-ups with retail chains have been done by many organisations.

Case Study 4.1 Sitara Microfinance Ltd.

In a recent board meeting, the investors of Sitara Microfinance Limited (SIMIL) expressed their displeasure about the meagre return on equity. As SIMIL had to write-off a large amount of bad loans during 2011-13, it was obvious that the profit would be a bit low. However, by now it was ready to take off. Last year, the company appointed Ms. Sudha, an experienced professional in the financial services sector, as the new Managing Director (MD). She assured the board that she would be able to provide an average growth rate of 20 per cent in the next three years. But fast growth would also mean more funds. Equity funds were difficult to find given the small profit; however, investors were aware of the prospects. One investor had committed ₹500 million. A private bank had also agreed to sanction a loan of ₹2000 million at 10 per cent interest rate. Ms. Sudha also came to know from government sources that as a part of a central government scheme, she can apply for a low interest (3% p.a) loan of ₹1000 million on the condition that this would be lent only to women SHGs at a maximum interest rate of 12 per cent per annum.

SIMIL is a non-banking finance company engaged in microfinance for the last 10 years. At present, the MFI has about 500,000 clients and has an area of operations covering 25 districts of three states of Eastern India. SIMIL has done commendable progress since its inception; however, on the face of losses during the microfinance crisis, it had acquired a significant amount of bad loans. But it was one of the few companies that could offset the losses incurred during the crisis. Last year, it reported profit after tax of ₹200 million and had a gross loan portfolio of ₹5000 million. The following shows the summary of financial statements of 2014-15:

Products

At present, SIMIL offers only loan and insurance products. The loan products are for agriculture (25% of total outstanding), dairying (15%), small-business like vending and shops (30%), household durable assets like TV, refrigerator (20%), and for meeting medical emergencies (10%). Although there is a lot of demand for consumption loans, loans for purchase of non-commercial vehicles like bikes and scooters, SIMIL has shied away from such loans because of the risks associated with them. However, moneylenders and other MFIs find this as an opportunity. Other than the loans, the company has loan-linked life and livestock insurance products. SIMIL markets and distribute these products on behalf of LIC (Life Insurance Corporation of India) and a private general insurance company. For selling and distributing these insurance products, SIMIL receives 15 per cent of the first years' premium and 5 per cent of the renewal premiums in the subsequent years.

The organisation offers finance for various purposes, such as:

- Agriculture, dairying and small business loans: 21% interest rate
- Loans for medical emergencies: 18% interest rate
- Loans for durables: 24% interest rate

(reducing balance basis and annual rate of interest)

Past records show that these categories of loans have an NPA of three, two and five per cent, respectively. Consumption loans, if given with due diligence, also have an NPA of about one to two per cent, (the company used to provide consumption loans before the microfinance crisis). The company also charges a processing fee of one per cent of the loan amount.

Ms. Sudha, the MD of SIMIL, believed that another 15 neighbouring districts could easily be covered without much hassle. Recently, she commissioned a study to understand the situation in these prospective 15 districts and found the following:

- There are sufficient SHGs in the area that could be targeted for lending.
- However, about 60% of SHGs have been formed in the last two years as part of a government programme. All of these SHGs have only women members. However, to fulfil the target, the groups were formed hurriedly. Internal lending started in the third month of formation and bank loan was provided in sixth month. A grading exercise done by a bank found that half of the SHGs did not come up to mark but under the pressure of the government, these SHGs had to be funded.
- However, the NGOs and government agencies who formed these SHGs said that records were maintained properly. Bad loan was not yet observed in significant way (barring a few instances).

Other than the expansion in the area of operation, Ms. Sudha took ideas from various staff members and consulted the Chairman also. They suggested going for new products including weather insurance, gold loan and housing loan. "This is where the future lies", said a senior official.

Discussion Questions

1. Is the existing product mix enough to meet the customer needs? Do you think the suggestions related to going for weather insurance, gold loan and housing loans make sense? Critically examine the existing product portfolio, product features, and suggest a better alternative.
2. In a recent move, IRDA has suggested that the insurance companies cannot pay a commission exceeding 10 per cent of premium (for the first year) and 4% of the premium for renewals. How will it affect SIMIL?

Summary

- Microfinance includes both financial as well as non-financial services. Financial services include savings, credit, insurance, remittance, pension and leasing, while non-financial services include services like institution building, technical services and business development.
- Savings are lifeline of poor, which can help them in relieving the stresses of disaster, planning for large investments; however, poor have a low propensity to save.
- Credit services are the most widely used financial service in microfinance. There are various kinds of loans, income-generating activity loans, consumption loans, loans for improving quality of life, loans for life-cycle events and emergency loans.
- There are three models of microinsurance, partner-agent, master policy and mutual benefit model. Microinsurance services are generally attached with business and other loans. However, in itself, insurance services are important for poor. IRDA has mandated the insurance companies for covering the social sectors.
- Micropension has been a new entrant to the product portfolio of the MFIs. However, it has a great potential simply because of the volume. Though, it needs skilled investment hands to manage pension funds.
- Remittance has been a basic service of microfinance sector. It can help expand the business of the MFIs.
- Microleasing has an unrealised potential in microfinance. There have been some experience in Bangladesh, Bolivia and Tanzania.
- Non-financial services are compliment the provision of financial services. These services, i.e. institution building, technical support and business development help in sustaining the financial services.

Exercises

A. Multiple-choice Questions

1. VimoSEWA is involved in
   (a) Microsavings
   (b) Microinsurance
   (c) Micropension
   (d) All of the above
2. Which of the following schemes helps in opening of bank accounts?
   (a) Pradhan Mantri Jan Dhan Yojana
   (b) Pradhan Mantri Suraksha Bima Yojana
   (c) Pradhan Mantri Jeevan Jyoti Bima Yojana
   (d) Atal Pension Yojana
3. Insurance is primarily a risk ________ mechanism.
   (a) Avoiding
   (b) Retaining
   (c) Transferring
   (d) All of the above
4. Which of the following products requires continuous periodic saving for a long term?

(a) Microsavings
(b) Microinsurance
(c) Remittance
(d) Micropension

5. Which of the following countries receives the highest remittance?
   (a) India
   (b) China
   (c) Indonesia
   (d) None of the above
6. Remittance can help in
   (a) Improving product diversity of MFIs
   (b) Adding new customers
   (c) Both (a) and (b)
   (d) None of the above
7. The different types of institutions promoted as part of microfinance include
   (a) SHGs and SHG federations
   (b) Cooperatives for aggregation of produces
   (c) Marketing federations
   (d) All of the above
8. Suppose an MFI provides training on honey processing to a group of clients who have taken loans. This would be in the nature of the service called
   (a) Institution building
   (b) Technical service
   (c) Business development service
   (d) None of the above
9. IRDA defines microinsurance as an insurance policy having a sum assured of ₹ _____ or less than that.
   (a) 10,000 (b) 25,000
   (c) 50,000 (d) 100,000
10. Microleasing can help in
   (a) Leveraging the small amount of capital available
   (b) Avoiding the need of huge collateral
   (c) Use of an expensive asset without having huge liability
   (d) All of the above

B. Review Questions

1. What are the different needs that can be fulfiled through microfinance products?
2. What are the four schemes floated by the Government of India for low-income groups. Do you think they help in ensuring financial inclusion?
3. How are the different kinds of microinsurance useful for MFIs/SHPIs?
4. 'Remittance is no more an appropriate product for the MFIs in the face of schemes like Pradhan Mantri Jan Dhan Yojana'. Comment.
5. 'When poor are striving to manage two square meals a day, it is foolish to design pension products'. Comment.
6. What is the relevance of standardised products in microfinance?
7. 'Standardised products are better than customised products'. Comment.
8. Remittance services have multiple effects. Justify the statement.
9. How is micro insurance different from regular insurance services?

C. Application-based Questions

1. You are working in an MFI. You want to launch some new savings products. How can you go for it?
2. An MFI offers products, such as agricultural loans, loans for household durables and loans on emergency requirements. Do you think the MFI has sufficient products to offer? Justify your statement.
3. You have joined an NGO which has an SHG programme. The Director asked you to suggest a set of various products which can be offered to the SHG members. Develop a portfolio of products based on the needs of the members.

Further Readings

- Ledgerwood's edited volume *The New Microfinance Handbook* has several chapters that would be useful for enhancing the understanding on the issues of microfinance products and services. The part three of this book (Chapter 8 to 13) describes various issues like savings, credit, agricultural finance, insurance, payment services and others.

- Ingrid Matthaus-Maier and J. D. Von Pischke's edited volume *New Partnerships for Innovation in Microfinance* has two chapters (Chapter 7 and 8) on remittance, two chapters on micropensions (Chapters 14 and 15) and a chapter on microinsurance (Chapter 16). These are useful readings for understanding the issues in greater depth.
- Two chapters from the book *Whose Sustainability Counts?* by Harper, Iyer and Rosser, detail out the integrated approach of microfinance that goes beyond the issues providing credit only approach. This provides a detailed understanding of how livelihoods approach is more important than the credit-only approach.
- *The Synergy of Microfinance* by Binod B. Nayak provides a detailed account of products in microfinance, in particular the issue of microleasing is provided. This is a recent addition to a critical appreciation of various products in microfinance.

CHAPTER

5

Delivery of Products and Services

Chapter Outline

Learning Objectives

After reading this chapter, you will be able to:

- discuss the elements of credit cycle.
- map the process of service delivery in microfinance.
- see what kind of structure is required for delivery of services.

Chapter 4 (the previous chapter) included discussions on various products and services in the context of microfinance. The most important part of these products and services lies in the delivery. Unless, the product or service is delivered effectively to the client, the task remains incomplete. This chapter discusses the process of delivery of various products and services.

5.1 Credit Process

Financial services are highly process-oriented; hence it is required that each of the steps of the credit process is followed meticulously. Before discussion of steps of credit delivery, it is important to know the principles of credit.

5.1.1 Five Cs of Credit

The popularly known five Cs of credit are character, capacity, capital, collateral and conditions. On a whole, these provide a conceptual guideline for making credit-related decisions. The first C, *character*, refers to the credit history of the borrower. This can be obtained from the information provided by credit bureau. The idea is to understand the repayment habits of the concerned person. The second C, *capacity*, is about the repayment capacity which can be understood from the existing and projected income and the expected repayment as a proportion of the income. Generally, it is seen that the debt repayment should not be more than one-third of the income. The third C, *capital*, is related to the equity contribution by the borrower. This is held as a security against moral hazard, as by not managing the enterprise, the borrower would also lose a substantial amount. In consumption or durables loan, this component is compensated by asking for a down payment. The fourth C, *collateral*, is used for securing the loan. The fifth C, *conditions*, is nothing but the terms of borrowing, such as interest rate, specification of purpose of loan, and other terms and conditions that allow the lender to monitor the effectiveness of utilisation of the loan (Kagan, 2019).

5.1.2 Credit Bureau

Credit bureaus play an important role in the financing ecosystem. When microfinance started decades ago, there was extensive financial exclusion, and people did not have recorded credit history. In the absence of such credit history, it was extremely difficulty to assess the creditworthiness of people. However, with the increasing coverage of bank accounts and use of online payment systems, more data is available now. Credit bureaus use this data to develop a credit score which becomes one of the important bases of credit appraisal. There are four credit bureaus in India, viz. Transunion CIBIL, Equifax, Experian, and CRIF High Mark. Credit bureaus are regulated by RBI.

Credit bureaus collect information on credit history, repayment behaviour, and borrowing patterns. Based on this information, they provide a score which ranges from 300 to 900, and ordinarily a score of 750 is treated as a good credit score (Kaur, 2024).

5.1.3 Credit in Microfinance

Credit process in microfinance is slightly different from that of standard bank credits because of one major problem that one of the five Cs, that is collateral, cannot be obtained here. At least 75 per cent of a Microfinance Institution's (MFI's) loan has to be in the nature of 'qualifying assets' which means that it must be without collateral. This affects the credit related decision significantly. Another problem that MFIs face is that unlike a bank they do not have the record of past banking habits of the person. Banks, having the deposit facility, are in a better position than the MFIs, as they already have some idea about their clients. Of course, if the MFIs lend to self-help group (SHG), they can use its records, but for Joint Liability Group (JLG) or individual lending, there is hardly any record for reference, other than the record of credit bureau. This makes the appraisal process of microfinance loan characteristically different from bank loans.

Some basic principles of microfinance credit processes are as follows:

- It is the household rather than the enterprise, for which the finance is being done. Unlike what the standard accounting principle says, it is very difficult to separate the enterprise from the owner in the context of poor. First, it is not easy to check whether the loan has been utilised for any specific purpose. If it is for consumption purpose, then there is no other way than to look at the household repayment capacity. In group loans, it is only taken by the face value of the borrower and for all practical purposes, it becomes a consumption loan. Second, if the loan is taken for the purpose of enterprise and there is hard evidence towards that, it is the household members who contribute the labour component. In such micro enterprises, the owner, who also carries out substantial tasks of the enterprise, does not actually charge for the family labour contributed. The net cash flow (income minus cost) does not include the labour payment, unless such labour is hired from outside, which is unlikely. Thus, the net cash flow does not exactly indicate the net income from the enterprise. Family labour also has to be accounted for. If the EMI/repayment is fixed without taking this into consideration, the family may starve.
- Repayment terms depend on the cash flow. Banks generally expect repayment in terms of EMIs, which means repayment would be received on monthly basis. But in MFIs, this may not hold. Majority of the MFI borrowers do not get a monthly salary. Their cash flows come on a daily or weekly basis. A rickshaw puller, betel shop owner, or a vegetable vendor earns his/her income every day. Asking for a monthly repayment may not be suitable here.

5.1.4 Credit Cycle

Credit cycle includes several steps starting with identification of customer to the closure of loan and feedback. Figure 5.1 provides an indicative diagram of the credit process.

It can be observed that the process does not start with loan application, which generally happens in the case of bank loans, rather it starts with the identification of customers. Microfinance has so far been a push market, where the loan process has been initiated by the lender rather than the borrowers. In this stage, which

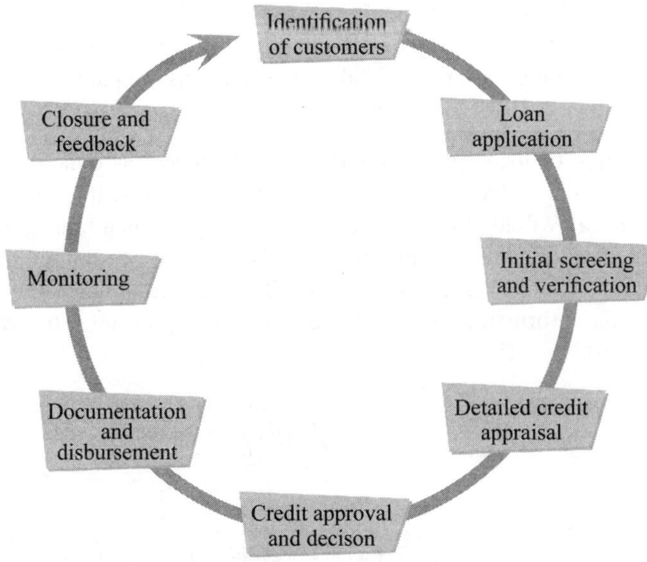

Fig. 5.1 Credit Cycle

Note: Adapted from FAO/FFM (2009) and George, Venkata. and Mugwang'a (2010).

generally includes visit to SHGs/locality, communication about the loan products and also taking a note of the general loan requirements of the customers as a whole is included. The objective of these contacts is to generate an interest in the potential borrowers. It may also be noted that the community may have some doubts and apprehensions because of the past experience like frauds, somebody running away with money, or similar problems. Here it is also required that the MFI/SHPI (Self Help Group Promoting Institution) makes an effort to build rapport with people. Conservative MFIs go one step further here. BASIX used to have an area appraisal before starting operations in any locality. The idea was to understand the financial needs of people, availability of credit institutions in the area (such as banks, cooperatives, etc.) as well as getting acquainted with the repayment habits of people. It may be noted here that the past banking habit does not necessarily mean it would continue for the MFI. Some people might have defaulted a repayment to a public sector bank. Such default often takes place with the expectation that government would write off the loans. One has to be careful in interpreting such information.

When people show their interest, the next stage is to seek loan application from the client. In this stage, the individual/SHG/JLG members makes a formal request to the MFI/SHPI that a loan is required. This application format is standard and provided by the concerned lender.

Upon receipt of the application, the lending agency screens the application and checks the basic eligibility of the applicant for providing a loan. This may include checking KYC documents, credit bureau score and the fitment of the loan sought with the products available with the organisation.

Once this stage is completed, a thorough credit appraisal is undertaken. This involves field visit, interaction with the customer, neighbours, other group members if he/she is a part of any group, and detailed assessment is undertaken regarding the need of the loan and repayment capability. Upon receipt of a favourable report, loan is sanctioned. Generally, loan sanction is undertaken by a credit committee involving the Credit Officer, Branch Manager and the field officials, where final decision related to size and repayment terms are also approved. Ideally, the person who has apprised the loan should not be a part of the approval process. Sometimes, such approval may require special sanction from regional or head office.

Upon the decision of credit approval, detailed documentation is carried out which requires signing on the loan agreement, signature of guaranteer if required and hypothecations. When these formalities are completed, the loan is disbursed.

After disbursal, the loan officers keep on monitoring the utilisation of loans and assure that the instalments are repaid timely. If there has been any delay or default, they follow up the reasons and if required, decisions related to restructuring and write-off are made. If all the instalments are paid, the loan is closed and with the feedback of customer, another cycle of loan starts.

Illustration An illustration of loan appraisal and approval process as done in Annapurna Microfinance Private Ltd is given in Figure 5.2. The whole process includes 10 steps. It starts with the recommendation by group members, appraisal by field officer; if found satisfactory, Branch Manager undertakes group rating and credit bureau check. Then the credit committee and risk team at head office look into it, if they find it viable, it is forwarded to the Chief Financial Officer (CFO), who further checks it and approves it. If at any stage it is not approved, the information is communicated to the applicant. The whole process takes about five to six days (AMPL, 2013).

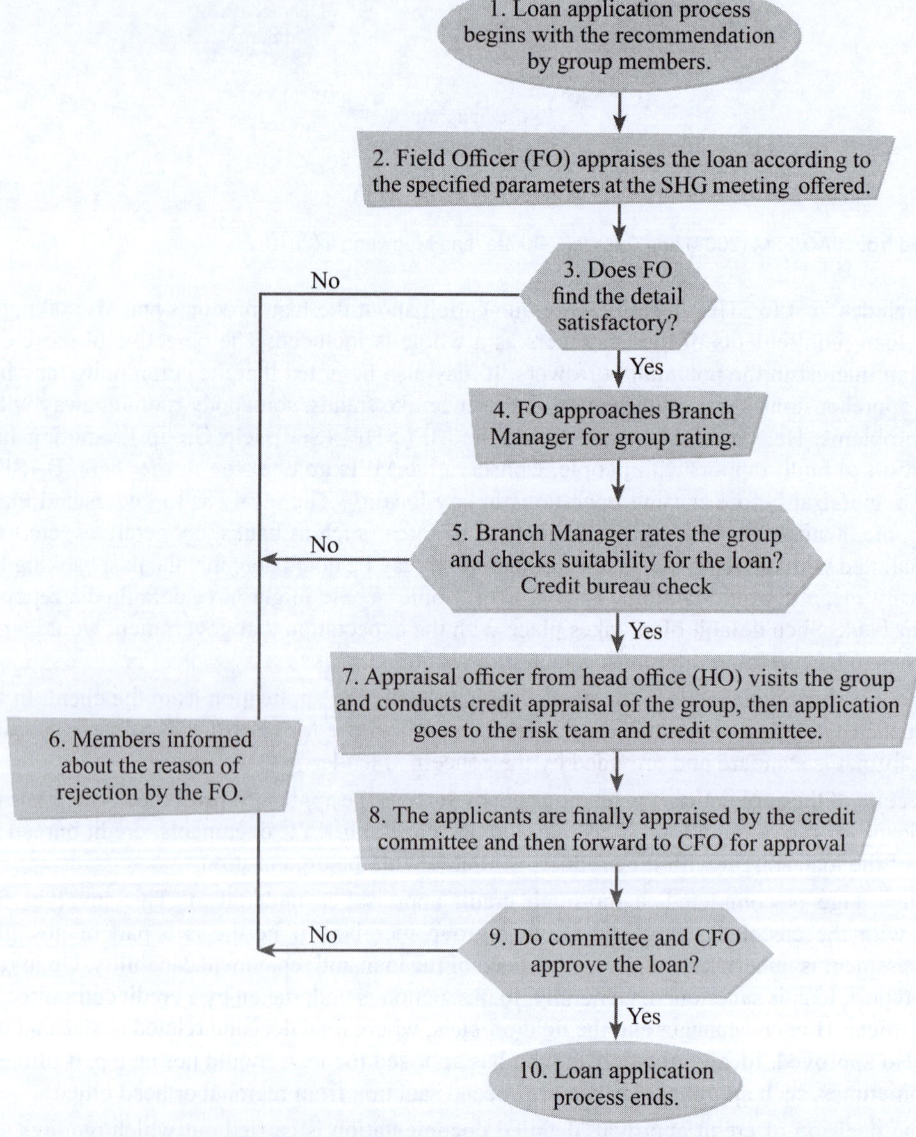

Fig 5.2 Process of Loan Appraisal and Approval (adapted from operational manual of Annapurna Finance Pvt Ltd (AMPL, 2013)

With the digital finance being used extensively and online payment system is followed, here is a typical process of how loan process goes through digitally.

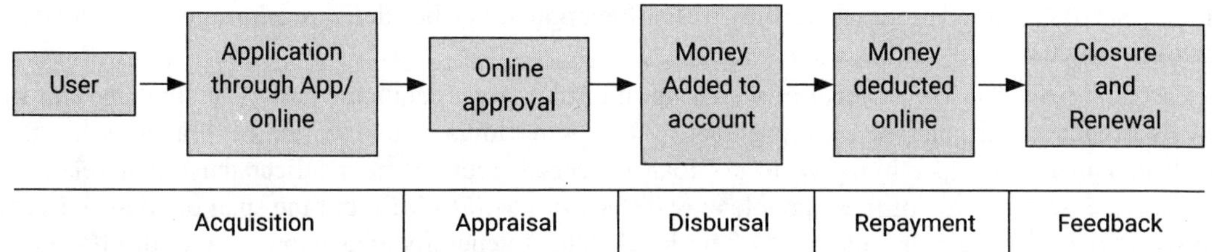

Fig. 5.3 Process of loan using online system and apps

5.1.5 Business Correspondence (BC)

Financial inclusion remains a critical goal in India, aiming to provide accessible and affordable financial services to the unbanked and underbanked populations. The Business Correspondent (BC) model, introduced by the Reserve Bank of India (RBI) in 2006, has been instrumental in extending banking services to remote and rural areas where traditional banking infrastructure is lacking.

Business Correspondents act as intermediaries between banks and customers, delivering a range of financial services at the grassroots level. Their key functions include:

1. *Account Opening and Maintenance* BCs facilitate the opening of bank accounts by assisting customers with documentation and KYC compliance, thereby simplifying the onboarding process.
2. *Cash Transactions* They enable customers to deposit and withdraw cash, thus providing essential banking services without the need to visit a bank branch.
3. *Loan Disbursement and Recovery* BCs assist in the disbursement of microloans and collect repayments, ensuring timely credit delivery and recovery.
4. *Financial Literacy and Advisory Services* They educate customers on financial products, savings, credit management, and insurance, promoting informed financial decisions.
5. *Technology Integration* Utilising devices like micro-ATMs and mobile phones, BCs conduct transactions securely and efficiently, even in areas with limited connectivity.

The advantages of the BC model are that of enhanced accessibility, cost-effectiveness, and customised services. BCs provide banking services at the doorstep of customers in remote areas, thus preventing costs and time loss. People often have to forego their day's wage labour in order to go to bank. Because of the BCs, the banking services becomes handy. From the point of view of banks, BCs are low-cost, and particularly in low density regions, it would not be viable to establish a branch. Employing BCs is more economical than running a branch. Finally, the BCs are part of the locality, and they know the people. They trust the person, and the BC also understand the local needs. This results in customised products and services, that enhances the customer satisfaction.

Despite their pivotal role, BCs encounter several challenges. First, the operational sustainability: as transaction volumes are low in sparsely populated area, the viability of BC is always a question. Second, the banking systems and regulations keep on changing continuously, this requires the BCs to be trained continuously and be updated about financial products and BC operations. Third, technological barrier and connectivity issues in remote areas can hinder in the BC's service delivery. Finally, adherence to everchanging banking regulations and maintaining data security are ongoing concerns.

The Business Correspondent model has significantly contributed to advancing financial inclusion in India by delivering microfinance services to underserved populations. By addressing operational challenges and enhancing support mechanisms, the effectiveness of BCs can be further improved, ensuring sustainable and inclusive financial growth.

5.2 Delivery Systems and Structure

Delivery of financial services is not just about products, but also about people, systems and organisation structure. A set of very good products can only realise their potential when delivered through the organisational systems and structure.

Let us start from the lowest level at which the microfinance operations start. The smallest unit of an MFI is its branch which may be covering about 20-25 Km radius at its location. A branch is headed by a branch manager and under him five to six loan officers/executives/field officers/customer relationship officers operate. Designation of these people may differ from MFI to MFI, but the span of control is around five to six. If the MFI has more number of field level staff, it generally adds another layer of officers, such as assistant branch manager or similar kind of designation. Branches of MFIs are the foundation stone of their businesses. These are profit centres and invariably contribute to the business of the organisation. A branch manager is responsible for the appraisal and delivery of all the products of the MFI. Loan officers/ field officers are responsible for making contacts with customers, making documentation and act as a liaison between branch and the customers. There may also be support staff like an accountant and/or an assistant. Generally, the branch manager and the support staff have to be in office, while the field officers or loan officers are in the field, unless they have a meeting to attend in the branch.

These branch managers report to an officer who is generally called area manager or some other designation. The responsibility of such a manager is to check weather the branches are being run properly or not. The area manager reports to a regional office, or state level office which is headed by a senior manager of the company (generally known as associate vice president or regional manager or zonal manager) who in turn reports to the head office.

Generally, the head office is staffed by various departments like operations, finance, marketing, human resources and MIS, each of which is headed by a very senior manager generally known as chief operating officer/ chief finance officer/ or may be something like general manager or vice president. These functional heads report to the managing director who runs the company on behalf of the Board of Directors. In larger companies, by statutory mandate, there have to be positions like company secretaries. Typically, the organisation structure of a mid-sized MFI is shown in Figure 5.4.

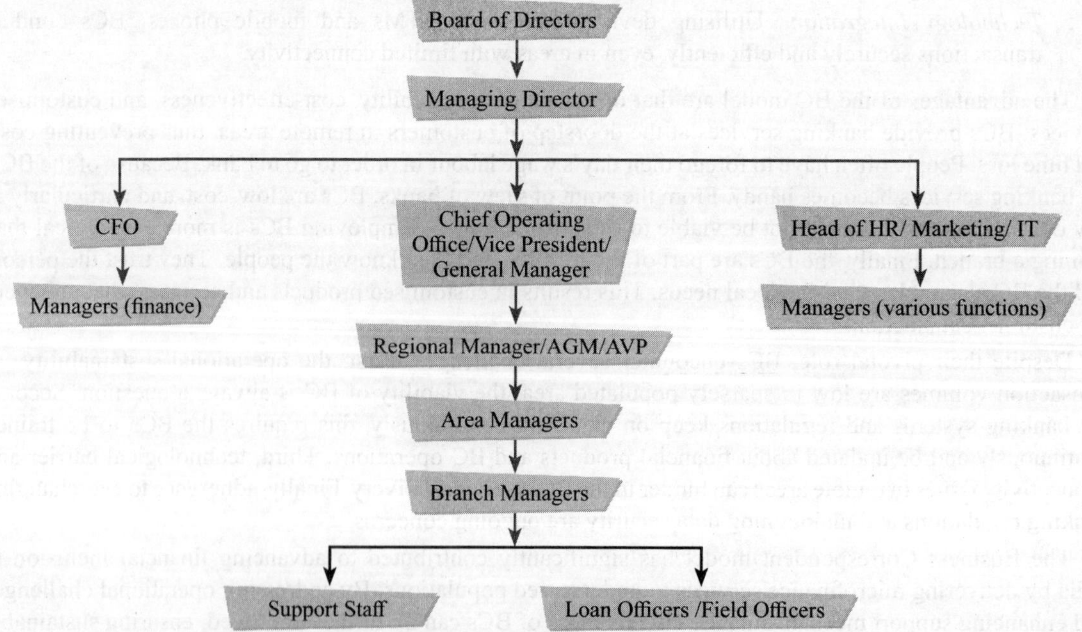

Fig. 5.4 Structure of MFI

In real life, many MFIs works as a part of holding companies, hence they may have a more complicated corporate office.

In the context of an SFB, the structure is slightly different. While the overall structure would be similar, they have to deal with the deposit function also. As a bank branch, it must have a counter through which it can deal with the customer. There are dedicated employees (Teller) for this purpose. The organisation structure of a typical SFB would be as shown in Figure 5.5.

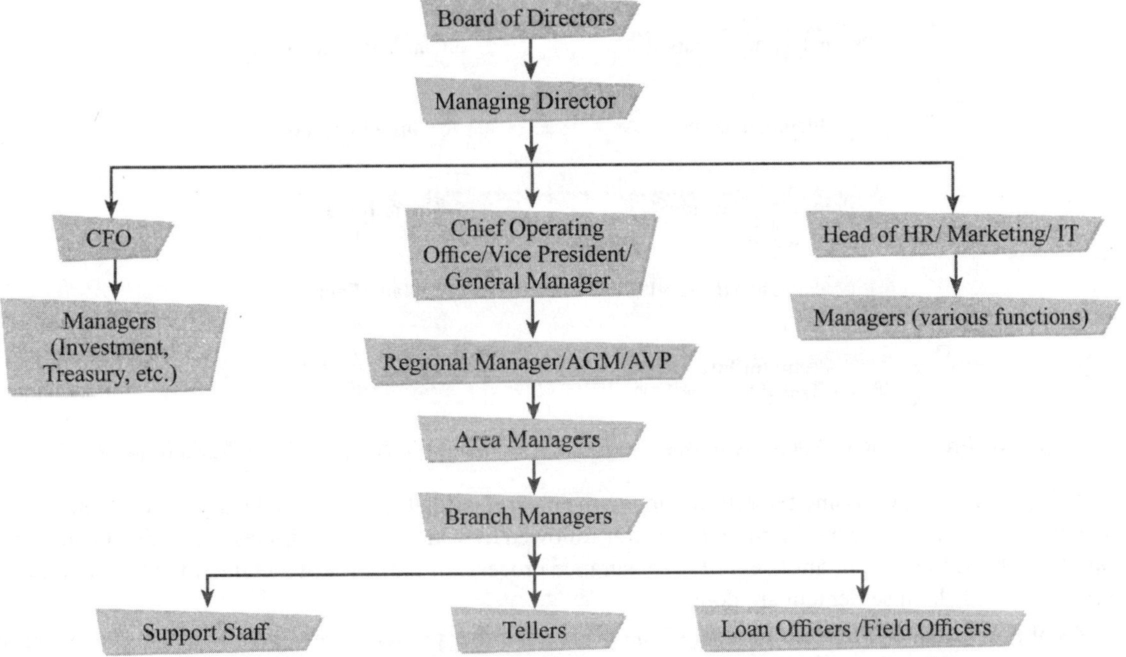

Fig. 5.5 Structure of an SFB

5.3 Redressal of Customers' Grievances

Customers' grievance redressal is an important function of MFIs. This has been insisted again and again, particularly since the onset of the Andhra Pradesh (AP) crisis. While the customer can walk into a branch and file a complaint; with increasing scale, this kind of mechanism does not work. Some MFIs have used advanced technology in this regard. A case in point is that of Annapurana Finance as given in Box 5.1.

Box 5.1 Customer Grievance Redressal in Annapurna Finance

Annapurna Finance Pvt Ltd has a Grievance and Customer Feedback Cell, which has implemented an interactive voice recording system (IVRS) for dealing with customer complaint and feedback. A team of technically qualified people are hired to handle this. Executives also routinely call customers to find if they have any grievances. Based on these inputs, actions are taken to resolve the problem (AMPL, 2017:41).

Customers can make a call to a toll-free number which is forwarded to the grievance cell. The team handling the cell attends the call. Grievances are recorded and classified based on various parameters, such as query, service request and complaint. This is forwarded to the concerned department; which must report in 24 hours on the status of whether the matter was resolved or not. It is also conveyed to customer on the same day. The status of the complaint (open or closed) is updated. Open cases are regularly monitored; in case they are not resolved in 15 days, the matter is escalated to the Grievance Redressal Officer (GRO). In case it is still not resolved in another 15 days, the matter goes to the General Manager, Department of Non-Banking Supervision, RBI for a final decision (AMPL, 2017: 42)

5.4 Delivery of Insurance Products

The delivery of insurance is a relatively simple process because the MFI does not make the product, rather only markets and distributes it. The first step is contact with customers, in which the field officers communicate about the need of the product and product's features. If the customer agrees to buy the product, then detailed risk assessment and documents are processed followed by which the premium is collected and records are maintained at MFI level.

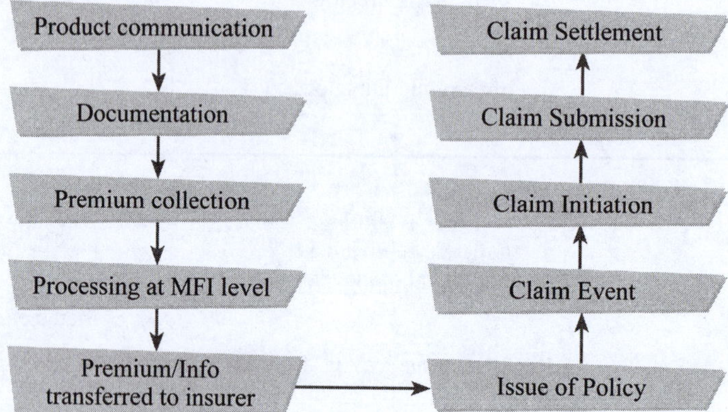

Fig. 5.6 Processing of Microinsurance Product through an MFI (Adapted from World Bank, 2005)

This is followed by passing the information to the insurer, as that is the original party insuring the client. Then the MFI transfers the premium to the insurer followed by which the latter issues policy document. This completes the second important event of the insurance process. In the event of a claim, the claim initiation, verification and claim settlement are done.

As of now, credit is the main product of the MFIs. All other products are generally bundled with credit products or are of limited scale.

Case Study 5.1 The Operations Manual

You have recently joined as a Manager in an MFI that provides loans and insurance related services to the low-income groups in rural areas. The organisation has recruited you primarily because you have long experience in running microfinance operations in reputed organisations. Upon joining the place, you met Mr. Narayan, Managing Director of the company, who told you that the company has 250 employees and 90 per cent of them are loan officers. As of now, they have a loan portfolio of ₹800 million and they have a plan to expand the operations fast. They have secured funding of another ₹500 million and expect that another ₹700 million in near future. However, the investors had some concerns about the processes, which had to be addressed if the funding was to materialise. Mr. Narayan suggested that for the first seven days, you understand the existing processes. Based on the suggestions, you investigated the processes at the head office and visited 10 branches selected randomly. The following were your observations:

- The organisation provides credit through the JLG-based system.
- Loan processes starts when the borrower expresses interest to take a loan from the company. The loan officer gets the application forms filled and submits the same to the concerned branch. The branch manager screens the application and checks the KYC, income level, occupation and credit history, if any. If found in proper order, all such applications are compiled and sent to the head office on the first working day of the next week, when the branch manager visits for a weekly meeting. At the head office, a committee, including the credit manager, branch manager, and the director, goes through the applications and approves the loan. Rejection of loan applications is usually not done, unless the applicant is a defaulter.

- Disbursement is done in cash to the concerned applicant. If the amount is more than ₹15,000, then payment is done by cheque. Instalment is received in cash. Incentives for the loan officer are based on the disbursal and repayment rate, and is paid at the end of the financial year.
- It has been observed that attrition of employees is highest in the month of May, after the annual incentives are released.
- Instances of theft are rare. This is because disbursal is done once every month, and on the day of disbursal, an armed security officer accompanies the loan officer and they travel by a four-wheeler. Instalments are also collected on the same day. Cash collected through repayment is added to the pool of funds to be disbursed to the approved loan accounts. Any surplus is carried back and deposited in bank (in the account of the organisation).
- In case there is a delay in payment for more than 30 days, branch manager and loan officer visit the customer. If the cause of default is genuine, then the loan repayment is rescheduled. Branch manger can approve a rescheduling of three months. If it is more than that, the case is forwarded to head office.
- There have been some instances of frauds recently. Some borrowers (five members of a JLG) took a loan of ₹5 lakh and disappeared. People say that they have migrated to a distant city for starting a business. Their phone details are not working. Their family members say they have no idea of where they are. Rumours have spread that one of them is in contact with the villagers and promised that they would repay the loan shortly as they expect a huge gain in their business. The concerned loan officer, who is from the neighbouring village, said that they had repaid the previous loan (₹10,000 each) regularly. He had no idea about their intentions. He said he made a mistake by recommending their loan, but he did it in good faith. He was unhappy that his incentive would be affected this year.
- Mr. Narayan heard these points next week. He said that the processes are heavily based on personal knowledge. This must be improved. 'Now that the scale of operations is about to grow, we must institutionalise the processes', he said. He expects you to prepare a manual of operations calibrated to the need of the locality.

Discussion Questions

1. What are the loopholes in the delivery process of the organisation?
2. What changes would you suggest in the process?
3. What additions are required in the operational mechanism?
4. How would you ensure that the new mechanism is implemented successfully?

Summary

- The five Cs of credit include character, capacity, capital, collateral and conditions.
- Rather than the cashflow from the enterprise, the cash flow from the household matters in microfinance.
- Repayment depends on the cash-flow; the repayment frequency should be decided accordingly.
- The credit cycle has various steps, such as identification of customers, loan application, initial screening, detailed loan appraisal, credit approval decisions, loan disbursal, monitoring and closure.
- Product delivery is undertaken by loan officers/field officers at the field level. The basic unit of the MFI is its branch which includes five to six such field officers and is headed by a branch manager.
- SFBs have an added vertical of bank teller that deals with the liabilities side (savings).
- Insurance services are delivered by the MFI functionaries at the field level on behalf of the insurer.

Exercises

A. Multiple-choice Questions

1. Which of the following 5 Cs of credit does not always apply to microfinance?
   (a) Character (b) Capital
   (c) Collateral (d) Conditions
2. Which of the following functions are not required for MFIs?
   (a) Loan officer
   (b) Teller
   (c) Branch manager
   (d) None of the above
3. Generally, a branch covers an area having radius of
   (a) 5-6 Km (b) 10-20 Km
   (c) 20-25 Km (d) 50-100 Km
4. Which of the following activities is not required in the credit delivery process?
   (a) Collection of application
   (b) Payment of premium
   (c) Field visit
   (d) Disbursal
5. Which of the following is TRUE for credit decisions?
   (a) Loan officer should decide whether the applicant should get loans or not.
   (b) Branch manager should decide whether the applicant should get loans or not.
   (c) Head office/Regional office should decide whether the applicant should get loans or not
   (d) The person carrying out appraisal should not be involved in decision making on whether the applicant should get loans or not.
6. Who has the ultimate responsibility of appraisal of the financial products of an MFI?
   (a) Branch manager
   (b) Loan officer
   (c) Teller
   (d) None of the above
7. Which of the following is not true with regard to customer grievance redressal?
   (a) Customer grievance should be recorded and forwarded to the concerned department
   (b) It should be resolved within 15 days, or it is forwarded to the GRO
   (c) If still not resolved in another 15 days, it is forwarded to RBI for final decision
   (d) None of the above
8. Which of the following activity is undertaken to check if the repayment is made in time?
   (a) Loan appraisal
   (b) Loan approval
   (c) Monitoring of loan
   (d) Closure of loan
9. During loan appraisal process, which of the following activity is not required?
   (a) Signing of loan agreement
   (b) Field visit
   (c) Understanding the cash flow of the applicant
   (d) Credit bureau information check
10. The role of loan officer/field officer is to
    (a) Act as liaison between branch and customer
    (b) Identification of customers and their needs
    (c) Documentation
    (d) All of the above

B. Review Questions

1. What are the important principles of lending in microfinance sector?
2. What are the differences between the processes followed for group lending and individual lending?
3. Who are the different actors associated with the loan approval process? Discuss their roles and responsibility? Who plays the most important role in this process?
4. Describe the delivery structure of the MFIs and SFBs.
5. How is the loan process different from the insurance delivery processes?

C. Application-based Questions

1. A loan officer reported that a group of gypsies, who are camping in his area of operations, are asking for loan of ₹200,000 for 15 days. They have some medical emergency to meet and they require money within three days. They say that they can provide enough gold as collateral. They have no problem with whatever interest rate charged. So far you have lent only to the SHGs (unsecured loans) in the area to an extent of ₹50,000 per SHG. What would you do?

2. While screening a loan application you found that the copy of Aadhar provided as KYC belongs to the applicant's husband. The purpose of the loan is to purchase fertiliser which is required quickly. Upon inquiry, you found that the applicant thought that the land title is with her husband, so she provided that Aadhar. The loan officer said it was an oversight. Assuming everything else is in place, should this loan be approved?

Further Readings

- Samar K. Datta's book, chapter on 'Systems and Processes of Credit Operations: The Case of BASIX' in the report Cases in Microfinance by Shylendra, Sen, and Panda, is a conversational account of discussions between the author and the officials of BASIX. This provides the nuances of how loan process is followed in the organisation.
- The National Federation for State Cooperative Banks, Navi Mumbai has published four-volume long operational manuals for Cooperative Banks covering the following topics:
  - **Volume I** Branches and Banking Operations
  - **Volume II** Functions of Head Office
  - **Volume III** Loans and Advances
  - **Volume IV** Inspection and Internal Audit

These manuals together comprise more than 2000 pages, which provide details of banking operations. Those interested in understanding the financing operations may go through it. For those interested in loans and advances, which is particularly useful for MFIs, volume III is a useful resource.

CHAPTER

6

Product Development in Microfinance

Chapter Outline

Learning Objectives

After reading this chapter, you will be able to:

- provide an understanding of the need of product development in microfinance.
- discuss the process of product development microfinance sector.
- provide an idea of various dimensions that one needs to consider when designing a loan product.

It is a fact in all businesses that products are formulated, launched, sold and finally withdrawn. The concept of product life cycle has been explained by Levitt (1965). He classified the life of a product into four stages, market development, market growth, market maturity and market decline. It means that any product that is launched is going to decline some day and someday, it would be withdrawn from the market. In this context, financial service organisations must recognise for product development and they must continuously innovate to meet customer needs.

Product development in financial services is a time-taking task. One problem with financial service-related products is that they do not have any unique characteristics and they can be copied easily. According to Cooper et al. (1994), product development in service sectors is influenced by several factors including the advantages of the products, such as its unique benefits, marketing support for the product at the stage of launching, nature of the marketplace including growth, customer loyalty, and competition, corporate environment and the nature of the process.

This chapter involves discussion on the product development process and illustrates some of the products that had been discussed in the Chapter 4.

6.1 Product Development Process

The process of product development goes through several steps. Figure 6.1. provides an illustrative diagram that depicts the various stages of product development. Description of each of these stages is given here.

6.1.1 Understanding Customer Needs

Earlier, in Chapter 4, discussion about various kinds of customer needs has been done. The Microfinance Institution (MFI)/Self Help Group Promoting Institution (SHPI) must understand the need of the customers in the specific locality. Given that microfinance business generally looks for standardised products, it is important that the common needs of people, of course without losing the sight of specific individual needs,

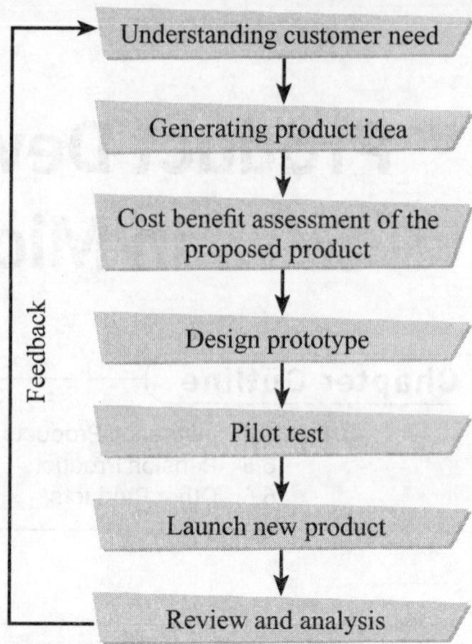

Fig. 6.1 Product Development Process (adapted from Cooper 1994, Edgett, 1996, IIBF, 2009).

should be looked into. In agriculture dependent area, the farmer would often need working capital loans during the beginning of the season. Once in a while, some of them may need financing for purchase of equipment and implements too. People who are involved in food processing (such as making pickle) would need substantial amount of working capital loan during the production season. Similarly, the repayment terms have also to be determined depending on the convenience of the customers. A housemaid receiving monthly payments would be happy to pay EMIs while a vegetable vendor would rather like to make daily or weekly payments.

To understand the customer needs, a few questions can be asked like What is the purpose of taking the loan? When does the customer need the loan? How much money is needed for the loan? Is it going to be a secured loan? Timing of delivery of loan is an important component, which many times the service provider forgets. In such a situation, the customer moves to another source of credit, and the MFI/SHPI loses a business opportunity. Moreover, the customer may end up paying a higher interest rate (see Box 6.1).

Box 6.1 Why Do They Pay Higher Interest?

In some parts of Alwar district, Rajasthan, which is populated substantially by Meo Muslim community, there is a great demand for goats during the bakr-id celebration. Such is the demand that a fully-grown goat can be sold at around `50,000 to `60,000 easily. The SHGs of the area have found a business opportunity in this market, and they purchase kids at an early stage and the rear them until they become marketable. They would require credit at the time of purchase of the kids. Any delay would result in two things, amount of initial investment would go up thus decreasing the expected return, and they may not get the quality of kid they want. When these SHGs approached the banks, the latter often took months together for processing such loans. MFIs provided loans in time, but they charged a higher interest rate. This was acceptable to the SHG members, who would otherwise take loans from the moneylenders at a much higher interest rate. According to the SHG members, the return from the investment is higher than the cost of the interest.

6.1.2 Generating Product Ideas

New product ideas are the basis of all products. Ideas should be brainstormed, discussed, and criticised in order to make them realise their potential. They are fundamental to the process of innovation and it is desired that no idea should be killed at the early stage. It is often seen that very innovative ideas often come from unexpected corners. In the organisations in which senior management do not encourage their people to come up with ideas, innovations take a backseat. This hampers the growth of the organisation and it ends up in stagnation and decline. A new idea can range from any point to any point, there is no limit to it. One may think of offering the products in a distant market, another may think of offering a completely new product which has no relation with the existing business, another may consider developing a product for a completely new segment of customers. Purpose of the loan is one of the important points on which ideas are generated.

6.1.3 Cost Benefit Assessment

Developing and launching a new product has its own costs and benefits. Not every product idea makes into the market. Not every product that makes into the market succeeds. The success rate is very low. Hence, before the product is developed, meticulous analysis of its costs and benefits is required. A typical cost of product development would include various cost items like market survey for need assessment, idea generation workshop, developing prototype, test marketing, product refinement, advertisement, and product launching event. These would need direct costs, such as cost of material, cost of survey, advertisement, cost of launching event, and indirect costs, such as time of employees and other experts spending for this purpose. A typical cost benefit format is given in Table 6.1.

Table 6.1 Cost Benefit Analysis of Product Development

Costs	Benefits
Brainstorming workshop	No. of units sold
Market survey	Price per unit
Cost of material used, if any	Amount realised
Test marketing	
Product refinement	
Launching event	
Advertisement	
Review workshop	
MIS modification cost to match the product needs	
Indirect costs (no. of person days)	
Total costs:	**Total benefits:**

A manager opts for product development if the expected benefits are higher than the expected costs. However, such decisions are never easy. Product development costs are sunk costs for the organisation; if the product fails, there is no way to recover the money. A manager can calculate the probability of success of such product development and accordingly make the decision. In any case, product development is a risky process and there is more chance of failure than success. However, the one that succeeds covers all the sunk costs. While the manager has to be aware of such issues, he/she must promote products which seem to have potential.

New products would also require arrangement of funding and board's approval (IIBF, 2009). Products also have to be developed within the mandate of long-term vision and mission of the organisation (Kapoor and Sinha, 2013)

6.1.4 Design Prototype

In the context of credit services, the prototype design would require various decisions, such as purpose of loan, amount of loan (range), tenure of repayment, frequency of repayment, interest rate and type, moratorium, and conditions attached with it. For savings product, the purpose, amount, tenure and interest rate are required. For insurance, the conditions and price are most important part, while for remittance, the place, price and speed of delivery matters.

6.1.5 Pilot Test/Test Marketing

In this stage, the prototype is offered to a limited number of customers. Their responses are recorded and necessary changes are made to the product. A refined product goes for the final launch.

6.1.6 Launch New Product

Product launching can be done through an event, or it can simply start on a particular day like a routine programme. Adequate advertisement or other forms of communications must be undertaken before and after the product launching. The launch of a new product requires the whole organisation to be synchronised to the product features. The MIS of the organisation must accommodate the new product features, otherwise there would be massive failure. This would need recalibration of the data collection formats; if they are online, it is required that the software or app is modified. The frontline functionaries (field/loan officers), and the branch managers must be trained on the new product's features and how it would be communicated to the customers. A set of frequently asked questions (FAQ) for the customers as well as the employees may need to be prepared. If the product features are new, it needs to be included in the operations manual too.

6.1.7 Review and Analysis

When the product launch is complete, the performance should be reviewed from time to time and the sales and repayment data should be analysed. If there is any specific feedback from the customers, it should be incorporated and the product should be continued. If the product does not succeed, it should be withdrawn from the market.

6.1.8 Feedback and New Product

If the product succeeds, it goes through the product life cycle of development, growth, maturity and decline. Throughout the life cycle the product should be observed, and clues should be taken for identification for further needs of customer which becomes the basis of new product development again.

6.2 Saving Product

Savings products are simple. As Non-Banking Financial Company (NBFC)-MFIs cannot offer this product, it is open for banks like Small Finance Banks (SFBs) and cooperatives. In savings products, one has to compete with the existing service providers. Saving products can be designed based on purpose, tenure and rate of return. Saving bank account carries low interest rate, such as 3.5 to 4.0 per cent per annum. Fixed deposits carry higher rate of return. Chapter 4 (Section 4.1.) includes the way return can be calculated. Interest rate of savings product is also influenced by the RBI-declared rates like that of repo.

6.3 Loan Product

In developing a new loan product, the manager has to take several decisions on various parameters, such as purpose of the loan, loan size, interest rate, tenure of repayment, collateral and moratorium period.

6.3.1 Purpose of Loan

The purpose for which the client asks for a loan and the MFI approves and disburses is of primary importance. This is also the basis of all regulatory constraints and pricing decisions. For example, if the loan is for consumption purpose, the MFI has to see if there is any assured cash flow (such as salary or business). If it is for productive purpose (like establishment of a new shop, working capital loan, buying of cow, etc.), then the cash flow from that enterprise becomes the primary point of analysis, although in practice the lending institution looks into the household cash flow. The purpose of loan has several implications for the product features (see Table 6.2).

Table 6.2 Purpose of Loan and its Implications

Type of loan	Implications
Agriculture loan	Working capital for purchase of seed, fertiliser, tilling, etc. (short term)
	Purchase of implements (medium-term)
Dairy loan	Purchase of cow, construction of shed (medium-term)
Non-farm loan	Trading activity (working capital loan) (short term)
	Establishment of new shop (medium-term)
Housing loan	Long term
Home improvement loan	Short term to medium term depending on the cost
Personal loan	Generally short term

Note: short-term loan is for a tenure of up to one year, medium-term loan is for a tenure up to five years. Long-term loans are repaid in a tenure of more than five years.

If the purpose of loan is to purchase a fixed asset, the lender may also insist upon bundling the loan with an insurance to avoid risk.

6.3.2 Loan Size

Loan size directly influences the instalment and tenure. The repayment capacity of the concerned person also needs to be looked into. The regulatory constraints are given in detail in Chapter 10. The MFI has to assure that the total indebtedness of the client does not exceed the ceiling (which is ₹1 lakh at present). Also, if the amount of loan is higher than ₹30,000 the tenure has to be more than 24 months.

6.3.3 Tenure of Loan

This refers to the term (duration) in which the repayment has to be completed and the frequency of repayment. A good product should be designed in such a way that it matches with the cash flow of the client. A farmer's income is realised seasonally, while a shopkeeper earns daily (IIBF, 2009). Technically, the repayment can be daily, weekly, fortnightly, monthly, or can even be a bullet payment (IIBF, 2009: 181). It may be noted here that the RBI guidelines allow weekly, fortnightly and monthly instalments, which means that the daily payments cannot be followed. At the JLG or SHG level, internally, this can be done as it would be independent of the MFI.

Instalment amount should be fixed prudently; a very high amount would make the client making frequent default, while a very low payment would affect the cash flow of the MFI negatively (IIBF, 2009).

6.3.4 Interest Rate

Interest rate is regulated by the RBI. An NBFC-MFI can charge a margin cap of 10 per cent (12% for small MFIs). Further, it cannot be more than 2.75 times the average base rate of the commercial banks. From the point of view of the lender, it must a sustainable rate of interest, the formula of which is as follows (IIBF, 2009:188).

Sustainable interest rate =

$$\frac{\text{Financial Cost+Loan Loss+Operating Expenses+Margin for future growth–Investment Income}}{\text{1–Loan Loss}}$$

(All of these are to be expressed in terms of percentage of average portfolio.)

Interest rate is generally expressed on annual basis, unless it is mentioned otherwise. However, for calculation of compounding and discounting, one must be careful that it should be converted into the per-period interest rate, as the formula includes number of periods. Interest rate is calculated in two ways.

- **Flat Rate of Interest** As per this method, the borrower has to pay the interest for the whole year at the specified rate irrespective of the number of payments made in that period.

  Illustration 6.1 Suppose, A has taken a loan of ₹12,000 from an MFI at 15% flat rate of interest per annum, which has to be paid within one year (12 EMIs). Total interest paid would be ₹1500.
  The EMI will be calculated as

  $$\text{EMI} = \{\text{Principal} + \text{Interest}\}/\ \text{No. of instalments}$$

  A loan repayment schedule for this will be as follows (see Table 6.3).

  Table 6.3 Loan Repayment Schedule for Flat Rate of Interest (amount in ₹)

Month	Principal outstanding in the beginning	Interest paid	Principal repaid	Repayment	Balance outstanding at the end of the month
A	B	C = (B × 0.15/12)	D	E	F = (A – D)
1.	12,000	150	1,000	1150.0	11,000
2.	11,000	150	1,000	1150.0	10,000
3.	10,000	150	1,000	1150.0	9,000
4.	9,000	150	1,000	1150.0	8,000
5.	8,000	150	1,000	1150.0	7,000
6.	7,000	150	1,000	1150.0	6,000
7.	6,000	150	1,000	1150.0	5,000
8.	5,000	150	1,000	1150.0	4,000
9.	4,000	150	1,000	1150.0	3,000
10.	3,000	150	1,000	1150.0	2,000
11.	2,000	150	1,000	1150.0	1,000
12.	1,000	150	1,000	1150.0	0

  We can see from Table 6.3 that the amount of interest remains the same irrespective of the amount of principal repaid.

- **Declining balance rate of interest** In this method, the client pays the interest on the amount of principal outstanding (unlike the flat rate where it is paid on the whole principal).

  Illustration 6.2 Suppose B has taken a loan of ₹12,000 at 24 per cent interest rate per annum on declining balance rate. It has to be repaid at 12 EMIs. Here, the amount of interest rate paid would continue declining.

  However, it may be noted here that the calculation of EMI in such case is relatively complex and it can be done by using the formula of present value of annuity.

  $$\text{Present value of annuity (A)} = \text{P} \times \{1 - (1 + r)^{-n}\}/r$$

  Where

  A = Present value of annuity (₹12,000)

  P = Periodic payment, (EMI)

  n = Number of periods (12)

  r = Rate of interest per period (2% per month); here, the EMI would be ₹1134.70.

Table 6.4 Loan Repayment Schedule for Declining Balance Rate of Interest (amount in ₹)

Month	Principal outstanding in the beginning	Interest paid	Principal repaid	Repayment	Balance outstanding at the end of the month
A	B	C = (B × 0.24/12)	D = (E – C)	E	F = (A – D)
1.	12,000	240	895	1134.7	11,105
2.	11,105	222	913	1134.7	10,193
3.	10,193	204	931	1134.7	9,262
4.	9,262	185	949	1134.7	8,312
5.	8,312	166	968	1134.7	7,344
6.	7,344	147	988	1134.7	6,356
7.	6,356	127	1,008	1134.7	5,348
8.	5,348	107	1,028	1134.7	4,321
9.	4,321	86	1,048	1134.7	3,272
10.	3,272	65	1,069	1134.7	2,203
11.	2,203	44	1,091	1134.7	1,112
12.	1,112	22	1,112	1134.7	0

It can be observed that the outstanding principal comes down over time, and hence interest payment goes down, while the principal payment goes up (EMI, by definition, remains the same throughout the tenure of payment). Further, in flat rate of interest, the client pays higher amount than the declining balance rate of interest.

In making the above calculations, one must take into account various other components, such as down payment, insurance and processing fee. In case any of these are paid, the amount to be repaid would be adjusted accordingly.

Illustration 6.3 Suppose X has applied for a TV loan, which costs ₹20,000. However, X said he can make a down payment of ₹5,000. Thus, the principal that has to be repaid will be treated as ₹20,000 – ₹5000 = ₹15,000.

Illustration 6.4 In addition to the above, suppose there is an insurance (5% of total cost of TV) and processing fee (1% of loan amount) is also charged on that amount. The client said that she does not have any more funds, and hence this should be added to the loan amount. The principal here will be treated as ₹15,000 + (20,000 × 5%) + (15,000 × 1%) = 15,000 + 1,000 + 150 = ₹16,150. EMI calculation will be done on the basis of this amount.

6.3.5 Tenure and Frequency of Repayment

This is determined depending on the size of the loan and the repayment capacity and convenience of the client. Short-term loans are repaid within a period of one year. If the repayment is in EMI, there would be 12 instalments; if it is to be repaid weekly, it would be calculated as 52 instalments.

6.3.6 Moratorium

Moratorium should be included in the terms and conditions of the loan, particularly if it is an asset-based loan, and the establishment of that asset would take some time. Suppose the customer wants to establish a turmeric processing plant, which needs procurement of establishment of plants and machineries and some construction also. It may take six months. It is clear that for the first six months, till the plant becomes operational, there would be no cash flow from the plant. Hence, a moratorium of six months would be useful here.

Traditionally, moneylenders often deducted the first instalment at the time of repayment. If this deducation is applied to Illustration 6.1, the client will receive only ₹10,850, which increases the effective rate of interest. Some MFIs had allegedly practised this. Hence, the RBI guidelines mandate that that first instalment cannot be recovered before a period equal to the frequency of payment. For example, if the repayment is in terms of EMI, the first EMI cannot be recovered before the end of the first month.

6.4 Insurance Products

Design of insurance products requires decision on various aspects, such as the object of insurance (purpose), claim parameters and premium. In case of livestock insurance, e.g. a cow, the object of insurance is the cow and the claim parameters would be death of the cow. In crop insurance, the object would be the crop and claim parameters would be loss of crop; in case of weather insurance, the claim parameters would be a sub-normal rainfall.

Premium calculation in insurance is based on the following:

Insurance premium = Risk premium + Operating cost + Profit margin – Investment income

Risk premium is calculated based on the expected claims. A simple example can be given here.

Illustration 6.5 You are a livestock insurer and you have insured 10,000 cows, each cow insured for ₹25,000. Past records say that out of the insured cows, about 2 per cent die and for these, you have to settle the claim. For running this business, you have an office and several employees, the cost of which is ₹5 million fixed cost and ₹100 per cow as variable component. This comes to ₹6 million, which is 2.4 per cent of the total face value of the insurance (i.e. 25,000 × 10,000 = ₹250 million). You expect a profit of ₹10 million, which means 4 per cent of the face value of the insurance. You generated an investment income of ₹1.25 million which is 0.5 per cent of total face value. Now the premium will be:

Insurance premium = Risk premium + Operating cost + Profit margin – Investment income

= 2% + 2.4% + 4% – 0.5% = 7.9%.

Thus, for every cow priced at ₹25,000, the customer has to pay a premium of ₹1,975.

An MFI, which operates as an agent, does not have to worry about such pricing details. The premium is generally fixed by the insurer. The commission part can be bargained for. Also, as it would be a bulk transaction, generally the MFI can bargain for a lower premium.

6.5 Pension Products

Pension products include two components, expected return (return from the total investment of pension fund) and management fee. Generally, management fee is charged as a fixed percentage and the net return becomes the basis for paying out to the pensioner.

For a customer, it is important that he/she knows what exactly he/she would be getting upon retirement. A simplistic calculation would be in the nature of annuity. Suppose, A, at the age of 30, starts investing in pension fund, making an annual contribution of ₹12,000. At the age of 60, if the fund pays eight per cent return, the value of pensionable fund becomes

Future value of annuity

$$= P\left\{\frac{(1+r)^n - 1}{r}\right\} = 12{,}000 \times \{(1.08)^{30}-1\}/0.08$$

= Approximately ₹13.60 lakh

Generally, an annuity is paid by the pension funds to the pensioners. Assuming that, this amount is reinvested for a monthly return at say 9% per annum, one can get ₹10,195 per month. Thus, by investing

₹12,000 per year (which comes to ₹1,000 per month) for 30 years, one can get expect a pension of about ₹10,000 per annum. It is assumed that the principal amount would be paid to the nominee upon death of the pensioner. There are several schemes of pensions in National Pension Scheme (NPS), as a part of which one can opt for continuing pension for spouse also.

This is, however, a relatively simplistic proposition, there are two issues here. Generally, people invest in pension funds in terms of proportions of existing salary, which increases every year (say by 5%). In such case, the pensionable funds would become about ₹23 lakh and accordingly, the pension would be higher (about ₹17,000 per month).

In India, there are strict regulatory provisions for who can manage funds. At present, companies/institutions like LIC, SBI Life, and HDFC Life are the annuity service providers as part of NPS scheme. An MFI can operate on behalf of such an institution and charge a commission.

6.6 Other Products

Design of other products, such as remittance and leasing, is done based on the operating costs of the specific product. It may be noted that such products are ordinarily bundled with loans and savings products. Revenue from such products also is miniscule. However, given that it adds to the product diversity, the MFI should take care that at least the operating costs of these products are recovered.

Case Study 6.1 Mohini Microfinance Ltd.

"In the last Board meeting, you complained of shortage of affordable funds. Now you have got a commitment of ₹1000 million (100 crore) from this private investor. You have to tell us how you would use this fund", said a non-executive board member of Mohini Microfinance Limited (MML).

The last Board meeting, held in early 2014, was a forum for hot discussion. Mr. Vinay Prakash, the MD, had requested the Board members to look for opportunities for new funds. He believed that one cannot depend purely on loan-based funds, which cost around 10-12 per cent per annum, to grow satisfactorily. Given that the interest rate is a sensitive issue, not just for the borrowers but also for the policy maker, there was a need for some equity funds. A few board members helped him in building contacts with some private equity (PE) firms and one firm agreed to provide ₹1 billion (100 crores), subject to having a viable business plan. The forthcoming Board meeting in July 2014 would have a presentation by Mr. Prakash on the business plan. If the Board is satisfied, it will be submitted to the PE firm.

Last financial year (2013-14), MML had a topline of ₹4.53 billion (90% as from loan products; rest from commission from selling insurance and other financial products) and a PAT of ₹310 million. Given that the microfinance market was slowly recovering, this was not an issue. After the industry-wide crisis in 2010-11, the company incurred a loss of about ₹300 million, which has already been written-off. The challenge is how to put it in a growth path. Since the crisis, banks have been quite conservative in lending to MFIs, and MML was no exception from this apathy. Still, it managed to get a ₹2.5 billion loan, the rest has been from equity funds. However, it being a loan-fund, the company had to shell out ₹280 million to interest in a year. Otherwise, the profit could have been higher. Being an NBFC, it was not in a position to take deposits from public. Hence the only option left for cheaper funds was PE. However, PEs were not coming forward after they had to suffer huge losses in the aftermath of the crisis. Hence, a PE getting ready to provide a huge sum of ₹1 billion was a big deal for MML.

Mr. Prakash began, "MML operates in 10 districts of Odisha and Jharkhand. It has about 36,000 clients. However, from a client base of about one lakh, it had not been able to tap into even two-third of them because it did not have the funds. Now that some funds have been received, it can serve more clients". But a few board members were not convinced. "You know that there are multiple MFIs working in the area. Going to new clients will increase that exposure too. I would rather suggest to focus on the existing clients. Earlier, you were mentioning that you were not able to meet the demands of existing clients. Why not focus on them?", said another board member.

Mr. Prakash tabled a report of a study conducted by a few interns on the financial needs of existing clients. Based on a sample survey of 300 clients, it found the following demand pattern:

1. For small business/vending (₹10,000-₹25,000) : 32%
2. For purchase of household assets (₹5,000-₹10,000) : 24%
3. For consumption (₹2,000-₹5,000) : 40%
4. For agriculture/dairy (₹10,000-₹20,000) : 15%
5. For marriage of daughter/son (₹40,000-₹75,000) : 5%
6. For other purposes (₹5,000-₹50,000) : 24%

(total would be more than 100% because of multiple responses)

Mr. Prakash added that this figure represented the actual demand, while MML could only fulfil the needs of first, second, and fourth categories (in part). As a policy, it did not provide consumption loan and non-productive loans. Presently, 60 per cent of its loans were taken for first category (business), but report said that many took loans for small business on paper, while the actual purpose was consumption. However, MML did not worry much about such aberrations as there was no problem in repayment. Bad loans (after the 2010-11 crisis) were quite less, as MML was quite cautious before sanctioning loans. This is to be noted that non-performing assets (NPAs) were to the extent of only 2.5 per cent (Agriculture: 2.2%, small business: 3.5%, and household assets, 1.5%).

The Chairman had another viewpoint. He said, "Mr. Prakash, you are only focussing on this billion-rupee funds. Look it from a five-year perspective, and your business plan for this particular funds should only be a part of it. I would rather like to listen from a loan officer who operates at the grassroot level on what could be the possibilities".

In the afternoon, a few loan officers were called for interaction with the Board. The officers said that because of the conservative approach of MML, a large part of the market was again captured by moneylenders (who lend at 36% to 48% interest p.a.) and a few other MFIs. They said the following loans were demanded by people, which MML did not consider:

- Purchase of second-hand motorcycle/scooter
- Top-up loans ranging from ₹ 2,000 to ₹ 15,000
- Purchase of new clothes just before Dussehra festival (₹ 5,000 to ₹ 10,000)
- Treatment of ailing family members (₹ 1,000 to ₹ 50,000)
- On occasions like child birth, marriage, death of a family member (up to ₹ 20,000)
- Payment of school fees and purchase of books during June and July (₹ 500 to ₹ 1,500)

When the board meeting started again at 4.00 PM, the members felt that there has to be some new products to increase market share. Particularly those clients who have a perfect record of repayment could be provided loans for various purposes, other than what are sanctioned at present. Where the risks are slightly higher, some assets can be attached, at least for the sake of formality, as the Board knew well that it would be difficult to sell such assets.

"I think it is time that we became a little pragmatic and recognise the real credit needs of people in a more realistic manner. Also, prepare a presentation of NPAs in the last three years (2011-14) on various types of products, and provide for bad loans and also provide information about the proportion of loan that has been restructured. The PE has to know the facts clearly. This will also help us in building a long-term relationship", said the Chairman.

Discussion Questions

1. What are the types of loan products that have been or can be used by MML?
2. What kind of products have been more effective than others?
3. Do you think any kind of product that has been left out?
4. Does the existing portfolio take care of the credit needs of the poorest?
5. Develop the right kind of product portfolio for MML.

Summary

- Any product has a life cycle, including the stage of development, growth, maturity and decline.
- In order to stay in business, an organisation must innovate continuously and develop its products.
- Product development starts with understanding the need of customers. This is followed by idea generation, assessment of cost benefit, development of prototypes, test marketing, refinement, product launching, product review, and based on customer feedback, again starting the product development cycle.
- Savings products are designed based on purpose, interest rate and tenure. Interest rate in savings is generally rigid and depends on repo rate and competitor's offers.
- Loan products are designed based on purpose, loan size, tenure and frequency of repayment, interest rate and moratorium. Interest rate can be of flat rate or declining balance rate.
- Insurance premium depends on risk premium, profit margin, operating cost minus return from investment. Pension products are long term. Generally, MFIs act as agents for insurers and pension aggregators, hence they can bargain for a commission. They also can bargain for insurance premiums.
- Products like remittance and leasing are incidental to the MFIs's core business and are ordinarily bundled with other products, such as loan. Such products should be designed keeping in mind that at least operating costs is recovered.

Exercises

A. Multiple-choice Questions

1. Product development in financial services does not include
   (a) Need assessment of customers
   (b) Generating product ideas
   (c) Pilot testing of the prototype
   (d) None of the above
2. Which of the following is TRUE about saving products?
   (a) Interest rate depends on competitors' and RBI's rates
   (b) It cannot be offered by NBFC-MFIs
   (c) Scope of tweaking with interest rate is small
   (d) All of the above
3. Design of loan product does not depend on
   (a) Loan officer
   (b) Purpose of loan
   (c) Amount of loan
   (d) Tenure of loan
4. Suppose a company offers loan at 24 per cent flat rate of interest. Later, it changed the terms to declining rate of interest. All other things remaining the same, interest income will be
   (a) Higher
   (b) Lower
   (c) Will remain the same
   (d) Cannot be determined
5. Which of the following is TRUE for pension products?
   (a) Pension products are like insurance products
   (b) Pension funds are managed by NBFC-MFIs
   (c) Pension products are long-term investments
   (d) None of the above
6. Ordinarily, which of the following products are directly offered by NBFC-MFIs as their own products?
   (a) Savings (b) Credit
   (c) Insurance (d) Pension
7. Insurance premium does not depend on
   (a) Risk premium
   (b) Profit margin
   (c) Interest rate
   (d) Return from investment
8. Repayment of a loan instalment cannot be expected before the
   (a) Completion of tenure of the loan
   (b) Agreed moratorium period
   (c) Client defaults
   (d) All of the above

9. A client wants to buy a used bike that costs ₹ 25,000. He said he can pay a down payment of ₹ 2,500. But he has to pay the cost of insurance which is ₹ 1000 and you charge a processing fee of ₹ 100. He has only ₹ 2,500 and cannot pay anything right now. For calculation of EMI, what would be the principal?
   (a) ₹ 25,000 (b) ₹ 22,500
   (c) ₹ 23,500 (d) ₹ 23,600

10. In determining loan size, which of the following is TRUE?
   (a) There are regulatory restrictions on tenure related to loan size
   (b) There are regulatory restrictions on interest rate related to loan size
   (c) There is no regulatory restriction related to loan size
   (d) None of the above

B. Review Questions

1. Describe the product development process for development of a loan product. Your target group is farmers from rural areas of your state.
2. Distinguish between declining rate of interest and flat rate of interest rate.
3. What are the important features needed to be covered in designing a loan product?

C. Application-based Questions

1. A loan officer received a loan application for ₹15,000 from a client. The loan was approved at 18 per cent interest rate per annum (reducing balance rate), with a one-time processing fee of ₹150. An insurance cost of ₹350 was also added. The client agrees to make a down payment of ₹3000. The loan would be repaid in 12 EMIs.
   (*i*) Prepare a loan repayment schedule in the format given below.
   (*ii*) If the terms of the loans are changed and the client would be charged a flat rate of interest, what would be the revised EMI?

   Note that

   $$\text{Present value of annuity} = \text{Periodic payment} \times \{1 - (1+i)^{-n}\}/i$$

   where i = rate of interest and n = number of periods in which payments will be made.
2. A loan officer received a loan application for ₹10,000 from a client. The loan was approved at 24 per cent interest rate per annum (reducing balance rate), with a one-time processing fee of ₹100. An insurance cost of ₹400 was also added. The loan would be repaid in 12 EMIs. By mistake, the loan agreement mentioned that it would be 24 per cent flat rate of interest. Prepare a schedule of payment sheet (in the given format) for each type of interest calculation and find out the differential in actual payment in the mistaken method of payment.
3. A loan officer received a loan application for ₹20,000 from a client. The loan was approved at 24 per cent interest rate per annum (declining balance rate of interest), with a one-time processing fee of ₹500. An insurance cost of ₹500 was also added. The client agrees to make a down payment of ₹3000. The loan would be repaid in 12 EMIs. Prepare a loan repayment schedule.
4. An MFI has an average loan portfolio of ₹1500 million, financial cost of ₹135 million, operating expenses are ₹90 million, loan loss of ₹15 million, it keeps a margin for future growth of 8 per cent and has an investment income of ₹50 million. Calculate the sustainable rate of interest for the MFI.
5. You are in the business of insuring small businesses like pan shop, grocery store and variety stores in rural areas and urban slums. In a year, you generally insure 20,000 such businesses for a face value of average ₹1 lakh. Past records say that there are about 1 percent claims. Your operating costs are about 2 per cent of the total face value of the insured amount. Assuming an expected profit margin of 2.5 per cent and investment income of 0.5 per cent of total face value, calculate the premium to be charged for the next year.
6. A group of SHG members asked you to calculate the amount of pension they can expect if they continue saving ₹500 per month. All of them are in the age of 40 now. They say they can deposit for another 15 years.

Further Readings

- Chapter 10 titled 'Financial Products and Services' of *Microfinance: Perspective and Operations* by the Indian Institute of Banking and Finance is a useful resource material for understanding various dimensions of products.
- The Microsave toolkit 'Product Rollout: A Toolkit for Expanding a Tested Product Throughout the Market' (by McCord et al) provides a step-by-step and extensive idea of product development in the context of microfinance.

PART III
Monitoring and Evaluation in Microfinance

CHAPTER

7

Impact Assessment and SHG-Grading

Chapter Outline

Learning Objectives

After reading this chapter, you will be able to:

- discuss the need of monitoring and evaluation in microfinance.
- provide an overview of the issues associated with impact assessment in microfinance.
- discuss and compare the different grading scales used for SHGs.

It was mentioned earlier in Chapter 3, that self-help groups (SHGs) are formed and strengthened in four stages, generally ranging over a period of 18 to 36 months. It is important to determine whether the SHGs have been making adequate progress or not and whether they are ready to move to the next stage, particularly to the stage of bank linkage. At this stage, it is required to conduct grading of an SHG. In this chapter, the SHG grading process and scale will be discussed.

Before we look into the grading issues, it must be underlined clearly that grading is only one of the component of monitoring and evaluation (M&E) of SHGs. Grading is a routine exercise and can be done by people with lesser experience. However, the result of grading has to be understood in the context in which the SHGs are formed. In this regard, there are several issues that need to be kept in mind.

This chapter includes a discussion on the issue of M&E in SHG programmes. Grading being an important aspect is the focus of this discussion.

7.1 Issues in M&E of SHGs

There are several issues associated with the M&E of SHGs in general and grading of SHGs in particular, such as purpose of SHG, need of the grading/evaluation exercise and the expectations from such exercise.

Self-help groups are not formed uniformly across the country; they have been formed in different communities, by different organisations and for different programmes. There are thousands of communities in India, hundreds of organisations working with these SHGs, and there are tens of programmes in the country. Considering that there would be some overlap and common characteristics between them, there still would be enormous variation. Scale of diversity in the SHGs is thus enormous. But there are some common themes. The most important theme is the purpose of formation of the SHG. At the first stage, any evaluator or somebody involved in grading of SHGs must understand the basic purpose of formation of SHGs.

In the early days, the purpose of SHG formation was to build community institutions, and the delivery of services was incidental. Nowadays, SHGs are formed for their instrumental values. Hence, the first task is to understand the basic purpose. If the evaluator is looking for solid institutions, specific achievements like 80 per cent attendance (why not 79%) can be relaxed depending on the context. But for instrumental objectives, such as bank linkage, specific parameters are seen with rigidity. For institutional values, the focus is on capacity building, while for the instrumental value, the priority goes to managerial decision making.

The second important concern in M&E of SHGs (and SHG programmes) is the purpose of the evaluation. Grading and evaluations are not carried out in silos, rather these exercises are embedded in the larger goal of the organisation or the programme. Organisations employ people, channel financial resources, and have to answer the donor or investor. They have to meet target and show progress to prove that they are efficient. Thus, they would like that a competitive space is built. A higher grade SHG gets priority over a lower grade SHG in getting funds. An executive promoting high grade SHGs get appreciated than others who could not attain such results. Evaluation and grading help in building this competitive space.

The third aspect of these exercises is related to what the expectations are. The expectations can be the same as the second point (progress, target attainment) given above. But ideally, such exercises are expected to provide deep insights into the way SHGs have been functioning. Given the nature of uneven power structure in rural areas, it is very much possible that the relatively influential people have control over the decisions and resources. There are several indicators like awareness among members, proportion of members taking loans, leadership rotation, etc., that show if the empowering feature of SHGs is realised or not.

7.2 Impact Assessment

There are several reasons behind the phenomenal growth of the microfinance industry. An important reason is the idea that microfinance can transform the lives of poor. This means poverty can be alleviated through microfinance. This idea has been propagated by various studies including frequently cited studies of Khandkar (2005) and Pitt and Khandkar (1998). There is no dearth of success stories published by Microfinance Institutions (MFIs) across the world on how the lives of the poor were transformed. A case in point is the Annual Report of SKS Microfinance of 2009-10, at that time it was preparing for the initial public offer (IPO), starts with a story of a woman, and the whole report carries many such stories. Several NGOs have also time and again published and presented similar stories. However, there have been questions on whether microfinance have such kinds of transforming influence on the poor? Unfortunately, some evidences show that the impact is not that deep.

The first criticism of the existing studies, saying that microfinance has done wonders, is that such reports are largely anecdotal. Here there may be a selection bias. Given that majority of such stories have been brought out primarily by the MFI themselves, selection bias is natural. There also have been faulty methodology, such as before-after comparison, without controlling the effects (Armendariz and Morduch, 2010).

Some critics have pointed out that there are mixed results when rigorous methods are followed. While there is no argument against the benefits of microfinance, a few findings really break the existing perceptions.

- Microfinance borrowers tend to be wealthier than the non-borrowers in the neighbourhood (Alexander, 2001)
- A study by Indian Market Research Bureau (IMRB) pointed out that after five years of operations, in BASIX operational area, about one-fourth of clients became poorer (BASIX, 2011)
- A study in Sri Lanka showed that microfinance-funded enterprises run by men provided significantly more. Returns than similar investments made by women borrowers (de Mel et al, 2008).

Thus, there has been some questions on methodological aspects of conducting impact assessment of microfinance. One way to solve this problem is the approach of randomisation, which can be used by randomised control trial (RCT) as a part of which selection bias can be avoided and it will provide a rigourous framework for evaluation too.

7.3 Grading Process, Principles and Indicators

Grading should ideally be undertaken by an independent evaluator and it is mandatory that the evaluator visits the SHG. The grading process involves interaction with the group members. The records of the SHGs also have to be checked by the evaluator. A participatory grading is better for the SHG, as in that case, the grading would be the result of the discussion between the evaluator and the group. Also, in this process, the SHG owns the scores provided in the grading and accepts the need of further improvement, which is the ultimate goal of such evaluations.

There are some basic principles based on which SHGs are evaluated or graded. These principles need not be the specific indicators, but overall they provide a set of guidelines for people engaged in grading and evaluations of SHGs and SHG programmes. A well-known set of principles is popularly called *Panchasutra* (literally meaning five formulae, but refers to five principles of SHG) in SHG based programmes, particularly in the National Rural Livelihood Mission (NRLM) programmes in India:

- There should be regular meeting in the group
- There should be regular savings by the members in the group
- There should be regular inter-loaning (internal lending) in the group
- There should be timely repayment of loans in the group
- Books of accounts of the group should be up to date.

These five formulae are the beginning point. As they can easily be memorised, they have been found to be known among the ground level staff members and animators. These are handy during the implementation of the programme. However, grading indicators go relatively in-depth.

There are several grading scales. Here discussion will be focussed on the grading by two organisations, Mysore Resettlement and Development Agency (MYRADA) and National Bank for Agriculture and Rural Development (NABARD). It must be noted here that these grading indicators have a lot of overlapping, which might be because MYRADA and NABARD worked collaboratively in promoting SHGs in India.

MYRADA uses two sets of formats for grading of SHGs (it must be noted here that MYRADA does not call the groups by that name, rather it maintains the name 'self help affinity groups', which are conceptually more rigorous than SHGs).

Format 1: used for assessing the SHGs to check if they are ready for linking with banks and financial institutions.

Format 2: used for deciding if the organisation's involvement can be phased out.

NABARD also uses two kinds of formats, first, for assessing the SHGs for credit linkage (Table 7.1), and second, for assessing the credit requirement of matured SHGs (Table 7.2).

The first format of MYRADA includes eight points (MYRADA 30B: undated):

(a) The SHGs should have credit transactions from its own common funds for at least 6 months
(b) Overdue of repayment of loans from common funds should not be more 15 per cent of total outstanding amount, and overdue should not be more than 12 months
(c) Loans should have been taken by at least 80 per cent of members
(d) Higher proportion of loans should be for production than consumption purpose (at least in equal proportion)
(e) Evidence of regular savings (minimum per capita savings of ₹300)
(f) Records should be properly maintained and should be done independently (external assistances for this should be paid out of group's own fund).
(g) Evidence of regular meetings with 80 per cent attendance
(h) Common funds should be in regular circulation with minimum balance maintained in bank account

Each of these points are measured through one of these three options: *i*) verified and found to be satisfactory, *ii*) verified and not found to be satisfactory, and *iii*) not verified. The evaluator has to add some qualitative comments too.

The first format of NABARD (Table 7.1) also includes some of the above points (meetings, attendance, savings, interloaning, repayment and record maintenance). In addition, it includes indicators like group size, homogeneity and neighbourhood also. It may also be noted that issues like purpose of loans (production or consumption) is not there in the NABARD format. On the issue of internal lending, the NABARD format is not as detailed as that of MYRADA format. NABARD format is, however, easy to fill up and does not include qualitative inputs of the evaluators (NABARD, 2018).

The second format of NABARD (Table 7.2) is designed for matured SHGs who have already availed loans for at least two cycles. For them the indicators of grading include a few new points, such as rotation of group leaders, refresher training programme, credit history, percentage of members taking income generating activities, utilisation of bank loan, audit and proportion of members utilising financial services. It does not include some of the basic information, such as group size, homogeneity, neighbourhood, etc.

The second format of MYRADA has a very different kind of focus. Through this exercise, the task would be to understand whether the group is independently managed by itself or not. Based on this information, the Self Help Group Promoting Institution (SHPI) can withdraw from the SHG management processes. This format has five sections:

- The first section includes basic information, such as members, funds, savings, interest, rates, etc.
- The second section includes 12 essential criteria, including regular meeting, attendance, availability of loans to all members, rotation of leadership, regular savings, repayment, overdue, maintenance of records, common funds, ratio of production and consumption loans proportion of members linked to regular sources of income and liaison with other institutions for technical and financial support.
- The third section includes eight optional criteria, including being trained in technical services, membership in federation, group income generation programme, experience of implementing community based programme and social activities, instance of prooting social justice to its members.
- The fourth section has information, such as liabilities with the promoting agency (SHPI), attendance in training, following of rules and sanction and control mechanism, collective decision-making and having clear vision and plan for the future.
- The fifth section includes calculation of results of second and third section (essential and optional criteria), qualitative observations and recommendations of evaluator on withdrawal (MYRADA 30C, undated)

Thus it is clear that the second format of MYRADA involves relatively complex set of indicators.

Table 7.1 NABARD Format Assessing SHGs for Credit Linkage

Sr. No.	Factors to be checked	Parameters	Maximum marks	Marks obtained
1.	Number of members	13-20*	2	
		10-12**	1	
2.	Composition of group homogeneity	Similar economic status	2	
		Different economic status	1	
3.	Residents of same neighbourhood	Members belong to the same village/ cluster of hamlets	1	
4.	Group meetings	Once in every week	3	
		Once in every fortnight	2	
		Once in every month	1	

5.	Average attendance of members in group meetings	More than 90% --- 75% or more and up to 90% --- 60% or more and up to 74%	3 --- 2 --- 1	
6.	Savings (percentage of members saving regularly)	More than 90% --- 75% or more and up to 90% --- 60% or more and up to 74%	3 --- 2 --- 1	
7.	Internal lending	Taking place among the members	2	
8.	Repayment rate of internal loans	More than 90% --- 70% or more and up to 90%	2 --- 1	
9.	Maintenance of records of SHG	Books are regularly maintained and up to date --- Book maintenance is not in arrears for more than one meeting and satisfactory in general	2 --- 1	
	Maximum marks		20	

*9-20 & **5-8 for NE in hilly tracts/districts of North Eastern Region and Himalayan Region (Jammu and Kashmir, Himachal Pradesh, Uttarakhand and parts of West Bengal)

Score of 12 marks and above: SHG may be considered for credit linkage.

Source: *NABARD*, 2018

Table 7.2 NABARD Format for Assessing Credit Requirement of Matured SHGs

Sr. No.	Factors to be checked	Indicators	Maximum marks	Marks obtained
1.	Rotation of group leader/s	Every year --- Once in two years	2 --- 1	
2.	Maintenance of records of SHG	Books are regularly maintained and up to date --- Book maintenance is not in arrears for more than one meeting and satisfactory in general	2 --- 1	
3.	Refresher training programme	SHG has undergone a refresher training programme on capacity building	2	
4	Repayment rate of intra-group loan	More than 90% --- 75% or more and up to 90	2 --- 1	
5.	Credit history (repayment of dues to bank)	If the SHG has never defaulted --- Default was subsequently cleared	2 --- 1	

6.	Percentage of members undertaking income generating activities (IGA)	75% or more 50% or more and up to 74%	2 1	
7.	Activity/business/ livelihood/ credit plan	Member-wise plan is prepared by SHG	2	
8.	Utilisation of bank loan	Bank loan is not divided equally among the members and disbursement is need based	2	
9.	Audit	Informal audit of SHG is done or account of SHG is checked by a third party other than the SHG and SHPI	2	
10.	Financial services, percentage of members who have availed at least one of the financial services like individual S/B accounts, insurance, etc.	More than 50% Between 30-50%	2 1	
	Maximum marks		20	

@ A matured SHG assumed as one that has availed at least two cycles of credit from a bank and repaid it.

Score of 12 marks and above: Higher quantum of credit (more than four times of the group corpus) may be considered for sanction to mature SHGs.

Source: *NABARD*, 2018

7.4 Interpreting Results of Grading

Any grading scale (NABARD format, MYRADA format, or any other) has its own criteria of cut-off marks. Based on this cut-off, the manager can think of whether to initiate bank linakage or nor and the bank also can make a decision on whether to lend the SHG or not. Similarly, the withdrawal related format provides inputs on whether the group is ready for phasing out or not.

Although there are quantitative cut-off, the interpretation of the information received form the grading process should in interpreted with caution:

- Grading and evaluation results are not just for the SHPI/bank's decision of bank linkage, but are for the improvement of the group also
- Sometimes, score on the grading scale does not properly represent the strength of the institution. SHGs are ultimately institutions of community empowerment and this has to be reflected in the evaluation or grading.
- Grading results have to be looked in relative terms and this might differ from place to place. An SHPI like MYRADA would not only build the capacities of the SHGs, but also build the value system of the group. From target based SHPIs, such value system is not expected.
- Certain genuine factors also might turn into problems like non-repayment. Continuous drought, job loss and death in a family are such problems. The evaluator must be aware of such contextual factors.

7.5 Limits of Grading

Initially, grading was just an event in the process of SHG management. The pre-2000 SHGs were focussed on institution building and then there was less stake involved in getting a lower grade. However, post-2000, the focus of SHG promotion changed and the instrumental value of SHGs started getting emphasised

(Fernandez, 2017). A lot more funds are now routed through than earlier, and hence every effort has been made to improve the grades.

Has this resulted in creating artificial institutions? Do the SHGs score high but are not good on institutional strength? Most likely. The way SHG programmes have been upscaled, it needed enormous number of skilled people who can promote such groups. Given the scale, the only way it could be done was standardisation of the processes. Institution building is a complex task and is difficult to attain.

But standardisation is a double-edged sword. It assures that the minimum standards are met, but does not assure about the larger goal of meeting needs of people. Interestingly, standardisation has shaped the whole microfinance sector. Strength of the institutions has been made measurable through the scales and formula, but it seems that the latter has superseded the original idea of creating institutions.

Case Study 7.1 Windfall Gains from Loans

Ms. Reena Shukla, the Managing Director of BCD Microfinance Ltd, was invited to an international donor's meet to speak about the company's success. She prepared a 30-minute presentation on the interventions of the company, results and impact on the society. Her presentation included the following points:

- The company keeps a mark up of 2.5 per cent above the cost of funds and the operating costs. This is one of the lowest in the industry for all companies having more than ₹5 billion loan portfolios.
- Ninety per cent of BCD's loans are given for enterprise purpose. Consumption loans are allowed only under exceptional circumstances. Such enterprise loans were either for working capital, or renovation of shops. Average loan size was ₹7500 (approximately USD 100) Such investments, according to a study, have provided 80 to 123 per cent to return to the borrowers. They happily pay the interest which is 18-21 per cent per annum.
- Seventy-five per cent of borrowers are women.
- The microfinance activity of BCD is an effort towards bringing people out of poverty.

Ms. Shukla received an applause when the presentation was over. There were a couple of questions for her which she answered. There was another question from a person, but due to paucity of time, the moderator stopped it and said that he could interact with the speaker later.

Ms. Shukla located the gentleman during the break and said she wanted to know what that person wanted to ask. He said that he had some concerns about the results of the study. "The 80-123 per cent returns are phenomenal! But it seems unrealistic.", he said. Ms. Shukla replied that it has been carried out by an independent consultant, also shared the methodology, which was a stratified random sampling.

"No! No! I am extremely sorry if I gave you an impression that I did not like the rigour of the study. I believe it must be excellent, otherwise the donor would not have invited you to present in such a place. I have certain other issue with the finding. I presume that all your loans must have been given to the poor people who did not have access to any other source of institutions finance", said the gentleman.

"That's right", replied Ms. Shukla.

"And such loans that you have given have the average size of one hundred dollar!", he said

Ms. Shukla nodded.

"With such a small capital, any sensible project would have a high amount of return. Next time, the loan size would be higher, but the return would be low. When you reach the loan size of about one thousand, the return would be marginally higher than the cost of borrowing. Sometimes it may be slightly lower also!", he told her.

This is a striking observation, Ms. Shukla thought.

"I appreciate the fact that all of the borrowers have paid back, that means you had a system in place for loan appraisal. But this kind of return would not be there forever. I suggest that you re-analyse the data to see how return from enterprises change with the amount of investment. Intuitively, it would go down, particularly when you start with very small amount" the gentleman continued.

"That's possible", Ms. Shukla said.

"You said that the loans were given for working capital or renovation of shop. This means they already had a business, and that the borrowers were selected meticulously. What happens to the people who are not involved in enterprising activities? They may be poorer than your borrowers", he asked.

"Most probably", she replied.

"Now you read my mind", smiled the gentleman.

"So, we have lent to people who are relatively well-endowed. And to bring these people out of poverty is easier than the task of alleviating the poverty of the people who are not part of our loan programme", she said.

"That statement would be slightly harsh. All I am saying is that you need to be careful in interpreting your findings. Well, I believe that you will take care of in future. Wish you all the best", the gentleman said.

Discussion Questions

1. What should be the right approach to evaluate the loan programme of BCD?
2. Do you agree with the points raised by the observer?
3. What strategies should be followed to avoid such kind of problem?

Summary

- The most important aspects of an SHG is the purpose for which it has been formed, purpose of the evaluation and the expectation of the organisation from such an exercise.
- Impact of microfinance has been said to be high, but most such evidences are anecdotal and others followed flawed methodologies. Rigorous studies have shown that the results are mixed in nature. RCT can help eliminate such biases in research.
- There are various indicators of measuring the institutional strength of SHGs. The main principles are known as panchasutra, regular meeting, regular saving, regular interloaning, timely repayment and record maintenance.
- Specific grading scales have been prepared by several institutions. Two important scales have been discussed here, MYRADA and NABARD scales.
- MYRADA scale is in two parts, one for bank linkage and another for withdrawal.
- NABARD scale is in two parts, one for initial credit linkage and another for matured SHGs which have taken at least two cycles of loans.
- The results of grading exercises should be interpreted in their context, rather than judging based purely on the quantitative outputs.
- Grading has its limitations too; it standardises the long-term processes of institutional strength which sometimes dilutes the original goal of institution building.

Exercises

A. Multiple-choice Questions

1. Initial studies saying that microfinance has a phenomenal impact were
   (a) Anecdotal in nature
   (b) Having selection bias
   (c) Not randomised
   (d) All of the above
2. Which of the following can help in reducing the selection bias?
   (a) Success stories
   (b) Before-after comparison
   (c) RCT
   (d) None of the above
3. MYRADA's grading for bank linkage includes
   (a) Repayment related information
   (b) Microenterprise related information
   (c) Information related to social justice initiatives
   (d) All of the above
4. NABARD scale for new bank linkage related grading does not include
   (a) Inter-loaning data
   (b) Group size related data
   (c) Rotation of leadership
   (d) None of the above

5. NABARD scale for grading matured SHGs include
   (a) Homogeneity related data
   (b) Group size related data
   (c) Rotation of leadership
   (d) None of the above
6. MYRADA's second scale is related to
   (a) Withdrawal of SHPI
   (b) First bank linkage
   (c) Bank linkage for matured groups
   (d) None of the above
7. MYRADA's second scale has ______ sections.
   (a) 2 (b) 3
   (c) 4 (d) 5
8. Which of the following is true about MYRADA's second grading scale?
   (a) It covers the essential features of SHG
   (b) It covers the optional features of SHG
   (c) It covers the essential as well as optional features of SHG
   (d) None of the above
9. Interpretation of the grading related information should be done on the basis of its
   (a) Results
   (b) Context
   (c) Hypothesis
   (d) None of the above
10. Which of the following is a limitation of grading?
   (a) Institutional processes have been converted into standardised information
   (b) Standardised processes have been converted into institutional information
   (c) No standards are followed in grading
   (d) None of the above

B. Review Questions

1. SHG programmes should be evaluated in their context; grading is just a tool. Comment.
2. What are the positive and negative impacts of microfinance?
3. What are the problems in impact assessment of microfinance?
4. What are the important features of NABARD's grading scale for initial bank linkages?
5. What are the important features of MYRADA's grading scales for assessing whether to phase out or not?
6. What are the differences between MYRADA and NABARD's scale?
7. Describe the process of grading of SHGs.
8. What are the limitations of grading?

C. Application-based Questions

1. The Government of India has been running the NRLM programme since 2011. This programme is being run across all parts of India, and it has been based on SHG-approach. Institution building is the foundation on which it operates. The programme would complete 10 years in 2021. Assume that the programme has been questioned on its impact by the donors, and government also wants to know whether it is worth continuing for another five to ten years. Develop an impact assessment methodology that helps in understanding the impact of the programme on the following:
   (a) Impact of the programme on livelihoods
   (b) Impact of the programme on institutions
   (c) Impact of the programme on women empowerment
2. Suggest the changes in NABARD SHG-grading formats that make us understand whether the SHG would be now able to operate independently (without the support of SHPI) or not.

Further Readings

- Chapter 9 titled 'Measuring Impacts' in the book *The Economics of Microfinance* by Armendariz and Morduch provides a detailed theoretical account and literature review of the various issues in the impact assessment of microfinance operations. This reading would help understand the complexity and difficulties of the issue.
- MYRADA and NABARD scales have been given in this chapter. There have been a lot of materials around these grading scales. Further, these scales keep on changing from time to time. Readers are advised to go through how these scales have changed over a period of time.

CHAPTER

8

Ratio Analysis

Chapter Outline

Learning Objectives

After reading this chapter, you will be able to:

- describe the application of various financial ratios in microfinance.
- critically analyse the utility of ratios in understanding performance of MFIs.

The performance of any for-profit organisation can be judged by the way it manages its finances. Generally, financial information can be found from several sources. One of the most important sources of such information is the financial statements of an organisation. Microfinance institutions (MFIs) are for-profit organisations and their performance can be found from their financial statements.

There are three important financial statements, balance sheet, income statement (also known as profit and loss statement) and cash flow statement. It must be noted here that there are other statements as well, such as statement of change in equity, notes to financial statements and various schedules which detail out the summarised data provided in the above three statements. For example, provision for loan loss is one single item provided in balance sheet, this may be described further in the schedules.

Audited financial statements are prepared by the management and can be accessed by both internal stakeholders (shareholders, employees) and external stakeholders (tax authorities, lenders, suppliers, industry analysts, and others). Hence, these statements contain important information. Generally, financial statements are prepared at the end of financial year. Listed companies are required to present audited financial statements every quarter.

One accepted way of analysing financial statements is ratio analysis. There are different kinds of ratios, such as profitability ratios, solvency and liquidity ratios, asset quality ratios, and efficiency and productivity ratios. The ratios described here have primarily been taken from two sources, Mbeba (2008) and SEEP (2010)

8.1 Profitability Ratios

Several types of profitability ratios can be calculated, such as operational self sustainability ratio (OSSR), financial self sustainability ratio (FSSR), portfolio yield, net interest margin (NIM), return on assets (RoA), and return on equity (RoE), financial expense ratio, operating expense ratio, and impairment expense ratio (Table 8.1). By calculating the ratio, one can understand the level of profit the organisation earns, and whether

Table 8.1 Profitability Ratio Formulae

Ratio	Formula
1. Operational Self Sustainability Ratio	$\frac{\text{Financial Revenue}}{\text{Financial Expenses + Provision of Loan Losses + Operating Expenses}}$
2. Financial Self Sustainability Ratio	$\frac{\text{Financial Revenue}}{\text{Adjusted Financial Expenses + Adjusted Provision of Loan Losses + Adjusted Operating Expenses}}$
3. Return on Assets	$\frac{\text{Net Profit}}{\text{Average Assets}}$
4. Return on Equity	$\frac{\text{Net Profit}}{\text{Average Equity}}$
5. Portfolio Yield	$\frac{\text{Interest, Fees and Commisison on the Portfolio}}{\text{Average Gross Loan Portfolio}}$
6. Net Interest Margin	$\frac{\text{Interet Income} - \text{Inerest Expense}}{\text{Average Earning Assets}}$
7. Cost of Funds (also known as Financial Expense Ratio)	$\frac{\text{Financial Expenses (Interest and Fees) on Funding Liabilities}}{\text{Average Gross Loan Portfolio}}$
8. Operating Expense Ratio	$\frac{\text{Operating Expenses}}{\text{Average Loan Portfolio}}$
9. Impairment Cost Ratio	$\frac{\text{Impairment Expenses}}{\text{Gross Loan Portfolio}}$

Source: *Mbeba* (2008), *SEEP* (2010)

it is considered to be adequate from various perspectives. It may be noted that some of the ratios mentioned earlier have been classified differently by Mbeba (2008), and SEEP (2010), but here the SEEP classification has been followed.

OSSR is the most common ratio used by the MFIs. This indicates to what extent the revenues cover all expenses. An OSSR of 100 per cent means operationally, the company has attained break-even. This is easy to calculate and can be done manually too. Further, it should be calculated every month to control the costs (Mbeba, 2008). This can also be calculated at branch or divisional level.

FSSR is nothing but another version of OSSR, however some adjustments are done in addition to the OSSR. While the numerator remains the same, the components of denominators are adjusted against various changes, such as subsidy, inflation, in-kind contributions and adjustments in provisions to meet the industry standards (Mbeba, 2008). FSSR helps in understanding whether the MFI is able to offset inflationary and other price distorting pressures. Suppose there is an MFI that receives some grants. Ordinarily, profitability would be high, but when adjusted with the grant amount, the real picture will emerge.

It may be noted that under the Microfinance Finance Reporting Standards (MFSR), OSSR and FSSR are not included, as the profitability is already indicated through other ratios, such as RoA and RoE (SEEP, 2010).

RoA and RoE are nothing but ratios that present the net profit as a proportion of the average assets and average equity of the company. Average assets means the average of the assets in the beginning and end of the year. Same formula applies in calculating the average equity too. These two are very important ratios. RoA indicates how well the company used its assets to increase earning, while the RoE is quite interesting for the investor. Investors are interested in earning more from their investment and that is what this ratio provides.

Portfolio yield ratio indicates if the MFI is able to generate interest, fees, and commission from its loan portfolio. An increasing yield is expected, decrease can mean change in pricing, or write-off of revenue.

Net interest margin is nothing but net interest income upon the earning assets. Earning assets refer to those assets which help in generating revenue. It includes gross loan portfolio, trade investments and other investments. This ratio helps in understanding how much is available to cover the expenses of the company. If it decreases over time, it means the company is squeezed to meet its costs (SEEP, 2010).

Cost of funds or the financial expense ratio is important even from the regulatory point of view. Pricing decisions have to depend on it meeting the interest rate cap. For deposit taking companies, the numerator would also include deposits.

Operating expense ratio (OER) is the ratio of operating expenses and the gross loan portfolio. This shows how efficient the MFI is. As portfolio size increases, it is expected that the OER decreases and this can have a bearing on the pricing. It may be noted that this has been brought to several debates. During 2006-10, when MFIs grew significantly, people expected them to decrease the rate of interest. But that did not happen, as the organisations had to report a higher profitability to attract private equity investors. The criticism was that the MFIs initially charged higher interest rate on the pretext of higher transaction cost, but did not pass it on to the client when transaction costs decreased.

Impairment expense ratio is·the calculated as impairment expense upon average gross loan portfolio. Impairment takes place when an asset does not recover its book value. For example, suppose a company owns a car whose book value is ₹250,000. When it was sold, it realised only ₹220,000. Here ₹30,000 will be impairment losses. In financial services, this can happen when there are changes in provisioning policies. For example, suppose, you have a portfolio of ₹5000 million and you have provisioned ₹50 million. The government mandates that the provisioning should be three per cent, i.e ₹150 million. There arises an impairment loss of ₹100 million.

Data for profitability ratios are easy to get, majority of them can be found in the balance sheet and income statement. For getting details of loan loss, one needs to look into cash flow statements as well. For impairment cost, one may need to look into the schedules.

8.2 Solvency and Liquidity Ratios

Solvency ratios include debt to equity, capital adequacy ratio and liquid ratio (Table 8.2).

Debt equity ratio is important to measure how far the company is internally prepared to cope with shocks. Financial services organisations are stressed in times of recession and other problems. Under such circumstances, a high debt would require paying a high amount of interest rate. Also, too much of leverage brings in a lot of risks. With a high debt equity ratio, the organisation is exposed to high risks.

Here long term debt to liabilities ratio can also be useful. While current liabilities are more of a liquidity related matter, long-term debt equity ratio provides an indication of the actual leverage from which the risk exposure can be gauged.

Capital adequacy ratio or capital risk-weighted adequacy ratio (CRAR) provides a measure of how ready the organisation is to handle its risk-weighted assets. It may be noted here that the capital here includes both tier 1 and tier 2 capital, while the denominator includes only risk weighted assets. Risk-free assets like investment in government bonds are not included here. At present, MFIs and NBFCs have to maintain a CRAR of 15 per cent. A good CRAR makes sure that the company survives the stressed times and continue its operations.

Liquid ratio or cash ratio provides an indication on whether the company is able to meet its current liabilities in a short term.

Table 8.2 Solvency Ratio Formulae

Ratio	Formula
1. Debt Equity Ratio	$\frac{\text{Total Debt}}{\text{Total Equity}}$
2. Long-term Debt Equity Ratio	$\frac{\text{Long-term Debt}}{\text{Total Equity}}$
3. Capital Adequacy Ratio (CRAR)	$\frac{\text{Total Capital}}{\text{Risk-weighted Assets}}$
4. Liquid Ratio (also known as Cash Ratio)	$\frac{\text{Cash + Cash Equivalents}}{\text{Demand deposits + Short-term Time Deposits + Short-term Borrowings + Interest Payable on Funding Liabilities + Accounts Payable and Other Short-term Liabilities}}$

Source: for serial no. 1, 2, 4: *Mbeba* (2008), *SEEP* (2010)

Data for calculating solvency ratios can be obtained from income statement and balance sheet. For finding out the risk weighted assets, one may go into the schedules.

8.3 Asset Quality Ratios

Asset quality ratios include portfolio at risk (PAR), write-off ratio, risk coverage ratio (Table 8.3). Portfolio at risk for more than 30 days (PAR>30) can be calculated as the proportion of gross loan portfolio. Renegotiated loans are also included in the numerator. Increasing PAR>30 means that there are repayment problems. The MASF standards, instead of PAR>30, include NPL30 which means non-performing loans greater than 30 days past due. This conceptually includes the renegotiated loans; hence it is calculated as NPL30/gross loan portfolio. It may be noted here that ordinarily 90 day past due is considered as non-performing loan, but in microfinance sector, because of the overwhelming short-term nature of the assets, NPL30/PAR30 becomes more relevant.

Write-off ratio is the actual amount of loan written off as a proportion of average gross loan portfolio. This is a recognition that the loan loss has been brought into books.

A more practical approach is to calculate the NPL30 + write-off ratio, which shows how much actual plus potential risk the company has to bear. A related ratio is the risk coverage ratio, which is the ratio of provision for loan loss and PAR>30. This shows to what extent one recognises the potential loss.

Table 8.3 Asset Quality Ratio Formulae

Ratio	Formula
1. Portfolio at Risk (same as NPL 30)	$\frac{\text{Portfolio at Risk > 30 Days + Renegotiated Loans}}{\text{Gross Loan Portofolio}}$
2. Write-off Ratio	$\frac{\text{Loans Written-off}}{\text{Average Gross Loan Portfolio}}$
3. NPL30 + Write-off Ratio	$\frac{\text{Average NPL30 + Loans Written-off}}{\text{Average Gross Loan Portfolio}}$
4. Risk Coverage Ratio	$\frac{\text{Provision for Loan Losses}}{\text{Portfolio at Risk > 30 Days}}$

Source: *Mbeba* (2008), *SEEP* (2010)

For asset quality ratio related information, balance sheet, income statement and some schedules would be useful.

8.4 Efficiency and Productivity Ratios

Efficiency ratios cover several non-financial aspects (Table 8.4). Portfolio to assets indicates the extent to which a company's assets are effectively utilised to have good quality assets. This ratio can indicate the requirement of funds (liquidity issues) or that the funds are lying idle.

Cost income ratio indicates the proportion of expenses to earn every rupee. This shows how efficiently one is operating.

Cost per client, borrower per loan officer, active clients per staff members are self-explanatory ratios. These are same to input output ratios, the higher the ratios, the greater the efficiency and productivity in the organisation.

The client turnover ratio (or client dropout ratio) indicates the proportion of clients who did not have transactions with the company. Loyal and satisfied customers are not expected to dropout, hence higher the ratio, the more the clients are considered to be satisfied.

Average loan disbursed and average outstanding loan size indicate the contribution to indebtedness of the company to clients, while average deposit related ratios indicated the liabilities toward the customers.

Table 8.4 Efficiency and Productivity Ratio Formulae

Ratio	Formula
1. Portfolio to assets	$\frac{\text{Gross loan portfolio}}{\text{Assets}}$
2. Cost income ratio	$\frac{\text{Operating expenses}}{\text{Total revenues}}$
3. Cost per client	$\frac{\text{Operating expenses}}{\text{Average no. of active clients}}$
4. Borrowers per loan officer	$\frac{\text{No. of active borrowers}}{\text{No. of loan officers}}$
5. Active clients per staff member	$\frac{\text{No. of active clients}}{\text{No. of employees}}$
6. Client turnover ratio (also known as client dropout ratio)	$\frac{\text{No. of active clients in the beginning} + \text{No. of new clients during the period} - \text{No. of active clients at the end of the year}}{\text{Average no. of active clients}}$
7. Average outstanding loan size	$\frac{\text{Gross loan portfolio}}{\text{No. of loans outstanding}}$
8. Average loan disbursed	$\frac{\text{Total amount of loans disbursed}}{\text{Total no. of loans disbursed}}$
9. Average deposit account ratio	$\frac{\text{Total deposits}}{\text{No. of deposit accounts}}$
10. Average deposit account balance per depositor	$\frac{\text{Total deposits}}{\text{No. of depositors}}$

Source: *Mbeba* (2008), *SEEP* (2010)

Efficiency ratios would need information, which is generally not available in financial statements. For example, number of employees, number of loan officers, number of borrowers, all such data would have to be brought from other records.

8.5 Which Ratios are Important?

According to Armendariz and Morduch (2010), five ratios, i.e. OSSR, FSSR, RoA, PAR>30 and Yield on Portfolio, are most commonly used in MFIs, and some of them are not found in standard accounting books.

Given that the NBFC-MFIs have grown substantially and they have a significant amount of portfolio, one needs to understand the financial strength comprehensively. Hence it would be difficult to segregate if any particular ratio is important. It may be noted that the interpretation of a ratio becomes different from situation to situation and from organisation to organisation.

Summary

- Ratio analysis is an important tool to understand the financial health of organisation.
- Ratio analysis can be done based on the information provided in the financial statements, such as balance sheet, income statement and cash flow statement. For some ratios, details in the schedules and non-financial information like data on employees and clients are also required.
- There are four kinds of ratios, profitability ratios, solvency ratios, asset quality ratios and efficiency ratios.
- In general, there is an agreement on the formula, however, sometimes there are different names for various ratios.

Exercises

A. Multiple-choice Questions

1. Which of the following ratio is not related to profitability?
   (a) OSSR
   (b) RoA
   (c) PAR30
   (d) All of the above
2. Which of the following ratios are not applicable for small finance banks?
   (a) RoA
   (b) RoE
   (c) Average deposit account balance
   (d) None of the above
3. Which of the following ratio can be calculated using only the income statement?
   (a) Debt equity ratio
   (b) Return on equity
   (c) Cost income ratio
   (d) None of the above
4. Which of the following does not need any information from balance sheet?
   (a) Cost per client
   (b) Debt equity ratio
   (c) Liquid ratio
   (d) None of the above
5. In comparison to last year, OSSR increased. This means
   (a) It is not good for the company
   (b) It is better for the company
   (c) It does not matter
   (d) Cannot be determined
6. Suppose an MFI decided that the interest rate will be decreased. Everything else remaining the same, the cost per client would
   (a) Increase
   (b) Decrease
   (c) Will not be affected
   (d) Cannot be determined
7. You are required to calculate two ratios, NPL30 and NPL30 + write-off ratio. Which of the following is true in this regard?
   (a) NPL 30 is always higher than NPL30 + write-off ratio
   (b) NPL 30 is always less than NPL30 + write-off ratio
   (c) NPL 30 is not less than NPL30 + write-off r atio
   (d) NPL 30 is not greater than NPL30 + write-off ratio

8. For calculating cost of funds of Small Finance Banks, which of the following data are required?
   (a) Interest and fee expenses, and gross loan portfolio
   (b) Interest and fee expenses and deposits, and gross loan portfolio
   (c) Interest and fee expenses and deposits
   (d) Deposits and gross loan portfolio
9. Operating expense ratio has decreased significantly over the last three years. You can think of?
   (a) Increasing the interest rate
   (b) Decreasing the interest rate
   (c) Keep the interest rate same
   (d) The above ratio has no bearing on interest rate decisions
10. Which of the following ratio is used specifically by MFIs?
   (a) OSSR
   (b) Debt equity ratio
   (c) CRAR
   (d) None of the above

B. Review Questions

1. Distinguish between operational self sufficiency ratio and operational efficiency ratio.
2. What is the importance of leverage ratio like debt equity ratio for a financial services company?
3. If you have to choose five ratios that are most important for assessing the financial health of an MFI, what would those be? Why?
4. Which of the ratios discussed in the chapter would be useful for a not-for-profit MFI?
5. Can ratios provide the real picture of a financial services company? Critically analyse the practice of using ratios in understanding the performance of a company.

C. Application-based Questions

The balance sheet and income statement of Utkarsh Microfinance Ltd for the year 2014-15 are given below.

1. Calculate all the ratios based on the data available in the given two statements.
2. Which ratios cannot be calculated based on the information provided? Which statements and schedules are required to calculate all these ratios?
3. What do you interpret about the financial situation of the company based on the these ratios?

Table 8.5 Balance Sheet for the Financial Year ended on 31 March 2015

	As on 31.3.15 (in ₹)	As on 31.3.14 (in ₹)
EQUITIES AND LIABILITIES		
Shareholders' fund		
Share Capital	501,444,530	258,637,030
Reserves and Surplus	1,115,451,559	484,115,741
Subtotal	1,616,096,089	742,752,771
Non-current Liabilities		
Long-term Borrowings	4,212,548,269	1,837,586,599
Other Long-term Liabilities	9,865,170	5,011,247
Long-term Provisions	16,706,171	7,297,289
Subtotal	4,239,119,610	1,849,895,135
Current Liabilities		
Short-term Borrowings	180,000,000	317,361
Other current Liabilities	3,329,688,472	2,042,079,414
Short-term Provisions	62,750,819	23,849,986
Subtotal	3,572,439,291	2,066,246,761
Total	9,428,454,990	4,658,894,667

ASSETS		
Non-current Assets		
Fixed Assets		
(i) Tangible Assets	31,377,995	15,403,480
(ii) Intangible Assets	1,074,644	1,042,252
Deferred Tax Assets, Net	371,266	190,206
Gross Loan Portfolio	1,476,879,884	746,934,580
Less-managed Portfolio	160,230,933	122,281,930
Loan Portfolio	1,316,648,951	624,652,650
Long-term Loans and Advances	127,302	307,218
Other Non-current Assets	571,220,934	304,939,385
Subtotal	1,920,821,092	946,535,191
Current Assets		
Current Investments	1,013,639	452,593
Trade Receivables	40,977,722	10,225,970
Cash and Bank Balances	2,367,779,905	1,319,762,842
Gross Loan portfolio	5,804,029,967	2,809,160,770
Less-managed Portfolio	886,405,834	587,864,092
Loan Portfolio	4,917,624,133	2,221,296,678
Short-term Loans and Advances	94,596,166	70,255,305
Other Current Assets	85,742,333	91,266,088
Subtotal	7,507,733,898	3,713,259,476
Total	9,428,554,990	4,659,794,667

Table 8.6 Statement of Profit and Loss for the Year ended on 31 March 2015

	For the year ended on 31.3.15 (in ₹)	**For the year ended as on 31.3.14 (in ₹)**
Revenue		
Revenue from Operations	1,254,874,354	634,567,749
Other Incomes	94,744,425	68,699,611
Total Revenue	1,349,618,779	703,267,360
Expenses		
Operating Expenses	129,669,218	62,799,244
Employee Benefits expense	279,584,336	141,666,688
Finance Cost	650,729,370	349,947,447
Depreciation/Amortisation	7,758,812	3,232,524
Other Expenses	17,078,536	9,763,188
Total Expenses	1,084,820,272	567,409,091
Profit Before Tax	264,798,507	135,858,269

Tax Expenses		
Current Tax	104,775,598	53,660,000
Deferred Tax Expense/Benefit	(181,060)	(44,883)
Profit After Tax	160,203,969	82,243,152
Earning Per Equity Share		
Basic	5.26	3.36
Diluted	4.77	3.36

Source: Audited Financial Statement (2014-15) of Utkarsh Microfinance Ltd

Further Readings

- Textbooks on corporate finance or financial management provide an account of ratio analysis. These books would not be specific to the context of financial services organisations; however, they provide the detailed explanations of each ratio and its rationale. Examples of such books are
  - *Fundamentals of Corporate Finance by Ross, Westerfield, and Jordan; Fundamentals of Financial Management by Van Horne and Wachowicz Jr.*
  - Sa-Dhan's *Tracking Financial Performance Standards of Microfinance Institutions: An Operational Manual* is also a useful book for understanding ratio analysis.

CHAPTER

9

Responsible Finance and Social Performance Management

Chapter Outline

Learning Objectives

After reading this chapter, you will be able to:

- discuss the need of responsible finance.
- describe the different ratings followed in microfinance industry.
- provide an idea about the principles and practices of assessing social performance management in an MFI.

9.1 Need of Responsible Finance

Ratio analysis discussed in the previous chapter (Chapter 8) helps in understanding the financial performance of a company. To some extent, it can indicate something for the future performance also. However, all said and done, ratio analysis can primarily make one understand the financial aspects of performance. But performance is not limited to financials only, there are other aspects as well. These days, when people talk about sustainable development, they are talking about not just profits, but also about the triple bottom line, which includes people, planet, and profit. Thus, one must consciously make efforts to not just being profitable, but also to be prudent in terms of social and environmental outcomes of a business. The financial industry does not directly produce environmental hazards (unlike manufacturing companies), but it still can contribute negatively if it funds such organisations. However, there are significant implications of financial services companies to social outcomes. There is enough news about frauds, cheating, imprudent decisions and misbehaviour by financial services companies. Corruption, money laundering, counterfeiting and terror financing are menaces to the whole world, which have been done in participation of some banks and other financial services companies. The ultimate result is that one really has to think twice if the financial services sector has contributed anything positive. But there are silver linings also. In Chapter 1, there was a mention of Professor Robert Shiller's work, which described how finance could contribute to the formation of a good society.

In this context, there has been wide acceptance of the view that financial services companies have to be responsible in terms of making financing decisions. Never before have there been such intensive calls for promoting transparency and accountability. There has been a fair amount of consensus about what exactly responsible finance means. According to the Social Performance Task Force,

Responsible finance means delivering financial services in a way that is transparent, fair, safe and likely to generate benefits for poor clients (SPTF, 2014:9).

Responsible finance has two components, client protection and social performance management (SPM). This chapter includes discussion on various aspects of client protection and SPM.

9.2 Rating Models and Their Shortcomings

Before we move into the space of SPM, it is useful to understand the way traditionally financial services organisations were assessed and rated. There have been some popular models of rating for MFIs, such as CAMEL, GIRAFE, PEARLS, MicroRate, and M-CRIL.

- CAMEL rating includes evaluating a company on various parametres like capital adequacy (C), assets (A), management (M), earning (E) and liquidity (L). Adopted initially by ACCION International for its internal use, it later became popular, and is known as ACCION CAMEL rating. This is done based on 21 indicators (8 quantitative and 13 qualitative indicators), which are then converted into a 0 to 5 rating and their equivalent letter grading (AAA, AA, A, BBB, BB, B, C, D, and not rated), (Salzman and Salinger, 1998). It may be noted that the original CAMEL rating in USA has already added another parameter sensitivity (S), hence known as the CAMELS model of rating.
  The process of ACCION CAMEL assessment is a month-long exercise, including 10-day field visit of a two or three member-team of analysts from ACCION's Bogota and Boston offices. Before this visit, a questionnaire is sent to the concerned MFI. During the visit, interviews with management, staff and clients are done. Preliminary results are shared with the management. It may be noted that the results of this rating are confidential and cannot be shared with others without approval of the client and ACCION International (CGAP, 2001).
- GIRAFE rating was created by PlaNet Rating and has been used extensively in rating microfinance institutions across the world. If the client agrees, it is made available online by PlaNet Rating (CGAP, 2001). It includes evaluating a company on various parametres viz. governance and decision-making processes (G), information and management tools (I), risks analysis and control (R), activities and loan portfolio (A), funding equities and liabilities (F) and efficiency and liability (E). The process of this rating involves a one or two week visit by a team, including a local consultant who is acquainted with the regional situation, who analyse the financial and non-financial documents, interact with employees and management, and finally award a rating to the organisation. Rating is done on 26 factors (14 qualitative and 12 quantitative factors) and a global rating of G1 (serious weakness) to G5 (outstanding performance), and based on this, recommendations are made on whether investment should be made in the company or not. http://www.gdrc.org/icm/rating/rate-3.html, retrieved on 6 April 2019).
- PEARLS rating includes evaluation of various components, such as protection (P), i.e. adequacy of provisions against loan loss, effective financial structure (E), asset quality (A), rates of return and costs (R), liquidity (L), and signs of growth (S). It was created by the World Council of Credit Unions, Inc. (WOCCU) in the 1980s. The rating system uses 44 quantitative financial indicators to understand the financial health of financial institutions (WOCCU, 2002). Generally, the PEARLS rating is used as an early warning system internally. This rating is disclosed to a limited number of participants, such as members of credit unions and national associations (CGAP, 2001)
- MicroRate rating is based on benchmarking against peers. It looks at three aspects, lending operations and portfolio quality, organisation and MIS, and financial performance. Management and governance aspects are also assessed and the opinion on creditworthiness, i.e. recommended, watch and caution is provided. This way this rating is less a rating and more of an opinion about the creditworthiness of the Microfinance Institute (MFI), (CGAP, 2001).
- M-CRIL rating is done using 30 indicators on various aspects like organisational and governance aspects, managerial and resource strength, and financial performance. This is undertaken through an 18-day exercise which includes a visit to the organisation and interaction which goes on for four to

five days. The M-CRIL reports are confidential and can only be shared with others if the client agrees (CGAP, 2001).

These rating models have been widely used to assess the performance of the financial institutions. However, as it can be seen from the dimensions of the rating models, they are heavily inclined towards financial aspects. These look at governance and management aspects, but there is essentially not much information on looking at the social impact of the MFI's operations.

9.3 Initial Efforts of Client Protection and SPM in Microfinance

The Andhra Pradesh microfinance crisis of 2010 was, in a way, an eye opener for the microfinance industry (more details in Chapter 12). Although the crisis was rooted in one state (Andhra Pradesh), it had substantial effect throughout the country. It took place at a time when MFIs had become complacent and focussed on profit rather than the social objectives. The prevailing idea was that MFIs operated in a market-based model; as these organisations did not receive any grants, they did not have to take care of the concerns of government and civil society. But the crisis showed that the opinion of government and civil societies did matter.

Such influences shaped the microfinance industry significantly. Apart from highlighting the operational and strategic mistakes and callous approaches of MFIs, the learning from the crisis also made people realise the importance of social aspects of microfinance. MYRADA's social capital helped in times of such crises, while the MFIs could not generate any support.

> *...when leading politicians from the party in power in Karnataka attacked Myrada in the mid 90s, it was the 18,000 SHGs in Myrada projects that decided to go against this party in the State elections.........There are several examples where genuine SHGs that still exist in some pockets took a stand in certain areas where some local politicians, in an attempt to gain publicity, had started inciting SHGs not to return loans. Unfortunately for them, the SHGs decided to call the politicians' bluff. Similar experience did not emerge with the groups formed after 2000. In fact, some eminent economists expected the groups which received loans from Non-banking Financial Company (NBFC)-MFIs in Andhra Pradesh (all belonging to the post 2000 model), to rise up against the government's action in 2010 to curb NBFC-MFI activities albeit on disputed grounds. Nothing like this happened. Obviously the groups did not have any stake which they considered worthwhile fighting for... (Fernandez, 2017:13).*

The message was loud and clear. The MFIs were moving away from their core mission of financial inclusion and poverty alleviation. MFIs needed to be more prudent and responsible and they had to build social capital if they wanted to survive in long run. In the meantime, there were signs of slow growth by 2012, and the banks wanted to renew their lending activities to MFIs. But they needed some assurance that things had started moving in a right direction.

In this context, the industry associations like MFIN and Sa-Dhan made efforts to enforce a set of code of conduct. The guidelines of RBI issued in 2011 (discussed in Chapter 10) also suggested that fair practices have to be followed and Self-regulatory Organisations (SROs) could play important roles in this regard. At that time, MFIN and Sa-Dhan had their own set of code of conducts. In December 2011, the two sets of code of conducts were merged to create a Unified Code of Conduct (Sriram, 2017). Adherence to the code of conduct became an acceptable way that would enable subsequent lending to the MFIs. This started the concept of preparing Code of Conduct Compliance Assessment (COCA) reports. With support of the World Bank, this project was implemented by Small Industries Development Bank of India (SIDBI).

The COCA reports were prepared by various agencies such as Access-Assist, ICRA Management Consulting Services (IMaCS), M2i Consulting, M-CRIL, and SME Rating Agencies (SMERA). These agencies were independent evaluators, which provided credibility to the assessment, hence many financers gave importance to this assessment. However, there were limitations of COCA too. The principles of COCA were the same, but specific tools differed from organisation to organisation. Weightage assignment, degrees of leniency in assessment were some of the problems (Sriram, 2017).

Another initiative, Responsible Business Index (RBIndex) was also used extensively. This included various parameters, such as disclosure to clients, client engagement, institutional process, transparency and history of violation of norms. It had 69 indicators having a total score of 100. The members of Microfinance Institutions Network (MFIN) used this extensively in 2012-13 (Sriram, 2017).

9.4 Social Performance Management

Practices like preparation of COCA reports, RBIndex reports, were done widely in the aftermath of AP (Andhra Pradesh) crisis. This was also the time things were evolving worldwide. The global economy had stared recovering from the credit crisis in USA and everybody was talking about changing the way in which financial services companies were assessed. Internationally, there were already initiatives like client protection assessment (CPP certification), and Smart Campaign. Social performance management (SPM), in this context, came up as an acceptable practice in which the performance of the MFIs can be assessed in a realistic manner.

In a way, SPM is not a new invention; it was already present in various disguises. Various scholars and practitioners had highlighted it in some or the other manner. It was like going back to the basics. Ultimately, the goal of microfinance always remained at financial inclusion and well-being of the poor.

Thus the intent of the MFIs was always clear. SPM required the integration of this basic goal into the performance assessment framework, as follows (Imp-Act:2005).

Intent and design → Activities → Output → Outcome/Impact

A major problem with the microfinance industry is that the market operates in a push mechanism and is supply driven. Hence, it is the MFIs which have surplus funds than there are demands, and as a result, there is overindebtedness among clients.

The approach of SPM is a relatively balanced one. It does not ignore the importance of financial performance, but it also recognises that social values must be created out of the microfinance investments. It takes care of the needs of various stakeholders of the microfinance industry. It results in greater transparency in the system and MFIs develop an understanding of the clients' needs (IFAD, 2006).

Motivations behind conducting SPM varies from organisation to organisation. Organisations from countries like Bosnia and Herzegovina, Croatia, Russia and Slovakia indicated the following reasons for carrying out SPM:

- Improve organisational systems and products
- Develop ways to learn from clients in a small institution
- Profile poverty and deepen outreach
- Address drop-out problem
- Address low demand and delinquency problem
- Segment the market and monitor impact (Imp-Act, 2005:13)

However, there is a lot of diversity among various SPM reports which range from client demand, poverty audit to education and various other social aspects (IFAD, 2006).

A typical SPM report included detailed description and analysis of various aspects, such as:

- Intent and design (mission, vision, goals, governance, planning)
- Market strategy (targeting of clients, geographical spread)
- Products and their delivery (credit, savings, insurance, non-financial services)
- Operational systems (HR, MIS, internal audit)

- Compliance to social responsibilities (avoidance of over indebtedness, transparency, responsible pricing, fair and responsible treatment of clients, privacy of client data, mechanism for complaints resolutions (Klus, 2013)

Social performance management is a complex process. It requires establishing a direct feedback mechanism for collection of social performance data. At the strategic level, the management has to ensure that while meeting its financial goals, it is not drifted away from its social goals, which determine its ultimate existence. Further, various stakeholders, particularly the investors and donors, must be informed so that their goodwill and future investment avenues are secured. Customer services need to be a differentiating factor, which can make the organisation competitive. Retention of staff and influencing regulations because of its positive practices and reputation can also make a good social performance (STPF, 2014).

Social performance management is sometimes compared with impact assessment. It may be noted that SPM is a process, which includes implementation of the social goals, while impact is the ultimate outcome achieved.

9.5 Universal Standards of SPM

Interestingly, SPM has been carried out in multiple ways. There is no single acceptable way in which SPM can be defined. This creates some confusion among the users. Another problem is that conceptually one can still zero in somewhere, but how does one implement such a complex system? Some efforts have been made in standardising the SPM processes. The Universal Standards for Social Performance Management (USSPM) is one such initiative, which has been developed through integrating the best practices in the industry and thorough consultations with various stakeholders. According to USSPM, there are six dimensions of SPM (STPF, 2014).

- At the first stage, the organisation defines its social goals and monitors how these are being adhered to.
- Then it ensures that the Board, management and employees adhere to such social goals. Appropriate communication is made so that all stakeholders have a shared understanding of these goals.
- In the next stage, the products and delivery models are designed to suit the needs of the newly established goals. The systems and processes like MIS and performance system are also aligned to this.
- The organisation treats its clients responsibly.
- The organisation treats its employees responsibly. Employees are the backbone of an organisation, as without their support and cooperation no organisation can succeed in its goals.
- Finally, balance between social and financial goals is maintained.

There is no formula for ensuring that the organisation meets the requirement of SPM. It can be done internally, it can be implemented internally while being guided by an external expert, or vice versa (SPTF, 2014). Further, there can be repetitions and iterations of various activities which can go back and forth. The ultimate goal has to be kept in mind.

For implementing the USSPM, a lot of details have to be followed, as given in Table 9.1.

Table 9.1 Dimensions, Standards and Essential Practices in USSPM

Dimension	Standards	Essential Practices
1. Define and monitor social goals	The provider should have a strategy to achieve the social goals and collect the relevant data in that regard.	Mission statement specifying the service to vulnerable and low-income groups, appropriate indicators to measure progress, appropriate products and their delivery mechanism, MIS and regular analysis of relevant social indicators.

2. Ensure Board, management, and employee commitment to social goals	Board holds the company accountable to its mission. Management assures the implementation of strategy in that regard. Employees recruitment and performance evaluation is based on financial and social criteria.	Board members oriented on SPM, Board holds the CEO accountable towards achieving social goals, and preserves sanctity of mission during change. Management operationalises the social strategy and addresses SPM related risks. Employee screening based on commitment for social goals, and performance incentives and promotion criteria are linked to these aspects.
3. Design products, services, and delivery channels that meet clients' needs and preferences	The provider understands the specific needs of different clients. Products and delivery channels are designed to meet the clients' needs and organisation's social goals	The provider seeks data on need, preference of clients and monitors the products and delivery channels to see their fitment with clients' needs. Appropriate products that suit clients' needs are delivered and employee behaviour while dealing with clients is monitored.
4. Treat clients responsibly	Clients are treated in ways such that there is prevention of over-indebtedness. Fair and respect treatment Privacy of data Complaint resolution mechanism	Having a well-document policy for loan approval, use of credit reports, and monitoring by senior management regarding overindebtedness. Code of conduct is monitored and enforced, discrimination avoided, loan collected by staff appropriately, system in place to detect fraud and insurance claim processed fairly and timely. Security and confidentiality in maintaining client data, and information to clients about how the data is used. Should have an effective system of client complaint receipt and resolution, and clients' should be informed in this regard. Feedback is used for improving products and their delivery.
5. Treat employees responsibly	Written HR Policy Employees communicate about their functions and terms Monitors employee satisfaction	Written policy compliant with state law, clearly mentioning compensation norms, meeting industry standards, employee grievance mechanism in place, and employer takes care of the health and safety risks of employees. Employee should receive clear communication of their job description and performance evaluation, and should receive job-specific training. Employee satisfaction analysed and employee turnover monitored, and actions taken to improve the conditions.
6. Balance financial and social performance	Monitors growth and institutional sustainability Investors, lenders, board and management aligned with mix of social and financial mix Prices set reasonably Compensation to senior management which is appropriate to the stated social goals	Sustainable growth targets are set, monitored and internal capacity is checked. Engagement with various stakeholders to set a reasonable expectation level from investors and having transparent financial structure. Pricing policy aligned with client's interests' financial ratios should not signal pricing issues. Compensation to senior management should be in line with the provider's social goals and should be disclosed to stakeholders. Difference between top levels' and field employees' compensation is analysed and matched with social mission.

Note: This is a summary version of the detailed standards and practices as mentioned in SPTF (2014)

Case Study 9.1 COCA Report for Bandhan Financial Services 2012-13

Undertaken by M2I Consulting

There were two components of this report, code of conduct and compliance. Code of conduct assessment included measurement of six dimensions, client origination and targeting (how a client is identified), loan pricing, loan appraisal, client data security, staff conduct (communication with client, and loan recovery process), relationship management and feedback mechanism, and integrating social values into operations. Compliance assessment included looking at the four parameters, i.e., approval, documentation, dissemination, and observation (ADDO), a framework developed by M2i Consulting. According to this framework, major decisions, in relation to the above parameters, should be approved by the board, guidelines and procedures emerging from the policy should be documented and disseminated across all levels in the organisation, and this should be observed in practice.

The exercise included discussion with management and employees, review of policy documents and operation manuals at the head office, sample visit to branch offices and discussion with staff there, interview with clients on sample basis, and review of loan files at branch office.

Table 9.2 Weights of Various Dimensions in COCA Report of Bandhan

	Weight					No. of indicators	Score obtained
	Approval	Documentation	Dissemination	Observation	Total		
Client origination	4%	4%	4%	7%	19%	24	20.9
Loan pricing	2%	1%	1%	7%	11%	15	13.8
Loan appraisal	3%	3%	2%	4%	12%	16	11.7
Client data security	1%	2%	1%	1%	5%	8	7.0
Staff conduct	5%	5%	7%	85	25%	35	34.4
Client relationship and feedback	1%	6%	4%	7%	18%	26	23.8
Integrating social values into operations	2%	2%	2%	4%	10%	14	13.8
Total	18%	23%	21%	38%	100%	138	125.3
No. of indicators	25	31	31	51	138		
Regulatory compliance (parameters)						12	12

Notes: Scores have also been calculated on various compliance parameters, which were as follows: approval (23), documentation (26.5), dissemination (30.9), and observation (44.9).

Source: *M2i Consulting (2012: 3 and 24)*

Overall, the company received a score of 91%. Based on the above analysis, it was concluded that the MFI had a sound grievance redressal system, sensitive recovery system, sound practice of well-treatment of clients, and good training mechanism. It was suggested that in loan appraisal process improvements were needed.

Discussion Questions

1. How is COCA report different from standard rating reports?
2. Does the COCA report fall short of a comprehensive SPM assessment report? How?
3. What changes should be added to COCA report to meet the needs of present day demands of donors and regulatory agencies?

Summary

- SPM is required, as there has been an increasing emphasis on responsible financing.
- There are five popular rating models extensively in microfinance, such as CAMEL, GIRAFE, PEARLS, MicroRate and M-CRIL. These ratings are predominantly based on financial aspects; some dimensions of management governance are also there.
- The Andhra Pradesh crisis of 2010 was a wake up call to the MFIs, who had started focussing on the financial aspects only. The industry associations, MFIN and Sa-Dhan were the first to enforce code of conduct.
- With support from the World Bank, SIDBI implemented the COCA project. This helped the banks who wanted a robust mechanism of assessment, before they could revive financing to the microfinance industry.
- SPM includes a framework, intent and design → activities → output → outcomes/impact
- SPM balances the needs of all stakeholders, creates transparency and helps understanding customers' needs.
- The USSPM has a common framework for implementing SPM. It has six dimensions, define and monitor social goals, ensure the commitment of Board, management, and employees to these goals, align the products and systems to the goals, treat clients responsibly, treat employees responsibly, and balance social and financial goals.

Exercises

A. Multiple-choice Questions

1. Which of the following rating results are ordinarily not disclosed to outsiders?
   (a) Accion-CAMEL
   (b) GIRAFE
   (c) M-CRIL
   (d) All of the above
2. Which of the following is more of an early warning system than a full-fledged rating?
   (a) GIRAFE
   (b) PEARLS
   (c) MicroRate
   (d) M-CRIL
3. Which of the following event was a wake up call for the MFIs for making way to responsible finance?
   (a) Nobel Prize to Muhammad Yunus
   (b) Malegam Committee Report
   (c) AP microfinance crisis
   (d) All of the above
4. The components of responsible finance are
   (a) Client protection and SPM
   (b) Regulation and SPM
   (c) COCA and SPM
   (d) None of the above
5. The first step in the process of SPM is to have an
   (a) Impact assessment
   (b) Plan for activities
   (c) Intent and design
   (d) All of the above
6. SPM helps in
   (a) Improving transparency
   (b) Understanding clients' needs
   (c) Both (a) and (b)
   (d) None of the above
7. Which of the following is not true about COCA reports?
   (a) It was implemented by SIDBI
   (b) It was funded by RBI
   (c) It was carried out in the aftermath of AP crisis
   (d) It includes assessment of how code of conduct is adhered to
8. Which of the following is common for COCA and USSPM?
   (a) Treating clients responsibly
   (b) Treating employees responsibly
   (c) Both (a) and (b)
   (d) None of the above

9. Social performance management does not require
   (a) Being the market leader in the industry
   (b) Balancing financial and social goals
   (c) Ensuring that the organisation does not drift away from its mission
   (d) None of the above

10. Social performance assessment is
   (a) Same as impact assessment
   (b) Includes impact assessment
   (c) Different from impact assessment
   (d) None of the above

B. Review Questions

1. Make a comparative statement of various rating methods, Accion-CAMEL, GIRAFE, PEARLS, MicroRate, and M-CRIL.
2. What are the major parametres on which COCA reports were prepared? Describe the pros and cons of COCA assessments.
3. Describe the basic principles of SPM.
4. What are the dimensions of universal standards of SPM?
5. Social Performance Management holds the key for future growth of microfinance institutions. Comment.

C. Application-based Questions

1. You have to assess the social performance management (SPM) of a microfinance institution. What kind of information would you require for making this assessment? List out the information required.
2. Go through the case study 'Annapurna Finance Private Ltd' (Annexure III). Visit the website of the company and download the latest audited statements and annual reports. Based on this, critically analyse the standing of the company regarding social performance management.

Further Readings

- SPTF's *Universal Standards for Social Performance Management, Im-pact's Social Performance Management in Microfinance: Guidelines,* COCA reports of various organisations, are useful documents. The *Microfinance India: Social Performance Report* was published in 2012 and 2013. These would make useful readings for greater understanding of the issue. Some companies also have their SPM report available in the public domain, these can aslo be referred to.
- Ledgerwood et al's Chapter 14 'Monitoring and Managing Financial and Social Performance' in *The Microfinance Handbook* edited by Ledgerwood details out on this issue.

PART IV
Regulatory Environment for Microfinance

PART IV

Regulatory Environment for Microfinance

10 RBI Guidelines on Microfinance

11 Other Regulatory Issues and Debates

CHAPTER

10

RBI Guidelines on Microfinance

Chapter Outline

Learning Objectives

After reading this chapter, you will be able to:

- provide an overview of RBI guidelines on SHGs.
- discuss the various provisions of RBI guidelines on NBFC-MFIs.
- discuss the provisions of RBI guidelines on Small Finance Banks and Payments Banks.

10.1 Introduction

For quite a long time, starting with 1990s to 2010, microfinance sector was unregulated. It does not mean that there was no regulation at all, instead there were regulatory provisions in bits and pieces. For example, Non-banking Financial Companies (NBFCs) were regulated by the Reserve Bank of India (RBI), while the state governments also had some control on various microfinance agencies as moneylending was a state subject, and hence there were laws enacted dealing with issues related to this activity. It was this overlapping regulatory scope that led to the crisis in Andhra Pradesh in 2010.

In the aftermath of this crisis, in November 2010, the RBI constituted a committee headed by Mr. Y. H. Malegam to prepare a regulatory framework for the microfinance sector. Based on the recommendations of the Malegam Committee, the RBI issued a set of notifications in December 2011 in the form of guidelines for microfinance institutions.

Other than this, the year 2015 was also significant because a new set of differentiated banks were licenced. There were called small finance banks (SFBs) and payments banks (PBs).

However, there are no statutory guidelines available yet. Twice there had been efforts to have a parliamentary legislation and microfinance bills were prepared, once in 2006 and later in 2012. However, the bills did not see the light of the day and expired as a proposed bill only

This chapter outlines the regulatory framework dealing with Microfinance Institutions (MFIs), SFBs and PBs. It also makes a critical analysis of the existing regulatory provisions.

10.2 Guidelines for SHGs

In 1993, the RBI issued a circular that self-help groups (SHGs), whether registered or not, were allowed to open saving bank (SB) accounts in banks[1]. This was a breakthrough, as earlier banks were reluctant to open accounts of SHGs. Since then, RBI has been issuing circulars from time to time.

1. DBOD. No. BC. 63/13:01:08/92-93, 4 January 1993, Reserve Bank of India, (source: NABARD's 'A Handbook for Self Help Groups'.

In 1994, a working group under the chairmanship of Mr. S. K. Kalia, then MD of NABARD, was constituted. The working groups viewed that 'linking of SHGs with banks is a cost effective, transparent and flexible approach to improve the accessibility of credit from the formal banking system to the unreached rural poor, which is expected to offer the much needed solution to the twin problems being faced by the banks, viz. recovery of loans in the rural areas and the high transaction costs in dealing with small borrowers at frequent intervals.' (RBI, 2017: para 3). Hence, it was suggested that formation and bank linkage of SHGs should be encouraged. This could be an opportunity for the banks.

Further, banks have been instructed to report the lending to SHGs as a separate segment of priority sector lending ((RBI, 2017: para 5).

The norms for KYC of SHGs have been simplified. KYC verification of SHGs has been a tedious task as reported by banks. Further, this also became a pretext on which loans have been refused. Hence, the RBI's master circular in 2017 mentions that KYC verification of the office bearers is sufficient and can be done at the time of opening of account. While lending, there is no need of verifying the same again (RBI, 2017: para 6).

Another problem was that sometimes some of the members of an SHG defaulted their loan repayment on an individual basis. This has been made a reason to not lend to the SHGs. The RBI clarified that such SHGs can still be provided loans, however, the concerned members may not be issued such loans (RBI, 2017: para 10).

10.3 RBI's 2011 Guidelines

10.3.1 NBFC-MFI as a Separate Category

The guidelines for MFIs were issued originally in 2011 and were updated on 20 April 2016 (RBI, 2016a). These make a separate category of NBFC-MFIs for the business of microfinance. According to the guidelines, an NBFC-MFI is defined as a non-deposit taking NBFC (other than a company licensed under Section 25 of the Indian Companies Act, 1956) fulfilling two conditions, i) it should have a minimum net owned fund (NOF) of ₹50 million (5 crore). This condition is relaxed to ₹20 million (2 crore) if the organisation is registered in the Nort-East regions of India; (para II.1 i) ii) it should have at least 85 per cent of its net assets[2] in the nature of qualifying assets. (para II. 1. ii).

When the guidelines were issued, an NBFC could be floated by having an NOF of ₹20 million. Hence the existing companies were given a phase-wise target of meeting the NOF of ₹50 million by 31 March 2014. Those registered in North-East region, earlier required an NOF of ₹10 million (1 crore), which they had to enhance to ₹20 million by the aforesaid date. For the new companies who wanted NBFC-MFI registration, there was no relaxation. They had to meet the NOF of ₹50 million and ₹20 million, as applicable, from the beginning.

10.3.2 Qualifying Assets

Thus, the guidelines bring in two new concepts. One, the idea of a unique category of organisations known as NBFC-MFIs, and two, the idea of qualifying assets. What exactly the guidelines meant by the latter? According to the guidelines, qualifying assets of the NBFC-MFI would mean the following (para II. 1 ii-explanations):

- Loan disbursed to a rural household having an income of maximum ₹100,000 (one lakh rupees) or to an urban household or a semi-urban household whose income is under ₹160,000 (one lakh and sixty thousand rupees)
- The loan amount should not be more than ₹60,000 in the first cycle and ₹1 lakh in the subsequent cycles.
- Total indebtedness of the borrower should not be more than ₹100,000. In calculating this amount, the borrowings towards educational and medical expenses are not included.
- If the amount of loan is more than ₹30,000, then the tenure of repayment should not be less than 24 months, and there should be no prepayment penalty

2. "Net assets" are defined as total assets other than cash and bank balances and money market instruments.

- No collateral should be asked for the above borrowings
- The proportion of loans extended towards income generation should not be less than 50 per cent of the total loans advanced by the MFI
- Loans can be repaid on weekly, fortnightly or monthly instalments as per the choice of the borrower.

'The income an NBFC-MFI derives from the remaining 15 percent of assets shall be in accordance with the regulations specified in that behalf' (para II. 1. iii).

How does it matter if the NBFC-MFI does not meet the 85 per cent qualifying criteria assets? The implication is that the NBFC would not be considered as an NBFC-MFI and it can advance loans to the microfinance sector only to the extent of 10 per cent of its total assets. (para II. 1 iv)

10.3.3 Prudential Norms

NBFC-MFIs are required to maintain a capital adequacy ratio (CAR) of 15 per cent of their aggregate risk weighted assets. For the purpose of calculating the capital, Tier I and Tier II capital may be used. Tier II capital should never exceed 100 per cent of the Tier I capital (para II.2.B.i).

It may be noted here that Tier I capital includes the core equity capital (paid up capital), statutory reserves, disclosed free reserves, and this can be used without shutting down the company. Tier II capital includes hybrid capital instruments, loan-loss and re-evaluation reserves, and undisclosed reserves. This can be used only when the operations are going to be closed down. Tier I capital, signifies the financial strength of an institution (for more details, see RBI Circular on Basel Framework)[3].

All new NBFC-MFIs shall maintain a capital risk-weighted adequacy ratio (CRAR) consisting of Tier I and Tier II capital which shall not be less than 15 percent of their aggregate risk weighted assets. The total Tier II Capital, at any point of time, shall not exceed 100 percent of Tier I capital. It may be noted that RBI has provisions for providing risk weights for on-balance sheet assets and credit conversion factors for off-balance items. Such guidelines may be referred to while making such calculations. For the year 2011-12, some relaxation was provided to the existing companies. For example, those having small asset size (less than ₹100 crore, i.e one billion rupees) were given the target of 15 per cent CRAR to be achieved by 1 April 2012. Similarly, given that some of the MFIs were hit hard by the microfinance crisis in Andhra Pradesh (AP), only for the year 2011-12, those having more than 25 per cent of their loan portfolio in the state of Andhra Pradesh were given a target of CRAR of 12 per cent. From the next financial year (2012-13), every company in the category of NBFC-MFI must maintain a CRAR of 15 per cent (para II.2.B.i.a-d).

Because of the AP crisis, the loan portfolio of MFIs in the state (AP) was significantly affected and there was hardly any recovery. It was provided by the guidelines that provisioning for the AP portfolio 'shall be notionally reckoned as part of NOF and there shall be progressive reduction in such recognition of the provisions for AP portfolio equally over a period of five years. Accordingly, 100 per cent of the provision made for the AP portfolio as on 31 March 2013 would be added back notionally to NOF for CRAR purposes as on that date. This add-back would be progressively reduced by 20 per cent each year, i.e. up to March 2017.' (para II.2.B.ii.b). CRAR of 15 per cent has to be maintained on the notional AP portfolio and the non-AP portfolio.

Provisioning and asset classification norms are regulated by the Non-Banking Financial (Non-Deposit accepting or holding) Companies Prudential Norms (Reserve Bank) Directions, 2007. There are two kinds of assets:

- **Standard Assets** These are the assets for which there has been no default in repayment of principal or interest. These also do not have a risk profile higher than the normal risks associated with the business.
- **Non-performing Assets (NPA)** If the principal or interest has remained overdue for a period of 90 days or more, it is called NPA.

The provisioning norms for NBFC-MFIs mentioned in the guidelines are, 'The aggregate loan provision to be maintained by NBFC-MFIs at any point of time shall not be less than the higher of (a) one per cent of the outstanding loan portfolio or (b) 50 per cent of the aggregate loan instalments which are overdue for more

3. Master Circular - Prudential Norms on Capital Adequacy - Basel I Framework, Reserve Bank of India, RBI/2013-14/71 DBOD.No.BP.BC.21/21.01.002/2013-14, 1 July 2013; https://rbidocs.rbi.org.in/rdocs/notification/PDFs/71BM21290613.pdf

than 90 days and less than 180 days and 100 per cent of the aggregate loan instalments which are overdue for 180 days or more' (para II.2.B.ii.b.). What this means is that for the standard assets, it must have a provision of one per cent, while for the NPAs, it should be 50 per cent of the 90-day overdue loan instalments and 100 per cent of the 180-day overdue loan instalments.

The AP crisis brought in a special situation. Hence the guidelines recognised that provisioning must reflect the true and fair picture of the financials of the NBFC-MFI in the balance sheet, and hence the AP portfolio should be provisioned according to the current provisioning norms for NBFCs.

10.3.4 Pricing of Loans

Till 31 March 2014, the margin cap for all types of NBFCs was 12 per cent. After that, the margin cap was defined considering the size of the NBFC-MFI. Large MFIs are those whose loan portfolio is more than one billion rupees (₹100 crore). For such large MFIs, the margin cap is 10 per cent. For others (i.e. for MFIs having loan portfolio up to one billion rupees i.e. ₹100 crore), margin cap is 12 per cent. (para II.2.C.a.i).

Based on these norms, the NBFC-MFI may charge an interest rate of cost of funds + margin of 10 per cent or 12 per cent as applicable, depending on the size of the loan portfolio. However, that's not all, there is a proviso to this clause. The base rate of banks also has to be looked into before the organisation decides the interest rate. It cannot be more than 2.75 times the average base rate of the five largest commercial banks. For determining the base average base rate, the base rates of the concerned banks, as advised by the RBI on the last working day of the previous quarter are considered (para II.2.C.a.ii).

Illustration 10.1 An MFI having a loan portfolio of ₹5000 million (500 crore) has its cost of funds at 12 per cent per annum. The average base rate of the five largest commercial banks on the last working day of the previous quarter is 8.5 per cent. The cost of funds+10 per cent is 22 per cent, and 2.75 times 8.5 per cent is 23.375 per cent. The lower of the two is 22 per cent. Hence the company can charge a maximum of 22 per cent of interest rate per annum from the borrowers.

For individual loans, the company may charge an interest rate exceeding 26 per cent, but it must maintain that the variance between the minimum and maximum interest rate for individual loans should not be more than four per cent. This maximum variance norms, however, are not applicable to the loans provided by the NBFC-MFC against the funding made by National Scheduled Castes Finance and Development Corporation (NSFDC). It may be noted here that the latter allows NBFC-MFIs to act as channelising agents of NSFDC, to engage in on-lending to individuals out of its funds. Such on-lending must be through direct credit to the respective borrower's bank accounts. This amount is not included in calculation of average cost of funds for arriving at the pricing of credit. Its record should be maintained, and it should be disclosed in the balance sheet (para II.2.C.a.iii).

Over and above the interest rate, the NBFC-MFI can charge a processing fee of one per cent of the gross loan amount. Further, the actual cost of insurance for group, livestock, life and health of borrower and his/her spouse can also be recovered. Administrative charges may also be recovered, subject to the IRDA guidelines.

Illustration 10.2 An MFI provided a loan of ₹25,000 to a dairy farmer for purchase of a cow. The interest rate is 20 per cent per annum. The insurance of cow costs ₹1,000 for the first year. Other than this, the MFI charges a processing fee of ₹500 flat on the loan. This violates the guidelines as the processing fee exceeds 1 per cent of the gross loan amount.

10.3.5 Fair Practices in Lending

One of the major allegations against the MFIs during the AP crisis was that the there was no transparency in fixing the interest rates. Further, there were multiple lending that led to a vicious cycle of borrowing. Finally, exploitative practices were followed to recover the dues. The guidelines had provisions for meeting all these problems as follows (para II.2.C.b.I).

- The pricing of loan in microfinance has always been a contentious matter. It was alleged that the MFIs have many hidden costs. The guidelines stipulate that there can only be three components in pricing of MFI's loans, interest rate, processing fee and insurance premium (including the administrative charges for insurances).

- The MFIs cannot charge any penalty if the customer makes a delay in payment.
- The MFIs cannot collect any kind of security deposit/margin from the borrowers
- Loan agreement should be in a standard format. This would help in interpreting the laws in case of a dispute as banks and financial services companies often cite special clauses.
- The NBFC-MFI has to issue a loan card wherein the things mentioned are, such as effective rate of interest charged, all other terms and conditions, information which adequately identifies the borrower, acknowledgement of all instalments and final discharge. All entries should be in the local language.
- Finally, to ensure transparency, the guidelines mandate that the effective interest rate charged should be prominently displayed in NBFC-MFI's offices and also in the content provided in its website.

For curbing multiple lending, over-borrowing and ghost-borrowers, the guidelines prescribe that a self-help group (SHG)/joint liability group (JLG) should have unique member. This means that a person cannot be member of two or more SHGs or JLGs. However, if an individual borrower is not a member of any JLG/SHG, the NBFC-MFI can lend to him/her. Further, not more than two MFIs can lend to the same borrower. Another problem used to be that the first instalment often got deducted along with the loan disbursal. In order to stop this, the guidelines mandate a minimum period of moratorium between the disbursal and the due date for first instalment. This period cannot be less than the frequency of repayment. It has also been provided that recovery of loan given in violation of the regulations should be deferred till all prior existing loans are fully repaid. In order to avoid door-to-door recovery, it has been prescribed that disbursal and recovery should be done at a central location where other people are also present. Such processes should be closely supervised (para II.2.C.b.II).

The guidelines also provided that the MFIs must comply to the credit information requirement. It should be a member of credit bureaus, use such information, take self-certification of borrowers, and make due-diligence, such as local enquiries and other details about the capacity of the borrower, household income, and capacity to repay.

Regarding non-coercive methods of recovery, the guidelines specifically state that, "Recovery should normally be made only at a central designated place. Field staff shall be allowed to make recovery at the place of residence or work of the borrower only if borrower fails to appear at central designated place on two or more successive occasions". Other than this, the code of conduct specified for NBFCs (as issued in 2006) must be adhered to. This included the recruitment, training and supervision of field staff.

10.3.6 Corporate Governance

Regarding this, the Master Circular for NBFCs on corporate governance issued by the RBI[4] applies. This includes constitution of Audit Committee, Nomination Committee and Risk Management Committee. It also deals with issues like disclosure, rotation of partners of statutory auditors of the audit firm in every three years, and framing of internal guidelines for corporate governance.

Other Issues The guidelines also mention the following issues:

- There have been a lot of discussions on decreasing cost of operations of MFIs as this has a direct bearing on the interest rate charged. The guidelines suggest the NBFC-MFIs to "Review their back-office operations and make the necessary investments in Information Technology and systems to achieve better control, simplify procedures and reduce costs". (para II.d.)
- Bank loans to MFIs will be guided by the priority sector related norms issued by RBI.
- MFIs can act as channelising agents for central and state government agencies. Such loans disbursed would be treated as a separate business segment. However, all such loans would have to be reported to credit bureaus.

4. Notification No.DNBR.019/CGM (CDS)-2015 dated 10 April 2015, Reserve Bank of India. https://rbidocs.rbi.org.in/rdocs/notification/PDFs/M632AB80F7FAF3704D728FBC264BDE048268.PDF, retrieved on 27 March 2019.

- The NBFC-MFIs must be prudent and responsible in their lending activity besides educating their borrowers on the dangers of wasteful conspicuous consumption. Thus, the guidelines mandate the MFIs to contribute to the cause of financial literacy too.
- During the AP crisis, the concentration of MFIs' portfolio in the state caused a lot of problems. Hence the guidelines provided that the Boards should fix internal exposure limits in specific geographical locations.
- All NBFC-MFIs should be members of at least one self-regulatory organisation (SRO) recognised by the RBI and comply with the code of conduct as prescribed by the SRO. The role of the latter has been emphasised by the RBI in ensuring compliance with the regulatory framework. The RBI also suggests that banks lending to this sector should also monitor the NBFC-MFIs regarding compliances. However, it further insists that the primary responsibility of such compliances lies with the MFIs themselves.

10.4 RBI Guidelines on Differentiated Banks

The need of differentiated banks has been highlighted frequently in various policy documents. A discussion paper of the RBI titled 'Banking Structure in India – The Way Forward' released in 2013, and subsequently, the Nachiket Mor Committee suggested that for attaining financial inclusion, localised and small-scale banks of different kinds were required. Earlier, we had the practice of Local Area Banks (LAB), but that mode did not take off. Based on the previous experience and keeping in mind the need of the present day, the idea of two kinds of banks, Payments Banks (PBs) and Small Finance Banks (SFBs) was mooted. This was given a concrete shape through policy statements which the Finance Minister stated while presenting the Union Budget 2014-15.

> *After making suitable changes to current framework, a structure will be put in place for continuous authorisation of universal banks in the private sector in the current financial year. RBI will create a framework for licensing small banks and other differentiated banks. Differentiated banks serving niche interests, local area banks, payment banks, etc. are contemplated to meet credit and remittance needs of small businesses, unorganised sector, low-income households, farmers and migrant workforce.*

This was followed up and in August 2015, in-principle approval was accorded to 11 PBs. In September 2015, 10 SFBs were given in-principle approval as given in the Table 10.1.

Table 10.1 In-principle Approval Given to PBs and SFBs in 2015

Payments Banks	Small Finance Banks
Aditya Birla Nuvo Limited	Au Financiers (India. Ltd., Jaipur
Airtel M Commerce Services Limited	Capital Local Area Bank Ltd., Jalandhar
Cholamandalam Distribution Services Limited	Disha Microfin Private Ltd., Ahmedabad
Department of Posts	Equitas Holdings P Limited, Chennai
Fino PayTech Limited	ESAF Microfinance and Investments Private Ltd., Chennai
National Securities Depository Limited	Janalakshmi Financial Services Private Limited, Bengaluru
Reliance Industries Limited	RGVN (North East) Microfinance Limited, Guwahati
Shri Dilip Shantilal Shanghvi	Suryoday Micro Finance Private Ltd., Navi Mumbai
Shri Vijay Shekhar Sharma	Ujjivan Financial Services Private Ltd., Bengaluru
Tech Mahindra Limited	Utkarsh Micro Finance Private Ltd., Varanasi
Vodafone m-pesa Limited	

10.4.1 Payments Banks

The role of PBs is to augment the cause of financial inclusion 'providing (i) small savings accounts and (ii) payments / remittance services to migrant labour workforce, low-income households, small businesses, other unorganised sector entities and other users, by enabling high volume-low value transactions in deposits and payments / remittance services in a secured technology-driven environment. (para II.2.). Existing non-bank prepaid instrument (PPI) issuers, NBFCs, corporate business correspondents (BCs), mobile telephone companies, super market chains, real sector cooperatives, that are controlled and owned by residents, and public sector entities are eligible to set up such a PB (para II.3). In order to establish a PB, one must have a minimum paid up capital of ₹1 billion (100 crore). Further, CRAR of minimum 15 per cent of risk-weighted assets must be maintained (para 6). For these banks, the mandate of 25 per cent of their branches in unbanked rural areas is not required, but they must have physical access points (including BCs) in their rural centres (para 13i).

According to para 4 (i) of the Guidelines for Licensing of "Payments Banks" 27 November 2014, payments banks can accept all kinds of demand deposits, such as current account deposits, savings bank deposits, and such deposits can be received from individuals, small businesses and other entities. However, such banks cannot receive deposits from NRIs. The idea is that these banks will cater to the needs of low-income group, and hence there is no point in allowing them to accept NRI deposits. Deposits in the PBs are covered under the deposit insurance scheme of the Deposit Insurance and Credit Guarantee Corporation of India (DICGC).

There is a ceiling of taking deposits. Maximum balance for the individual customers can be up to ₹100,000. This seems to be a temporary ceiling as the guidelines mention that this limit may be raised by the RBI depending upon the performance of the PBs. In maintaining this ceiling, the RBI has allowed deposits of higher amount for pooled remittances but at the end of the day, the balance must not exceed one lakh rupees.

Payments banks cannot extend credit services.

KYC norms for the accounts are allowed to be simplified if they fall under the definition of 'small accounts' which primarily means that aggregate of all withdrawals in a month is not more than ₹10,000 and balance is never more than ₹50,000. The other provision of small accounts, i.e. aggregate credit in a financial year should not be more than one lakh rupees, is not applicable for PBs, as they do not extend loans.

Payments banks can issue ATM/debit cards (para 4 ii), and provide payment and remittance services through branches, ATMs, BCs and mobile banking (para 4 iii). However, they cannot issue credit card (para 4 iii) (as they are not allowed to provide credit services). Cash-out at point of sales terminals can also be permitted for the PBs. They can issue PPIs and can provide services like payment of utility bills on behalf of the customers (para 4x). They may also send or receive remittances through RTGC/NEFT/IMPS (para 4 vii), including carrying out cross-boarder transactions (para 4 viii). In this regard, PBs need to be technology savvy to be operationally efficient. Hence internet banking services are allowed for them which can help them provide low cost services. They are, however, not expected to act as branchless banks (para 4v).

Payments banks are allowed to act as business correspondents of other banks (para 4vi). Such activities do not require any capital investment. Similarly, distribution of mutual funds instruments and pension products, which are simple financial services, do not require taking risks. For undertaking such activities, they need prior approval of the RBI and need to comply with the sectoral regulators as applicable (para 4 ix).

Regarding ownership structure, as these PBs are not allowed to engage in extending credit, a diversified ownership structure is not required. However, for the first five years, the promoters should hold at least 40 per cent of the paid-up capital (para 7). Foreign shareholding is allowed as per the FDI norms; at present, allowed up to 74 per cent (49 per cent through direct route and after that upon approval). Residents, at any point of time, must hold at least 26 per cent of paid up capital (para 8).

10.4.2 Small Finance Banks

A major problem for the MFI is that they do not have easy access to capital, hence they depend on the debts. And by nature, debts are expensive, which increases the cost of funds and hence they have to charge a relatively higher interest rate. One demand of the MFIs is that they should be allowed to keep deposits. This is not allowed in India. However, considering the concern being genuine, a mid-way has been found in terms of Small Finance banks. As mentioned earlier, the RBI issued in-principle licence to 10 SFBs in 2015. However, by allowing them to take savings, it did not mean that they turn into full-fledged banks. This is visible from the guidelines for licensing SFBs (RBI, 2014b) as issued by the RBI.

> *The objectives of setting up of small finance banks will be to further financial inclusion by (a. provision of savings vehicles, and (ii) supply of credit to small business units; small and marginal farmers; micro and small industries; and other unorganised sector entities, through high technology-low cost operations (para i).*

An SFB can be promoted by resident individuals/professionals having 10 years of experience in banking and finance, and even by companies/societies owned and controlled by residents. Existing NBFCs, MFIs, Local Area Banks, which are controlled and owned by residents, can also convert themselves into SFBs. The guidelines clearly mention that the promoters must have a sound track record in their business for the last five years. (para ii).

In terms of scope of activities, SFBs are allowed to undertake the basic banking activities like taking deposits, and lending to unserved and underserved sections of society. The target groups can include small businesses, small and marginal farmers, micro and small industries and organised sector entities (para iii). SFBs can operate anywhere, there is no restrictions in terms of area.

In order to float an SFB, one needs to have a paid-up capital of minimum ₹1 billion (100 crore) (para iv). Promoter's contribution should at least be 40 per cent and should be diversified slowly and over a period of 12 years from the commencement of business, it should bring down the promoter's holding to 26 per cent of paid up equity capital (para v). Foreign shareholding is allowed as per the FDI norms, which is allowed up to 74 per cent (49% through direct route, and 74% through approval route (para vi).

The SFBs are primarily banks. Hence, they must maintain the cash reserve ratio (CRR) and statutory liquidity ratio (SLR) norms. They have to follow all prudential norms as applicable to commercial banks. However, they have to meet a target of 75 per cent of their loans (Adjusted Net Bank Credit) to the priority sector. Further, at least 50 per cent of their loan portfolio should be of loan size up to ₹25 lakh (para vii).

If the SFB wants to convert it to a universal bank, it has to maintain the required paid up capital, net worth requirement as required for such universal banks, and has to prove a satisfactory track record as SFBs, and would have to apply to the RBI (para viii). Such conversion is subject to RBI's approval.

10.5 RBI's 2022 Guidelines

The Reserve Bank of India (RBI) issued the "Master Direction – Reserve Bank of India (Regulatory Framework for Microfinance Loans) Directions, 2022" on March 14, 2022, effective from April 1, 2022. These guidelines aim to harmonize regulations across entities offering microfinance loans, ensuring borrower protection and responsible lending practices (RBI, 2024).

Applicability The directions apply to all Commercial Banks (excluding Payments Banks), Small Finance Banks, Local Area Banks, Regional Rural Banks, Primary (Urban) Co-operative Banks, State Co-operative Banks, District Central Co-operative Banks, and Non-Banking Financial Companies (NBFCs), including Microfinance Institutions (MFIs) and Housing Finance Companies. These institutions are termed as Regulated Entities (RE).

Definition of Microfinance Loan A microfinance loan is defined as a collateral-free loan provided to a household with an annual income not exceeding ₹3,00,000. The household includes the borrower, spouse, and unmarried children. These loans can be for any purpose and must not be linked to a lien on the borrower's deposit account. Repayment schedules should be flexible, based on the borrower's preference.

Assessment of Household Income Regulated Entities (REs) are required to have a board-approved policy for assessing household income, considering factors like household composition, income sources, and expenses. This assessment ensures accurate determination of the borrower's repayment capacity. REs must report household income data to Credit Information Companies (CICs) and reconcile any discrepancies with borrowers before updating records.

Limit on Loan Repayment Obligations To prevent over-indebtedness, the total monthly repayment obligations of a household should not exceed 50% of its monthly income. This includes all existing loans, both collateral-free and collateralized. REs must use data from CICs, borrower declarations, bank statements, and local inquiries to ensure compliance. New loans should not be extended to households exceeding this limit until their obligations fall within the prescribed threshold.

Pricing of Loans In a substantial departure from the past approach of having an interest rate cap (cost of funds + 10/12% or 2.75 times the base rate) as was there in 2011 guidelines, RBI in the new regulation deregulated the pricing. As per the new regulation an RE can decide its own interest rate but it must establish a board-approved policy outlining the methodology for determining interest rates, including components like cost of funds, risk premium, and margin. Interest rates and other charges should not be usurious and are subject to RBI's supervisory scrutiny. Borrowers must be provided with a standardized, simplified factsheet detailing loan pricing, fees, and repayment schedules. Prepayment penalties are prohibited, and any penalties for delayed payments should apply only to the overdue amount.

Conduct Towards Borrowers REs are required to adopt a Fair Practices Code (FPC) approved by their boards, ensuring transparent and respectful interactions with borrowers. Loan agreements and loan cards should be in a language understood by the borrower, detailing loan terms, repayment schedules, and grievance redressal mechanisms. Issuance of non-credit products must be with the borrower's explicit consent, and their purchase should not be a precondition for obtaining a loan.

Recovery Practices REs must identify borrowers facing repayment difficulties and provide appropriate guidance. Recovery should occur at mutually agreed-upon locations, with field staff visiting the borrower's residence or workplace only if the borrower fails to appear at the designated place on two or more occasions. Harsh recovery practices, such as the use of abusive language, persistent calling outside of 9:00 a.m. to 6:00 p.m., harassment, or threats, are strictly prohibited. REs must have a dedicated mechanism for addressing recovery-related grievances.

Engagement of Recovery Agents A significant observation in the past was the engagement of recovery agents. While it cuts down the costs of recollection and decreases the default rate, there comes a basic problem. The recovery agents are not the employees of the organisation, and they are only concerned with recovery, often leading of coercive methods. The new guidelines says that REs engaging recovery agents must conduct due diligence, including police verification of agents' antecedents. Borrowers should be informed about the recovery agents assigned to them, and agents must carry proper identification and authorization letters during recovery visits. Details of engaged recovery agencies should be publicly available on the RE's website.

Qualifying Assets Criteria NBFC-MFIs are required to have at least 75% of their total assets as microfinance loans, aligning with the revised definition. Other NBFCs can extend microfinance loans up to 25% of their total assets, an increase from the previous 10% limit.

Exemptions for 'Not for Profit' Companies 'Not for Profit' companies engaged in microfinance activities with assets of ₹100 crore and above are no longer exempt from certain provisions of the RBI Act, 1934. Such companies must register as NBFC-MFIs and comply with applicable regulations.

Net Owned Fund (NOF) Requirement Existing NBFC-MFIs must adhere to a phased increase in NOF: ₹7 crore by March 31, 2025, and ₹10 crore by March 31, 2027. For NBFC-MFIs operating in the North-Eastern Region, the requirements are ₹5 crore and ₹10 crore, respectively.

These comprehensive guidelines aim to foster a responsible and inclusive microfinance sector, ensuring borrower protection and financial stability.

Table 10.2 Comparison between 2011 and 2022 RBI guidelines

Feature	2011 Guidelines	2022 Guidelines
Interest Rate Caps	Cost of funds +10 or 12% and an interest cap of 26% per annum for loans classified as priority sector loans.	No specific interest rate cap, but mandates transparency in disclosing interest rates, fees, and other charges. Board approved policy is a must.
Loan Eligibility	Income of rural household at 100,000 and semi-urban households at 160,000	Defines microfinance loans as collateral-free loans to low-income households (annual income up to ₹3,00,000).
Borrower Protection	Focused on ensuring MFIs comply with interest rate caps, particularly for loans classified as priority sector.	Requires household-level assessment of income and indebtedness, including a limit of 50% on monthly loan repayment obligations as a percentage of household income. Provides for prompt redressal of recovery-related grievances.
Transparency	Fair practices were applicable, such as not charging penalty for delay in payment, collection of security or margin, standard loan formats, and use of local language, display boards about interest rate.	Mandates disclosure of minimum, maximum, and average interest rates, all charges, and details on websites and in literature.
Scope of Regulation	Primarily focused on NBFC- MFIs.	Applies to all lenders, including banks and NBFC-MFIs, for microfinance loans.
Recovery Practices	No specific guidelines on recovery practices beyond ensuring compliance with interest rate caps.	Includes guidelines on recovery, including a dedicated redress mechanism for recovery-related grievances, and prohibits coercive recovery tactics.

10.6 Regulatory Intervention by RBI in 2024

In October 2024, the Reserve Bank of India (RBI) implemented stringent regulatory measures against four MFIs: Asirvad Micro Finance Limited, Arohan Financial Services Limited, DMI Finance Private Limited, and Navi Finserv Limited. These entities were directed to cease and desist from sanctioning and disbursing new loans effective October 21, 2024, due to significant non-compliance with established regulatory frameworks.

10.6.1 Identified Regulatory Breaches

The RBI's action was precipitated by multiple supervisory concerns First, the MFIs were found to be charging interest rate that was considered having excessive spread over their cost of funds. This contravened the RBI guidelines that suggested fair pricing. Second, the bone of contention was the evaluation of household incomes and existing repayment obligations of borrowers, that lead to the inference about eligibility and qualifying assets and over-indebtedness. Third, there were instances of evergreening of loans where the borrowers were extended loans to repay the existing loans, but it was shown as a new loan. Finally, non-compliance with fair practices code like disclosures and transparency norms.

Following the imposition of restrictions, the affected MFIs undertook corrective actions to align with regulatory expectations, including reforms in practices, revamped processes and systems, and remedial measures. As a result, the restrictions of Navi Finserv, Arohan, and Asirvad were lifted during December 2024-January 2025.

10.7 Performance of Differentiated Banks

The policies regarding small finance banks and payments banks look to be quite logical. However, in practice, not everything goes on very well. While initially there was a lot of enthusiasm about PBs, three players (Cholamandalam DS, Dilip Sanghvi, and Tech Mahindra) withdrew from the process before they could commence the business. Further, Vodafone and Idea merged later, and this left only seven PBs in the market (Sriram, 2018). Later, a few changes took place and as of now, seven PBs are operating: [5]

(a) Airtel Payments Bank Ltd
(b) Fino Payments Bank Ltd
(c) Aditya Birla Idea Payments Bank Ltd
(d) NSDL Payments Bank Ltd.
(e) India Post Payments Bank Ltd
(f) Paytm Payments Bank Ltd
(g) Jio Payments Bank Ltd.

There have been some problems in the space of PBs. The first problem was that of raising capital. The limit of 49 per cent foreign holding means that one has to raise domestically sourced capital to the extent of minimum ₹510 million (51 crore). This was a difficult task.

The second problem was in the revenue model. Being PBs, these are solely dependent on the margins available from the difference between the interest they pay on deposits and the revenues they earn from investments. The operating guidelines (RBI, 2016) say that they have to maintain 75 per cent of their demand deposits in government securities which are safe but low yielding. Hence there is a demand that this limit should be brought down to 50 per cent (Sriram, 2018).

Another problem is that they have to compete with full-fledged banks and in this endeavour, some of them have increased the interest rate on deposits, which further cuts down their margins (Sriram, 2018).

Some irregularities have also been observed. As mentioned earlier, payments banks have to have a limit in terms of savings and maximum balance. There have been instances of violation of this rule. The RBI has taken a note of this and instructed the FINO PB to stop opening new accounts till it upgrades its processes. Similarly, Paytm PB also had to stop taking enrolling new customers because it failed to meet the KYC norms. Similar restrictions have been put on Airtel PB which kept upon opening accounts of customers without a clear consent from them (Livemint, 2018). It may be noted that applicants of mobile connections were enrolled as account holders of Airtel PB without the customers' explicit consent. Many did not know they held a bank account with this PB.

Regarding SFBs, all 10 of them have started operating. In general, there have been positive impression about SFBs. A recent report by Investment Information and Credit Rating Agency (ICRA) on SFBs projected that these banks can have a high growth rate in terms of diversified loans and deposits. According to the report, SFBs can grow at a compound annual growth rate (CAGR) of 25 to 30 per cent (Economic Times, 2019). Some of them have gone to the public to raise the funds. Ujjivan had a successful initial public offer (IPO) (Roy, 2018).

10.8 Conclusion

The RBI's decisive intervention underscores the critical importance of ethical lending practices and strict adherence to regulatory frameworks within the microfinance sector. By addressing issues such as exorbitant interest rates, inadequate assessment of borrowers' repayment capacities, and lack of transparency, the central bank aimed to protect vulnerable borrowers and ensure the stability of the financial system. The subsequent

5. Source: https://www.rbi.org.in/CommonPerson/english/scripts/banksinindia.aspx#IB

compliance by the NBFCs and the lifting of restrictions highlight the effectiveness of regulatory oversight in promoting responsible financial practices.

Overall, the new guidelines marked a significant step towards ensuring ethical lending practices in the microfinance sector. While the intentions were to protect borrowers and promote transparency, the implementation revealed challenges, particularly concerning interest rate deregulation and income assessment methodologies. The RBI's enforcement actions against non-compliant NBFCs underscore the need for continuous monitoring and potential recalibration of regulations to balance financial inclusion with borrower protection.

Summary

- The RBI has mandated that banks have to open the accounts of SHGs, even if it is an unregistered body. Further, some members being past defaulters is not a barrier for the bank linkage of SHGs.
- The 2022 RBI guidelines cover all kinds of banks excluding Payments Banks, NBFCs and they are called Regulated Entities (RE).
- By 2027, all Existing NBFC-MFIs must adhere to a phased increase in net owned fund to ₹10 crore.
- A microfinance loan is defined as a collateral-free loan provided to a household with an annual income not exceeding ₹3,00,000.
- Total monthly repayment obligations of a household should not exceed 50% of its monthly income.
- There is no specified interest cap. RE can decide its own interest rate but it must establish a board-approved policy outlining the methodology for determining interest rates, including components like cost of funds, risk premium, and margin. Interest rates and other charges should not be usurious and are subject to RBI's supervisory scrutiny.
- Fair practices should be followed while engaged in lending practices.
- There are two kinds of differentiated banks licenced by the RBI, Payments banks, and Small Finance banks. This has been brought out to enhance financial inclusion.
- Payments banks can operate all kinds of savings and payment instruments like bank account opening, issuing cheque, PPIs and ATM/debit card. They can also operate as BCs for other banks. However, they cannot extend credit services and related instruments like issue of credit cards. As of now, seven PBs are working in India. A capital of ₹ 100 crore (one billion) is required to initiate a PB.
- Small Finance banks can undertake the basic banking services like keeping deposits and providing loans. They also need ₹ 100 crore (one billion) of capital to begin with.

Exercises

A. Multiple-choice Questions

1. According to RBI directives, to open a bank account an SHG can be
   (a) Be a registered body
   (b) Be an unregistered body
   (c) Either registered or unregistered
   (d) None of the above
2. It requires net owned fund of ₹_______ million to start an NBFC-MFI (registered in Odisha)
   (a) 100 (b) 200
   (c) 500 (d) 1000
3. In order to qualify for microfinance loans, a household should have a maximum income of ₹
   (a) 100,000 (b) 160,000
   (c) 300,000 (d) 500,000
4. According to 2011 guidelines, for the pricing of microfinance loans, NBFC-MFI should follow:
   (a) Cost of funds + margin cap
   (b) average base rate of 5 largest commercial banks
   (c) lower of the above two
   (d) higher of the above two
5. Payment Banks are NOT allowed to
   (a) Open savings accounts
   (b) Provide remittance services

(c) Issue debit card
(d) Offer credit services

6. Small Finance Banks should cater to the priority sector lending to the extent of ________ per cent of their adjusted net bank credit
   (a) 75
   (b) 85
   (c) 50
   (d) 15
7. The maximum interest rate charged should be, according to the 2022 guidelines:
   (a) 24% per annum
   (b) 26% per annum
   (c) 36% per annum
   (d) As per the board approved policy
8. Tier II capital of NBFC-MFI should
   (a) Be equal to Tier I capital
   (b) Be more than Tier I capital
   (c) Not more than Tier I capital
   (d) None of these
9. Which of the following withdrew before operating the PB
   (a) Airtel Payments Bank Ltd
   (b) Fino Payments Bank Ltd
   (c) India Post Payments Bank Ltd
   (d) Cholamandalam Distribution Services
10. Which of the following cannot accept deposits?
   (a) Payments Banks
   (b) Small Finance Banks
   (c) NBFC-MFIs
   (d) Self-help Groups

B. Review Questions

1. What do you mean by 'qualifying assets' of an MFI?
2. Distinguish between Small finance banks and Payment banks.
3. What are the problems associated with Payments banks?
4. What problems do you think the small finance banks would face initially?
5. Do you think the Small finance banks would contribute much to the cause of financial inclusion? Justify.
6. 'Small Finance banks and Payment banks are going to be the greatest competitors of MFIs.' Do you agree with this statement? Explain.
7. Critically analyse the provisions of RBI guidelines? Does it help in maintaining financial prudence in the microfinance sector?
8. What role did the Malegam Committee play in shaping up microfinance policies?
9. Write three points about the code of conduct that an MFI should follow.

C. Application-based Questions

1. Suppose you want to start an NBFC that works in microfinance sector. What are the requirements for operating in the space of commercial microfinance?
2. An NBFC-MFI charges 24 per cent interest rate from its customers. Its cost of funds is 9 per cent and it has a loan portfolio of ₹10 billion. It may be noted that the average base rate of the five largest banks is 8 per cent. Evaluate the interest rate.
3. How much net owned fund/paid up capital is required by an MFI operating in Arunachal Pradesh, an MFI operating in the poorest districts of Tamil Nadu, a payment bank and a small finance bank?

Further Readings

- Updated versions of RBI Guidelines on NBFC-MFI, RBI guidelines on licensing of Payment Banks, RBI guidelines on licensing Small Finance Banks, RBI's operating guidelines on Payment Banks and RBI's operating guidelines on Small Finance Banks would be useful readings for better understanding of the chapter.
- *Inclusive Finance India Report 2017* by M. S. Sriram is an update on some of the areas of microfinance regulations. This would be a useful reading.

CHAPTER

11 Other Regulatory Issues and Debates

Chapter Outline

Learning Objectives

After reading this chapter, you will be able to:

- discuss the regulatory issues other than RBI guidelines of microfinance.
- highlight some relevant debates in the field of microfinance.

RBI Guidelines are just one aspect of regulating microfinance. There are several other regulatory issues and debates. In this chapter, discussion on some of these aspects has been done.

11.1 Self-Regulatory Organisations

There are two self-regulatory organisations (SRO) in the microfinance sector in India, Sa-Dhan and Microfinance Industry Network (MFIN). Description of each has been given below.

11.1.1 Sa-Dhan

Sa-Dhan is one of the industry associations in the field of microfinance. It has memberships of 193 institutions (56 Non-banking Financial Company (NBFCs), 113 societies and trusts, 13 cooperatives and 31 Self Help Group Promoting Institutions (SHPIs)), banks, rating agencies and capacity building agencies. The organisation represents all kinds of legal forms and microfinance models. As on March 2019, its membership network reached 33 million clients covering about 90 per cent districts of India. Sa-Dhan is an SRO recognised by the RBI. Its mission is read as:

> *Sa-Dhan's mission is to build the field of community development finance in India, to help its members and associate institutions to better serve the low-income households, particularly women, in both rural and urban India in their quest for establishing stable livelihoods and improving the quality of life.*[1]

The objectives of the organisation include providing a platform for advocacy in microfinance, making timely and reliable information available to members, research, promoting initiatives for informing and educating various stakeholders and providing technical and marketing support.[2]

1. http://www.sa-dhan.net/about-us/ retrieved on 6 April 2019
2. http://www.sa-dhan.net/about-us/ retrieved on 6 April 2019

11.1.2 MFIN

Microfinance Industry Network (MFIN) was established in October 2009. It received the RBI's recognition as SRO in June 2014. It was the first SRO in microfinance sector. The organisation works for a larger goal of financial inclusion and for this, it facilitates dialogue among various stakeholders. Its mission is read as:

> *..to work towards the robust development of the microfinance sector, by promoting: responsible finance, client protection, a supportive regulatory environment, and good governance.*[3]

Initially, MFIN was an association of MFIs. Subsequent to the 2022 guidelines of RBI, MFIN included banks, small finance banks, and other NBFCs also. Hence the name was changed from Microfinance Institutions Network to Microfinance Industry Network.

There is a characteristic difference between MFIN and Sa-Dhan. The latter has membership from all types of organisations and models operating in microfinance sector. However, MFIN is particularly focussed on the for-profit NBFC-MFIs only. It is believed that the need for MFIN came up because for profit, MFIs felt that Sa-Dhan did not represent their concerns properly (Sriram 2012).

In order to achieve its mission, MFIN strives to nurture its members in making them compliant to various rules and regulations, such as RBI guidelines, fair practice code, industry code of conduct and MFIN's own directives and advisories. The interest and welfare of customers have been looked after by the organisation by encouraging suitable products, transparent processes, following respectable interaction with customers, maintaining privacy of customer data, and providing a responsive customer centric grievance redressal mechanism. The main activities of MFIN have been in the area of framing rules and standards, to develop capacities, monitor and enforce the rules and codes and redress customers' grievances. Its six-member team for customer grievance redressal handles about 5000 calls every month.[4]

Before the AP (Andhra Pradesh) crisis, it was clear that there was something brewing in the governmental circle against the MFIs. MFIN was quick to come up with a code of conduct and voluntarily declared that its members would adhere to it (Sriram, 2012).

In the last eight years, both MFIN and Sa-Dhan have contributed to the sector. Other than monitoring various compliance aspects of members, they have also intervened in conducting dialogues at various level during the time of crisis. While the role of MFIN as an SRO in the commercial MFIs has been substantial, Sa-Dhan has a larger group of members to address, but given that its role becomes too broad to attain any landmark results. SROs have their own limitations. They are industry associations and not typical regulators, many times they do not have much power. Further, they have so far not been successful in getting a proper legislation passed. However, in any financial market, SROs play an important role, particularly in complimenting the role of regulator. Given that the RBI does not have time and resources to go into the details of the transaction intensive business of microfinance, SROs can make substantial contribution. However, there are limitations to their activities. According to Mary Schapiro, Former Chairman of the US Securities and Exchange Commission, SROs can be effective subjective to:

- SROs are well-funded
- They are technologically advanced
- There is government oversight
- They are held accountable
- They act within their authority
- They are structured to avoid conflicts of interest. (Voss, 2014)

During 2024-25, MFIN has compiled all the directives and advisories in the form of a compendium and has published a set of guardrails to help its members.

In August 2024, MFIN brought its members to agree on restricting the number of microfinance lenders to a borrower to a maximum of 4 and limit the total microfinance indebtedness to ₹200,000. With nearly 80% of

3. http://mfinindia.org/about-us/ retrieved on 6 April 2019
4. http://mfinindia.org/our-work/self-regulation/ retrieved on 6 April 2019

the loans having a tenure of 1.5 years or more, a limit of ₹200,000 effectively ensures much lesser repayment obligation than the permissible regulatory limit.

Following the RBI's actions on four MFIs on 2024 due to non-compliance of the latter, MFIN announced measures to promote responsible lending. From January 2025, MFIN members agreed to limit a borrower's exposure to three MFIs and cap total indebtedness, including unsecured retail loans, at ₹2 lakh.

However, MFIs have expressed concerns over the stringent regulations, arguing that the shift from net assets to total assets for qualifying loans restricts their ability to diversify and manage risks effectively. They have requested the RBI to reconsider certain provisions to allow more flexibility in lending practices.

11.2 Interest Rate Debate in Microfinance

A reputed industrialist walks into a bank for a loan, the bank would offer him/her a comfortable place to sit and because of the sensible project proposal, it would approve the loan at a bargained price (low interest per annum). The same bank, when dealing with an MFI (which in turn would lend it to a poor marginal farmer) would make a hard bargain for an interest rate ranging from 12 to 16 percent. The MFI would add its operational costs and a margin over it and lend the same to the farmer at a rate ranging from 20-26 per cent per annum. Before the regulatory ceiling was enforced, the MFIs often charged about 24 to 36 percent per annum.

This is a fictitious story, but we can find similar phenomena in real world too. Whatever the background might be; the ultimate result is that the poor gets a loan at a high interest rate.

What should the government do here? If the government puts an interest cap it harms the growth in the sector. If it does not, it indirectly allows usury.

11.2.1 What is the Debate About?

There is no second thought about the issue that is debated about interest rate. Earlier, interest rate charged by MFIs ranged from 20 to 36 per cent per annum. Nowadays, there is an interest rate cap of 26 per cent per annum, but that also can be relaxed in case of individual lending (see chapter 10). This is significantly higher than the prime lending rate or base rates of banks. Only credit cards charge higher; but the latter had a free-of-charge use for the initial 30-50 days. At its face value, it looks to be extremely high. Further,

- The clients of MFIs are poor, sometimes extremely poor
- Microfinance emerged primarily to 'serve' the poor
- This interest rate is charged even as the repayment rate is extremely high (to the tune of 99 per cent and above).

Given the above facts, it can easily be argued that the high interest rates are unfair. Hence interest rate cap is justified. Now let's look at the other side of the debate. The high interest rate charged by an MFI is justified because:

- The cost of capital is high. The MFIs cannot mobilise savings, and thus the major source of funds are the bank loans. As the cost of capital is equal and sometimes higher than the prime lending rate, it is natural that the on-lending rate, which includes the cost of capital, operating cost and a profit margin, would be much higher.
- Loans in microfinance are transaction intensive. An average loan size of commercial banks is several times higher than that of the microfinance sector; in 2009, it was slightly higher than ₹5000 (M-Cril, 2009). This leads to higher administrative cost. Apart from the bargaining power of the rich, the low interest is probably because of the loan size.
- This in turn increases the cost of loan processing and loan recovery. Unlike a commercial bank, the field official of the MFI has to collect it door to door. Recoveries are also as frequent as weekly.

The debate becomes complex when in principle there is an agreement on high interest rate; but given that the idea is to serve the poor, charging high interest rate would be unfair. In simplistic economic terms, interest rate increases when the demand for loans is high. This means there is not enough supply of credit in the area where MFIs operate. Let's also see the opportunity cost. The local moneylender charges a much higher interest rate and the client has to go through many exploitative terms and conditions in the process of getting the loan. Despite the high interest rate, the microfinance market has grown exponentially; it proves that there is a demand for such loans and there are not available adequately in the market.

In the event of having a strict interest rate cap enforced, the immediate outcome will be that the market will no more be lucrative, and it will hit the industry negatively. We have proven records in this regard that in Nicaragua, after an interest rate cap, the growth rate of the sector decreased from 30 per cent to 2 per cent (CGAP, 2004). This in turn will hit the poor for whose favour the interest rate cap was put as a policy measure. Irrespective of the interest rate, this is an accepted fact that microfinance has improved the access to financial products.

Does the justification of high interest rate mean that there is no exploitation? The initial argument was that at a small scale of operation, the costs are high; costs would come down as microfinance scales up. Unfortunately, such trends are not visible and when the profits rise, the MFIs do not pass it on to the customer. In spite of the high rate of growth in the microfinance sector, the interest rate has changed only marginally. However, there are issues like exceptionally high return (in the form of salary or other benefits), that also add to the cost. In one example, the remuneration of the MD of a successful MFI was as high as 15 per cent of the personnel cost (Sriram, 2010). It is clear that with increasing profits, personal motives have gained importance over the organisational mission of serving the poor.

11.2.2 Is There a Solution?

If there should be no interest cap, what is the way out? There is no doubt that this is possible. This could be done through two ways, increasing competition and building a transparent system.

There are a handful number of MFIs who hold more than 80 per cent of microfinance market in India. There is a need to enable competitive forces so that new players can flood the market till it gets saturated. The government or banks like NABARD can build a fund to promote such new entrants.

The second issue is about building transparency. One important issue about interest rate, forgotten in the debate, is that MFIs only quote the nominal rate to be 20 to 36 per cent. But the effective rate could be much higher that includes processing fees, frequency of collection, method of collection, etc. (Fernando, 2006). As per the estimates of www.mftransparency.org, the quoted rate of three per cent per month can result in an annual percentage rate of 36 to 96 per annum. Hence rather than pressing for the issue of interest cap, transparency as an issue seems to be much more effective. A public disclosure of cost of loan could actually be a desirable regulatory measure. The microfinance industry itself could take some self-regulatory measure in setting examples.

11.3 Commercial Microfinance Vs. SHG-Bank Linkage

The AP crisis was a direct result of the conflict between two models of microfinance, SHG-bank linkage model, which has been promoted by state and its arms, and commercial microfinance (MFIs) which operate on market-based model. There is an influential group of people who believe that the MFI model is not suitable for poverty alleviation, and hence it should be stopped, or its wings should be clipped.

What is the merit in this argument? The SHG-Bank Linkage model is primarily grant based. However, in long-run, it is beneficial. On the other hand, the MFI-driven model does not focus on building institutions, rather it takes a short-cut and lends to Joint Liability Groups (JLGs), which are nothing but a kind of mutual guarantee. This has helped the MFIs to expand very fast.

The problem with the commercial MFI model is that when it expanded so fast, it had to seek the investments from private equity sources. The initial funding came from social investors, but it could not continue for long. When one depends on private equity, it also comes under pressure to perform and provide high return on investment. This leads to cost cutting, compromising on robust processes, and ultimately lead to providing poor services to customers. In the business of moneylending, this means several things, such as aggressive selling, aggressive and insensitive recovery, and anything but customer satisfaction.

The problem with SHG-Bank model is that while it creates robust institutions, it creates a dependency syndrome. The way SHGs and SHG-based federations have been used by politicians for meeting their political ends, they do not look like financial inclusion related institutions, rather they look closer to vote banks. Another problem is that, not all SHGs are of the same quality. An SHG formed by Mysore Resettlement and Development Agency (MYRADA) is way different from an SHG formed by a government agency. In the past, it has been seen that weak SHGs have not been able to continue their works after the withdrawal of SHPI. There have also been cases of on-paper SHGs, which are controlled by a handful of people.

Thus, there are problems on both sides. In a vast country like India, it is very difficult to say that any one model will meet the diverse needs. We have to find the suitable model for every place. The role of government should be to regulate the activities and see that the ultimate mission of financial inclusion and poverty alleviation is not violated.

11.4 Should MFIs be Allowed to Accept Savings?

One of the major reasons behind the high rate of interest in microfinance is that they do not have access to the savings products, which would have decreased the cost of capital. If that is the situation, why does not the government allow them to take savings? Why should there be such restrictions over this?

When we talk of savings, we have to keep in mind that we are not talking about savings of a private party. A bank deals with the savings of public, and in this context, it becomes the custodian of people's hard-earned money. If it is a demand deposit, the depositor can ask the money back any time; if it is a fixed deposit, the depositor would expect the amount on the day of maturity. Under some circumstances, he/she may also like to foreclose the agreement of deposit and withdraw the amount. The understanding is that the bank has kept the money in safe hands, and it would be available any time it is required. In other words, the bank should invest the depositor's money in safe places so that it can return the money with interest and meet its own operating cost as well as earn a profit margin for itself and its investors.

Unfortunately, such deposit boxes have not been so safe. There have been several frauds and companies have run away with money deposited by depositors. In particular, Ponzi Schemes and some Chit Funds have done severe damage. It is in this context that government has been careful to not allow NBFCs to accept deposits, unless stringent requirements are met.

It is not necessary that the safety of deposits can be questioned only in terms frauds and cheating. A company with a positive intent also can lose money and can default when the payments are due to its customers. This can happen under two situations, when the economy takes a hit in the business cycle and when some of the management or strategic decisions go wrong. Unexpected policy decisions like demonetisation also can put a company under severe stress. The point here is that, in such an event, the company is not able to pay when the customer demands his/her deposit back and there the trouble arises. It may lead to situations like bank run. It can have a ripple effect on the economy. Not to mention, the depositor's life also would be in scrambles.

This makes the business of savings an uneasy one. Hence the government (or say central banks) has been conservative in giving licences to take deposits. In particular, the RBI has come down heavily on those companies who were taking deposits without explicit approval. As a bank, a company needs high amount of capital (minimum ₹5 billion, i.e. ₹500 crore), and lending is to be done within the limits of permitted leverage and capital adequacy.

However, in order to help the cause of financial inclusion, the RBI has recently come up with a mid-path. Differentiated banks like PB and SFB have been floated. This is, all said and done, still distant from allowing the MFIs to accept deposits.

11.5 With Schemes Like PMJDY in Place, Do We Need Microfinance?

Today, we have several schemes like PMJDY (savings), PMJJBY (life insurance), PMSBY (health insurance) and APY (pension) making efforts to meet the need of poor. Given that PMJDY is a kind of SB account, it can also be used for sending remittances. Thus, through these schemes we have a range of financial products and services that the poor can avail. A question arises here, do we still need microfinance?

The missing element of financial inclusion, i.e., lack of access to bank account, has been solved here. This is one of the contributions of PMJDY. And this account has multiple benefits, as discussed earlier in Chapter 4, which are linked to overdraft, insurance, and remittance possibilities also.

But there are a few concerns as well. The above-mentioned are standard products and do not meet the customised need of people in the diverse conditions of India. PMJDY accounts have several limitations like the amount of transactions that can be done. The most important thing is that it does not meet the credit needs of people.

It still does not replace the services of microfinance sector, because microfinance sector provides door-step delivery and unsecured loans. No banking sector, without the support of microfinance related actors, can go into the remote areas. Hence, PMJDY and the related schemes do not make microfinance obsolete, rather it can build a synergy here. Disbursements can be done directly to the PMJDY accounts, making the transactions cashless. Hence, it would rather boost the microfinance sector rather than reducing its scope and coverage.

11.6 Is the Repayment Rate in Microfinance Real?

Why do people stop making payment in the event of crises? Microfinance is known for it high rates of recovery which ordinarily is in the range of 98 to 99 per cent. How come all of a sudden, this repayment dips to an unbelievable level? There could be several reasons for this situation. One may not be able to pay because of liquidity problems, as happened during the demonetisation. One may also expect that there is a loan waiver waiting somewhere nearby, hence better not to repay. Another possibility is that there has been a deliberate political campaign not to make repayments.

There is a fourth problem, which stops the borrower from making repayments, even if he/she really wants to make one. This is a crucial problem inherent in microfinance. The borrower did not pay simply because she did not receive the next round of loan. In quite a significant number of places, this model of repayment is followed. A cycle of loan is repaid by another cycle of loan. During crisis, the subsequent disbursement stops. Hence, the borrower does not repay; in other words, they simply are not able to pay.

This circulation of loan is a major menace for the long-term health of the industry. While the industry strives on the promise of high rates of recovery, the real recovery rate is not known. How much of this repayment is due to circulation of loans? Even if this proportion is small, say 5 to 10 per cent, it makes a large dent on the promise of 99 per cent repayment! This generally happens in a supply driven market and when the investors push for a very high rate of return. The MFI management, in turn, pushes its employees to distribute more and more loans.

Thus, the repayment rate in microfinance industry must be taken with a pinch of salt.

11.7 Is the Regulation of MFIs Effective?

The RBI guidelines of 2011 was a step forward to regulate the unregulated space of microfinance. These guidelines fill the vacuum. Has it been effective? It has been more than seven years since the NBFC-MFI guidelines were issued in 2011. There are opinions that this was a significant step in regulating the MFIs, while many others say that it was far from the desired level of the requirement.

A regulation is judged by the level of clarity it has. In practice, no regulation can ever be perfectly clear to everybody. There can only be degrees of clarity. In a good regulation, there is less scope of confusion, and less chance of being interpreted differently.

But the microfinance related policies deal with ambiguities. The guidelines start with issues like qualifying asset, which in principle means loans to the poor households. Given that poor people generally work in informal sector, how does one see whether a household is poor or not. There will always be people who can be held on both sides of poverty lines. The second problem with the guideline is that it fixes a level of indebtedness and multiple lending beyond which the NBFC-MFIs cannot lend. This is where a major problem lies. The restrictions have been put and can be enforced for NBFC-MFIs. Banks still can lend the same persons through BCs or even directly. And it is possible for an MFI to operate as business correspondent (BC).

There are two issues here, one is that the regulations can be circumvented at larger level; and two, the idea behind the regulations ultimately lay in preventing over-indebtedness of poor borrower, this basic intent has not been met. Second aspect is that many MFIs have now received SFB licences and now, they would not come under the NBFC-MFI guidelines. They can go beyond such restrictions.

Overall, it can be said that while the RBI regulations on microfinance were a positive start, a lot of things have changed since then. Hence, slowly these regulations have started being less effective.

Case Study 11.1 The Right Interest Rate

"The government has decided that the MFIs cannot charge an interest rate of more than 12 per cent from the SHGs", announced the representative of the government in a press conference. It was a much-awaited press conference, held after a cabinet meeting of the state government. "It is understood that the MFIs are charging high rate of interest because of high cost of funds. To curb this problem, the government has the pleasure to announce that it would provide funds to the MFIs at a subsidised rate of 6 per cent per annum", added the government representative.

This particular cabinet meeting was a well-known event. Recently, there was strong criticism of the government for allowing microfinance companies to operate in the state. An opposition leader had said, "You allow the vultures to prey on our people, are you getting a share of the corpses!" But the government was of the view that stopping microfinance would increase private moneylending, which would not be a good situation. The government made some consultations after this and was of the opinion that cost of funds of MFIs was really high. Hence, it wanted to contribute.

But this government decision hit the MFIs hard. Also, there was some ambiguity. "Does it mean that we can still lend as usual to JLGs and individuals?", asked an MFI head. "Does it mean that we are now indirectly barred from lending to SHGs?", asked another.

The state has about 250,000 SHGs, having four million members. It has been estimated that 60 per cent of these SHGs take loan from the MFIs. Average loan by SHGs from MFIs was about ₹ 100,000. This means that about ₹ 150 billion (₹ 15,000 crore), which is way below the funds available for government's budget for the relevant department (Women and Child Development)

"It is possible that the government may simply fund the interest subsidy", said an analyst. "If the government funds the interest rate subsidy, assuming that the banks at present lend the MFIs at 12 per cent per annum, there would be subsidy of ₹ 9 billion every year to fund this idea."

"But this is so bizarre! Now market is not regulated by the government, rather it would simply be controlled by bureaucrats!", said another analyst.

Discussion Questions

1. What are the pros and cons of the government decision of subsidised loans to MFIs?
2. Suppose the government directs the banks to lend MFIs at 6 per cent and it would compensate an equivalent amount. What is your take on this?
3. Do you think there would be a rush among non-SHG members to form new SHGs after this decision?
4. What could be the alternatives with government rather than going for this interest rate subsidy?

Summary

- Self-regulation is an important issue in microfinance industry, as the regulators do not have the capacity and time to look into the compliance issues.
- There are two SROs, MFIN and Sa-Dhan in India in the microfinance industry. MFIN is for NBFC-MFIs, while Sa-Dhan has membership of all types of organisations involved in microfinance.
- Interest rate in microfinance is higher than banks because the transaction costs are high and they are not allowed to take savings.
- Commercial microfinance and SHG-Bank Linkage Programme are the two ends of financial inclusion model. Both of them have their pros and cons. Hence, both models should operate as long as they meet the objectives of financial inclusion and poverty alleviation.
- Allowing the MFIs in accepting deposits will help them in decreasing their cost of capital and thus they can decrease their lending rate. However, savings is a risky business. Due to factors like frauds, Ponzi Schemes, and sometimes due to recessions, depositors have lost their money. Hence, unless stringent conditions are met, banking licences are not granted.
- Schemes like PMJDY and other government initiatives have made significant contribution to the cause of financial inclusion. However, they cannot replace the services of microfinance that offers door-step delivery of services and collateral free loans.
- Microfinance industry is known for its high rate of repayment (such as 99%). However, this may be due to the circulation of loan. Hence, real repayment rate would be at least slightly less than what is stated.
- Regulation in microfinance is dented because there are scopes of circumventing it. The RBI guidelines focus only on NBFC-MFI, the same players without breaking the guidelines can add to the indebtedness and multiple lending when they operate as BCs.

Exercises

A. Multiple-choice Questions

1. Which of the following is not an SRO in microfinance?
   (a) MFIN (b) BASIX
   (c) Sa-Dhan (d) None of the above
2. Which of the following is true about SROs in microfinance in India?
   (a) Sa-Dhan'a members are NBFC-MFIs only
   (b) MFIN represents all kinds of models and organisations in microfinance
   (c) MFIN has members only from NBFC-MFIs
   (d) Sa-Dhan does not have any NBFC-MFI members
3. Savings product would help an MFI in attaining
   (a) Decrease in cost of funds
   (b) Increase in cost of funds
   (c) Decrease its loan portfolio
   (d) None of the above
4. The risk of MFIs offering savings product is
   (a) Stress situations can lead to bank run
   (b) MFIs do not have adequate capital to manage stress situations
   (c) It needs a high level of trust to manage public savings
   (d) All of the above
5. Commercial MFIs have not, in general
   (a) Passed on profits to customers
   (b) Grown fast
   (c) Attracted investors
   (d) None of the above
6. SHG-Bank Linkage Programme has the following problem
   (a) SHGs are subject to political influence
   (b) SHGs do not have homogenous quality
   (c) Both (a) and (b)
   (d) None of the above
7. Which of the following is not true about PMJDY?
   (a) It helps in improving financial inclusion
   (b) It meets all the credit needs of poor
   (c) It helps in linking with remittance services
   (d) It is used for direct benefit transfer of government schemes

8. In crisis situations, repayment tumbles in microfinance because
   (a) People do not have money
   (b) People do not want to pay
   (c) People do not get the next cycle of loan
   (d) All of the above
9. Circulation of loans (repayment out of next round of loan) in microfinance is a result of
   (a) RBI guidelines to comply to the rules
   (b) Pressure of investors for high RoI
   (c) Greed of MFIs
   (d) None of the above
10. What is/are the discrepancies found with the RBI guidelines on NBFC-MFI
   (a) BC and SFBs do not come under it
   (b) NBFC-MFI do not obey it
   (c) SROs do not enforce it
   (d) All of the above

B. Review Questions

1. Interest rate cap does not help the poor. Do you agree with the statement? Why?
2. What are the roles of self-regulatory organisations in the context of MFIs?
3. What are the risks of allowing MFIs to offer savings products?
4. Given that commercial microfinance focussed on profit rather than poverty alleviation, it should not be allowed to operate. Comment.
5. Financial inclusion cannot be ensured by government schemes like PMJDY. Comment.
6. Why do not the repayment rates in microfinance reflect the real repayment rates? What are the implications of this discrepancy?
7. Do you think the RBI regulations on NBFC-MFI are foolproof? Justify your statement.

C. Application-based Questions

You are the representative of an SRO for microfinance sector, and you have to meet the RBI Governor, who has invited the NBFCs to discuss certain important issues. An issue in discussion was that in the face of everybody having bank accounts (at least a PMJDY bank account) and the presence of payment banks everywhere, money transfer services offered by non-banking companies would be disallowed henceforth. Prepare an argument against this proposal.

Further Readings

CGAP keeps on publishing debatable issues on microfinance. These papers may be referred to from time to time. Some recent ones are *Does Financial Inclusion Impact the Lives of the Poor* by Mayada El-Zoghbi and *Should Funders support Switches for Mobile Payment Interoperability* by Alice Negre and William Cook.

PART V
Strategic Issues in Microfinance

CHAPTER

12

Crises in Microfinance

Chapter Outline

Learning Objectives

After reading this chapter, you will be able to:

- To provide a historical background of the AP microfinance crisis.
- To describe the provisions of the AP ordinance and its impact.
- To describe how demonitisation affected the microfinance industry.

12.1 Introduction

With a humble beginning in the early 1990s, microfinance activities took shape of an industry in less than two decades. By 2010, it was already an established business, with not only private equity being pumped in aggressively, but even the public investors also became aware of this business. When the initial public offer (IPO) of SKS Microfinance was oversubscribed tremendously in 2010, it was a kind of landmark event. In a way, the microfinance sector changed to a more business oriented one. These changes brought in a number of transformations in the microfinance sector. Not only it affected the way business was carried out, it affected the fundamental character of the operations and governance too. It was this transformation of the fundamental character of the business where the seed of crisis was also sown.

It was mentioned in Chapter 1 that initially the NGOs played an important role in initiating microfinance. The SHG-Bank Linkage Programme (SBLP) of National Board of Agriculture and Rural Development (NABARD) was primarily successful because of the contribution of NGOs. The self-help group (SHG) approach was so successful that it stormed into the major programmes of government. Even in programmes like natural resource management, health and livelihoods, the SHG approach was incorporated in some or the other way. The greatest recognition of SHG in government programmes was made in 1999, officially, when the Swarnajayanti Gram Swarozgar Yojana (SGSY) programme was mandated to be implemented in group approach. For the last eight years (since 2011), the revamped version of SGSY, the National Rural Livelihood Mission (NRLM) follows the same approach. Thus, SHG-based microfinance has become a cornerstone of the flagship livelihood promotion scheme of the government.

While the governmental programmes were implemented extensively, in the mid-1990s, a group of entrepreneurial minded development professionals found the grant-based approach to be slow. There were also problems in government led programmes which suffered from red tapes, corruption and political interventions. They saw that poor people needed capital and for that there was no institutional source of finance. Further, the informal sources charged high interest rates and quite often, it was exploitative too.

It was a win-win proposition that kick-started the commercial microfinance. The tested models of SEWA, Grameen Bank and many others were already there. BASIX was initialed in 1996. In about five years, it grew steadily and proved that microfinance could be grown professionally, sustainably and it really could address the issue of poverty (Harper et al, 2011).

What followed was the crowding in of a number of players in microfinance sector. In this process, the original mission of poverty alleviation was also diluted. This outcome lay at the heart of the crisis that occurred. This chapter provides a description of such crises, the most important of which occurred in 2010, in Andhra Pradesh. These crises were internal to the microfinance sector. There was also an instance where the sector faced a crisis not because something happened to the specific business, but the whole country came under its influence. The demonetisation of 2016 was that event. Like any crisis shapes the future trajectory in a markedly different manner, the aforesaid crises also affected the sector in both negative (immediately) and positive ways (in long-run). This will be discussed in the following sections.

12.2 The Small Crises: Precursors to the Disaster

Although the crisis of 2010 is the greatest setback in the history of microfinance, it was not the first time such a thing happened. In a way, it can be said that there were enough warnings already made to the people involved in the sector. And such warning was not just visible in Andhra Pradesh, but in other areas too. Three smaller crises have been documented well in this regard, which are also known as 3K. These three 'K's referred (Wright and Sharma, 2010) to three places in three different parts of India, Krishna (Andhra Pradesh), Kanpur (Uttar Pradesh) and Kolar (Karnataka).

The Krishna crisis took place in the year 2006, when the district administration closed down 50 offices of MFIs, particularly that of Spandana, Asmitha, and SHARE. The allegation against them was related to client poaching and usurious interest rates. There was allegation that 10 borrowers committed suicide. The then Chief Minister of the state wanted strict action against the Microfinance Institutions (MFIs) stating that MFIs were worse than moneylenders and charged interest rate of more than 20 per cent (*The Hindu,* 18 March 2006 cited in Shylendra, 2006). After this, the MFIs took some damage control measures. The central bank also intervened and as a result, the closed branches were reopened (Wright and Sharma, 2010).

This was considered as a typical state-civil society conflict; popularity of MFIs was a major contention for the political masters! Given the high transaction costs, it was natural that MFIs would charge interest rate of more than 20 per cent. However, MFIs were also to be blamed because of their lack of transparency in charging interests (Shylendra, 2006).

A fallout of the Krishna crisis was the partnership model in which the MFIs acted as the agent of the ICICI bank. This was a huge volume of transaction, covering about 1.2 million of customers and loan portfolio of USD 227 million. This also was an off-balance sheet transaction for the MFIs thus relaxing them from the capital adequacy requirement. As a part of this, a large number of SHGs were given loans, which was considered by the bureaucrats as client poaching. This model of lending had to be closed, as it violated the KYC norms (Wright and Sharma, 2010).

In Kanpur and its vicinities, in the year 2009, a local MFI (Nirman Bharati) defaulted. This was a clear mismanagement on the part of the MFI, which neither had any systems nor processes to monitor to whom lending had been done (Roy, 2018; Wright and Sharma, 2010).

Kolar, in 2009, faced a similar kind of situation. This was a relatively complex phenomenon (Wright and Sharma, 2010) in which the non-repayment was a result of a mix of rapid expansion, multiple lending and increasing repayment amounts, added with the decreasing income avenues in the wake of global recessions in the year 2008-09. There were a few attempts of suicide followed by which Anjuman Committees, which because of the Islamic beliefs traditionally opposed the practice of usury, banned microfinance in the area. The communal angle provided to this issue was exploited by quite a few people (Roy, 2018).

The MFIs understood clearly that there were problems. In 2009, forty-three MFIs (NBFCs) got together to form an apex body called Microfinance Institutions Network (MFIN) that tried to regulate the issues of transparency and pricing (Wright and Sharma, 2010). It was a modest attempt only, which showed that the microfinance industry people were aware that something wrong was going to happen. In a way, the three crises were precursors to the full-blown disaster that took place a year later. It cannot be said that the crisis was not expected. It was well known that the microfinance bubble would burst. And people believed that it was not a distant phenomenon. It was going to take place soon. What nobody knew was how it was going to burst.

12.3 The Crisis of AP in 2010

By 2010, commercial microfinance was already a fully bloomed industry. It had shown enormous growth. MFIs had started expanding like anything. Even relatively conservative organisations like BASIX had hired a hardcore banker to shape their expansion agenda. However, the highlights of new age expansion came from some other players like SKS Microfinance, SHARE, Asmitha and Spandana Sphoorthy. Incidentally, all of them were based in Andhra Pradesh.

These MFIs always boasted about their high recovery (near 100%) record (Sriram, 2012), which helped them in gaining credibility in the market. However, in an effort to maintain such repayment rates, allegedly coercive recovery methods were adopted. The MFIs (particularly Mr. Vikram Akula of SKS) repeatedly denied such acts, however Mr. Vijay Mahajan, who headed MFIN at that time, made a cautioning note about such allegations (Sriram, 2012). It may be noted that overindebtedness was proved by facts; the average borrowing in the sector in India was ₹7700, while in AP, it was ₹65,000 (CGAP, 2011).

Fuels were added to fire by reports that highlighted that MFIs had been earning money at the expense of borrowers. A report by Sriram (2010) highlighted several lapses in governance of some MFIs, in which the promoters had amassed huge sums money which did not make ethical sense.

The allegations of usurious interest rate and client poaching were nothing new. It was there during the Krishna crisis also, that took place about four years ago (in 2006). But this time, something else was there in the agenda. The political class was not happy with the way microfinance industry was behaving. There were allegations of coercive recovery, which led to suicides of MFI borrowers. A government run programme, Indira Kranti Pratham had documented 40 cases of suicides and it was reported to be caused by overindebtedness (Sriram, 2012).

On 15 October, 2010, the Government of Andhra Pradesh brought in an ordinance to curb the MFIs in the wake of the alleged suicides of microfinance clients. The motive of the ordinance was very clear from its description:

> *An ordinance to protect the women Self Help Groups from exploitation by the Microfinance Institutions in the State of Andhra Pradesh and for the matters connected therewith or incidental thereto.*

It further mentioned two ways in which the private MFIs exploited the poor women, usurious interest rates and coercive means of recovery, which lead to their impoverishment and even suicides. The ordinance provided the following measures to curb such acts:

- Registration of all MFIs with the district authorities
- Without such registration, no disbursal or recovery can be done
- Such registration can be done by the district authority for a period of one year, which can be renewed subject to the process of renewal given in the ordinance
- Prior approval of registering authority was required for granting second loans to SHGs and its members
- Registering authority were given enormous power to seize the document, search the premises and summon the officials of MFIs
- Coercive recovery would be punishable by imprisonment of one to three years, or fine of one lakh rupees, or both
- Pricing of interest rates, transparency, recovery methods were also mandated in the ordinance. A toll-free number for complaints was also provided.

The ordinance was interpreted conveniently by the borrowers and the MFI had no way to do anything.

Visits by MFI staff to the residence or workplace of the borrowers for recovery could be construed to be a coercive practice, so instead they had to sit in a central place hoping for borrowers to come there (Mahajan and Navin, 2013:10) .

The clauses of the ordinance ensured that there was an immediate stoppage of the MFIs operations. Some of them went to the district for registration, but interestingly, the district authorities had no clue on what is to be done. Apparently, there was no communication to the district authorities on the modus operandi of such registration. This ordinance was coupled with informal communication that there was no need to make repayment. As a result, borrowers stopped paying. According to Srinivasan (2011), repayments came down from 99 per cent to 10 per cent in the state. MFIs knocked the door of court, but to no avail.

Although the ordinance was promulgated in one state, the message spread like wild fire. In other states also, the repayment rate came down. There was an apprehension that the industry was going to melt down.

12.4 The Aftermath

Within a couple of months of the above ordinance, it was introduced as a bill in the AP state assembly and soon it became law. However, the message was spread to the whole country and there were a lot of discussions at regulatory level. In view of the emergency, the RBI sprung to action and appointed the Malegam Committee to look into the issue and suggest a regulatory framework. The committee had consultations with several stakeholders and in January 2011, submitted its report. The RBI circular of NBFC-MFIs was primarily based on this committee report, with some modifications.

For the MFIs, the AP crisis of 2010, brought in doomsday. The AP based MFIs, which used to be the high growth organisations, were hit hard. Their profitability took a deep plunge. They had to resort to several mechanisms like corporate debt restructuring and unprecedented level of downsizing of the staff. The microfinance wing of BASIX, which was ordinarily not considered to be one of the exploiters could not take off again, even till now. SKS Microfinance had a great turmoil in its Board and ultimately its Founder, Dr. Akula had to leave the organisation. Spandana, Asmitha, and SHARE were also hit. The impact on the AP based MFIs can be gauged from the fact that when in 2015 the licences for SFBs were called for, not a single of these organistions made it to the list. Organisations that did not have exposure to AP, particularly those who had good systems and processes, revived slowly. It took about three to four years to see signs of recovery in the microfinance sector.

12.5 A Critical Analysis of Crises in Microfinance

What was the root cause of the AP crisis? Did it have to happen in the manner that it happened? A lot has been written on this issue. The most important rhetoric was the greed of the MFI promoters. While the people who promulgated the ordinance and press always highlighted this, it was not a baseless allegation. A study by Sriram (2010) published months before the AP crisis highlighted that promoters amassed a lot of wealth, which might not be illegal, but defied the standard practices. Issues like disproportionate remuneration to directors and their relatives, allocation of shares to promoters and independent directors beyond any logic and conversion of holding of shares by Trusts to family-based holding were highlighted (see Chatper 13 for details).

However, if the sole responsibility of this crisis is fixed on the greed of promoters, it would be quite simplistic. The responsibility goes to the management of microfinance institutions (here one needs to distinguish between the shareholder and the management). Microfinance institutions ignored various important parametres like a robust MIS and capacity building of human resources.

> *In fact, as early as April 2009, MicroSave had raised the red flag while conducting a Loan Portfolio Audit (LPA4) of one of the large MFIs. The MIS was clearly inadequate for the scale of operations, and (probably as a result) the reporting of non-performing loans was inconsistent at various levels.*

Furthermore, there was a marked absence of control systems over the maintenance of cash and cheques; many branches where the entire staff had less than one year of experience and branch managers being transferred and replaced in less than a month; lack of properly documented policies in HR, Operations and Accounts; ... the list goes on. New field officers were being provided with 2 days of training followed by 2-3 weeks of exposure shadowing another field officer before being given the responsibility of managing a thousand clients or more (Wright and Sharma, 2010:).

Thus, in an overdrive for expansion, the MFIs neglected the information management and human resource management aspects. This also took place not without reason. Blaming greed to this would not be sufficient. There were some other root causes. Earlier, it was mentioned that by 2005, the microfinance sector was already taking off and everybody noticed it. Initially, the sector depended on grant funds, which were not sufficient for the unlimited expansions that the MFIs were going through. Some of them used external commercial borrowings (ECBs) which were banned on the aftermath of terrorist attack on parliament. This period also coincided with the transformation of NGOs into for-profit MFIs. Also, the RBI enhanced the CRAR requirement from 10 to 12 per cent. This required huge funds and the private equity (PE) funds provided a lease of life to such needy MFIs (Datta, Dutta and Bhaskaran, 2011).

By nature, the PE funds look for highly efficient operations. Such funds see the space for improving profitability in organisations, invest there, turn them around, book profit and exit. When such funds are invested in MFIs, they pressurised the newly transformed organisations (who used to operate as not-for-profits) to be more efficient, which led to cutting down processes and costs. The lapse in human resource capacity building was a direct result of this intervention.

But how did the cut down in capacity building affect the operations? It is well known that the primary goal of microfinance is to alleviate poverty. Without having this angle, microfinance has no existence. Now, in order to deal with poverty, one not only has to understand the critical steps of loan processes, but also has to understand the value system in which a development professional works. By having a longer period of training, such value systems could be communicated to the new employees. By cutting down this link, the new microfinance frontline workers became devoid of such values.

Thus, it is not that the MFI promoters and senior managers were always greedy. But to meet the need of expansion, they needed PE funds. To attract PE funds, they had to be highly efficient. It must be noted here that 2007-10 was also a period of crisis in the West. Hence many of MFIs were looking for avenues. According to Datta et al (2011), the initial investors were of the nature of social investment, which slowly changed to pure commercial interest. In an urge to be highly efficient, MFIs compromised on processes which led to issues like coercive recovery.

There are a couple of other issues that drove the sector to doomsday. The political economy of Andhra Pradesh (now it is divided into two, AP and Telengana) was controlled by several players like mining barons, moneylenders and so on. The latter category is alleged to provide a substantial amount of political funding, at least at the ground level. An outcome of the rapid expansion of microfinance directly hit their businesses, and they lobbied against the MFIs.

The last but the most direct cause of the ordinance being brought in was related to the competition between state run programmes and the MFIs. According to Srinivasan (2010), the commercial microfinance had clearly overtaken the SHG model that was promoted by the state. This was a cause of jealousy in the bureaucrats and their political masters. Further, the politicians had already tested that women's SHGs could be used as a political constituency (Mahajan and Navin, 2016), for them, the weakening of SHG based programmes was a kind of defeat.

This was not acceptable to the political class as they would lose hold over an important vote bank. The civil servants were in agreement with the political leaders as they would lose hold of a major programme and the related budget if MFIs occupied the dominant space. The hostility of the staff of the government sponsored Andhra Pradesh Society for Elimination of Rural Poverty (SERP) towards MFIs is largely based on this anxiety (Mahajan and Navin, 2016:8).

A point that can be taken from the crisis is that microfinance is not just a business but a complex platform for social, economic and political transactions. Managers of this business must be aware of this multidimensional arena. It may also be noted that the crisis, against all fears, did not die away and revived. However, in reviving, it imprinted great lessons. Many organisations took a lead from the crisis and do not try to make the mistakes like geographical concentration of operations. This clause, as mentioned in the RBI guidelines, has even entered into the guidelines of regulators.

12.6 Demonetisation

All the crises described earlier had one thing in common, they were all related to the business practices specific to the MFIs. By 2016, many such practices were corrected and microfinance had already moved into another phase of high growth. However, another cloud of crisis was hovering around, unexpected, unprecedented and unknown to anybody even a moment before it took place. It was like a high intensity earthquake. And this time, the crisis was not specific to microfinance sector in India; rather it hit the whole country. Microfinance sector, of course, was affected substantially. It was another phase of anxiety that the sector was going to be wiped out. This crisis, in the form of demonetisation, came up in November 2016.

The microfinance sector depended primarily on cash disbursal and cash collection. This was because the remote locations in which clients are located did not have proper banking facilities. When demonetisation was declared, the MFIs could not collect the EMIs because there was no cash available with the clients.

There were operational problems also. For example, initially it was allowed for any organisation to withdraw only ₹50,000. For an organisation like Ujjivan, it required about ₹10-12 lakhs. Hence cash holding at branch level was allowed, which was a very risky practice. There were instances of heist in that period (Roy 2018: 206). Confusions were also created by politicians who lauded the need for loan waiver (Roy, 2018: 197).

According to a report in Livemint, the following impacts were observed on the microfinance industry:

- Decrease in number of clients to the extent of 2 per cent over the quarter of demonetisation
- Decrease in disbursement in loan amount as well as disbursement in number of loans
- Average loan disbursed in the demonetisation quarter (₹20,981) was lower than the previous quarter (₹21,469)
- Portfolio at risk increased substantially. (Gaurav and Mankar, 2017).

Jain and Bakshi (2018) reported that 30-day PAR was about 0.3 per cent in September 2016, which increased to 14.1 per cent in March 2017, and by December 2017, it was as high as about 6 per cent. According to estimate, about ₹50 billion to ₹70 billion were expected to be written-off by the microfinance sector because of demonetisation (Business Line, 2018; Mondal, 2017). It was expected that the complete revival would take about 18-20 months (Business Line, 2018).

12.7 COVID-19 Impact on Microfinance Sector (2020–2021)

The COVID-19 pandemic had a profound impact on India's microfinance sector. Lockdowns and economic disruptions led to reduced incomes among borrowers, resulting in increased defaults and operational challenges for MFIs. The sector faced liquidity constraints and a decline in loan disbursements. In response, the Reserve Bank of India and the government introduced measures such as moratoriums on loan repayments, credit guarantee schemes, and liquidity support to assist the sector.

Despite these efforts, the pandemic underscored the vulnerability of the microfinance model to systemic shocks. The crisis highlighted the need for MFIs to adopt more resilient operational models, diversify risk, and enhance digital capabilities to withstand future disruptions.

12.8 Assam Microfinance Crisis (2021)

In 2021, Assam experienced a severe microfinance crisis characterized by widespread borrower distress, defaults, and social unrest. The crisis stemmed from multiple factors, including over-indebtedness due to multiple loans from various microfinance institutions (MFIs), aggressive recovery practices, and the economic fallout from the COVID-19 pandemic. The situation was further exacerbated by the lack of effective regulatory oversight and the proliferation of unregulated lenders.

In response to the crisis, the Assam government launched the Assam Microfinance Incentive and Relief Scheme (AMFIRS) in 2021. The scheme aimed to provide relief to over 20 lakh women borrowers by offering incentives for regular repayment and waivers for overdue accounts. The government allocated substantial funds to compensate lenders and restore creditworthiness among borrowers.

The Assam crisis underscored the need for robust regulatory frameworks, borrower protection mechanisms, and responsible lending practices to ensure the sustainability of the microfinance sector.

12.9 Karnataka Microfinance Crisis (2025)

In early 2025, Karnataka faced a microfinance crisis marked by rising borrower suicides, reports of coercive recovery practices, and widespread public outcry. Unregulated micro-lenders and aggressive collection tactics led to significant distress among rural borrowers. The crisis highlighted the vulnerabilities in the microfinance sector, particularly concerning borrower protection and ethical lending practices .

In response, the Karnataka government enacted the Karnataka Micro Loan and Small Loan (Prevention of Coercive Actions) Ordinance in February 2025. The ordinance aimed to regulate micro-lending activities and protect borrowers from exploitative practices. Key provisions included mandatory registration of lenders, transparency in loan terms, prohibition of coercive recovery methods, and stringent penalties for violations, including imprisonment and fines.

The Karnataka crisis emphasized the importance of regulatory oversight, ethical lending practices, and borrower education to prevent similar occurrences in the future. These crises highlight the critical importance of robust regulatory frameworks, ethical lending practices, and borrower protection mechanisms to ensure the resilience and sustainability of the microfinance sector in India.

Here is a comparative overview of the microfinance crises in Andhra Pradesh (2010), Assam (2021), and Karnataka (2025), highlighting key aspects of each:

Table 12.1 Comparison of AP, Assam and Karnataka Crises

Aspect	Andhra Pradesh (2010)	Assam (2021)	Karnataka (2025)
Primary Causes	• Over-indebtedness due to multiple loans • Coercive recovery practices • Lack of regulatory oversight	• Aggressive lending leading to borrower distress • Political promises of loan waivers affecting repayment behaviour • Economic impact of COVID-19 exacerbating defaults	• Overleveraging and sub-lending practices • Reports of coercive recovery methods • Implementation of stringent state ordinance affecting lender operations
Government Response	• Enactment of Andhra Pradesh Microfinance Institutions (Regulation of Money Lending) Act, 2010 • Imposition of strict regulations on MFIs	• Introduction of Assam Microfinance Incentive and Relief Scheme (AMFIRS) to provide relief to borrowers • Advisories issued against taking loans from MFIs	• Promulgation of Karnataka Micro Loan and Small Loan (Prevention of Coercive Actions) Ordinance, 2025, imposing penalties on coercive recovery practices

Impact on MFIs	• Significant decline in microfinance activities in the state • Loss of investor confidence • Shift of MFIs to other regions	• Temporary halt in loan disbursements by some MFIs • Need for MFIs to reassess lending practices and borrower assessment	• Operational challenges due to regulatory restrictions • Necessity for MFIs to adapt to new compliance requirements
Borrower Consequences	• Increased financial distress leading to borrower suicides • Reduced access to credit due to MFI withdrawal	• Confusion and uncertainty among borrowers regarding loan repayments • Potential for increased defaults due to expectations of loan waivers	• Legal protection against coercive recovery • Possible reduction in credit availability due to stricter lending norms
Long-term Outcomes	Catalyst for the establishment of national regulatory frameworks for MFIs Greater emphasis on borrower protection	Highlighted the need for balanced microfinance practices Emphasis on responsible lending and borrower education	Ongoing adjustments in microfinance operations to align with new regulations Continued monitoring of borrower welfare and MFI practices

12.10 Need of Studying Crises

Crises need to be studied because they teach a lot of things. They not only provide a long-term learning for the human society as a whole, but also bring in changes in modus operandi. What the World War II meant for world history and the Great Depression meant for economists, the AP crisis and demonetisation would mean for the microfinance sector in India. My opinion is that these are the landmark events in the history of microfinance.

Microfinance sector also learnt a lot of things from the crisis. The AP crisis made people aware about the complex set of interactions of the microfinance business with other domains of society, such as bureaucracy, press and politics. It also taught that companies should avoid things like concentration in a particular geography. It shows that the age old rule of maintaining diversity must be respected. From demonetisation, it was learnt that too much dependence on informal mechanism has its risk. Today, the sector boasts cashless transactions. While the outside world again reverted to cash transaction, microfinance industry swiftly switched to cashless mode.

Case Study 12.1 ABCML's Crisis

ABC Microfinance Limited (ABCML), is a reputed MFI working in some western Indian states. The organisation started in the year 2005 and by 2016, it has grown to be a reputed MFI operating in Madhya Pradesh, Gujarat, Rajasthan and Maharashtra. In these four states, the organisation has got 85 per cent of its operations. In rest of India, in 10 more states, it has recently started its business.

ABCML has a robust process of lending and has established risk management procedures as per industry standards. Its directors have long experience of working with banks and NBFCs and they have guided the management in building a solid operational system. By September 2016's quarter end, the organisation had an outstanding of ₹50 billion and in the previous financial year, it had reported the revenue of ₹11 billion and profit after tax of ₹2.1 billion. It has about 2500 staff members across all the places operating its 300 rural branches.

The organisation had several kinds of activities apart from microcredit. As a part of its welfare activities, it has provided support for health camps and scholarship for children. It had built a good relationship with the community.

In November 2016, the MFI was in a smooth position. It had plans to expand to other places. In the first phase, the plan was to enhance its presence in the existing states. In the second stage, it planned to expand in the eastern Indian states and in the third phase, it planned to expand in north India states. South India, because of its saturated record of microfinance, was not in the cards of ABCML at least in the near future. It was expected that all these expansions would require about ₹1 billion, which would be raised through debt and equity. There was also talks about issuing IPO in the year 2017-18. Meetings with investment banks and private equity firms were scheduled to be in the third and fourth week of November 2016, respectively.

At the close of office hour on 8 November 2016, the life of Mr. R. K. Diwan, MD of ABCML, was not out of stress. The upcoming meetings in the subsequent weeks were to be dealt with. The business plan needed to be strengthened. He thought that the next weekend would also be spent in office works. Operations at field level were moving smoothly and at the previous meeting, all the branch managers were given a hint that some significant expansion was going to happen.

He was on his way home around 8.15 PM and the CFO called him, "Mr. Diwan, did you hear the news?" "What news?", he asked. "Government has announced that the existing ₹500 and ₹1000 currencies will no longer be legal tenders. We have to stop all cash disbursement and receipt in these denominations immediately! You please come down to office immediately". Without any further question, Mr. Diwan returned to office. By the time he reached, the detailed announcement about demonetisation was already over. In the meantime, the Chief Operating Officer and some other managers that lived nearby had also reached the office. All the branch managers were informed immediately to close all disbursals and receipt with immediate effect. They were also asked to report by 11 AM next day about their observations regarding borrowers and the locality. It was decided that at 11 AM, a meeting of all staff would be held in head office. There was discussion with the Chairman of Board of Directors also. He told that at 4.00 PM next day, a skype meeting with all the available directors would be held.

At 11.00 AM next morning, the Chief Operating Officer presented his report compiled from the reports of branch managers:

- At present, 92 per cent of the disbursals and 99 per cent of the repayments take place in the form of cash.
- At 8.00 AM, there was a rush in front of the office of some branches to repay loans, however, all such repayments were being made in the banned notes. All the borrowers were told to go back, saying that on that date government has asked to close down the offices. Also, these notes could only be deposited in the bank accounts.
- In some areas, there were rumours that the government would waive off all the loans from MFIs.
- In some places, people wanted to exchange the invalid notes with the valid ones.
- Some borrowers were worried that they would not be able to repay and it would bring them into the defaulters list.

There was absolute mayhem among the staff members. Some branch level officials, including loan officers and branch managers had also come from nearby areas. They were not sure what would happen to their jobs as people were not going to repay. They believed that there would be no payment for the next two to three months. Some feared that asking money from borrowers would create severe backlash.

At 4.00 PM, the board meeting was held through skype. The board was worried about what would happen to the meeting with investment bankers and private equity firms. One of the directors said, "You must ask the PE firm to release funds immediately so that we can take care of the emergency needs of our loyal customers. It is a tough time for us. But it is tougher for people whom we are supposed to serve!" It was decided that in next 24 hours, Mr. Diwan would come with an action plan for the next three months.

Discussion Questions

1. What should be done with regard to recovery of dues so that the customer does not become angry and at the same time, the recovery is not written-off?
2. How would the willful defaulters be dealt with?
3. What should be done to boost the morale of the staff?
4. What action plan should be made so that the fund-raising activities are not affected?
5. Should the IPO plan be held up for some time?

Summary

- Microfinance sector faced several crises during the period from 2006-2016. The most draconian one was the AP crisis of 2010 which almost wiped out the industry. The demonetisation of 2016 also significantly affected the industry.
- The AP crisis of 2010 was not a standalone crisis. There were precursors to it in various places, such as Krishna (AP), Kanpur (UP) and Kolar (Karnataka).
- The AP crisis was caused by an ordinance to curb the usurious interest rate, coercive recovery and impoverishment and suicides of women SHG members. The ordinance was harsh on many aspects that led to defaulting of loans of enormous proportions (recovery came down to 10%).
- Although the ordinance was brought in AP, the whole of India was affected by it. The MFIs based in AP were, however, worst hit.
- In the aftermath of the crisis, the RBI appointed the Malegam Committee, the recommendations of which became the foundations for the subsequent RBI circular on NBFC-MFIs.
- Although the precarious and greedy practices of MFIs and its promoters are blamed for the crisis, there were other issues as well. The root cause was there in regulatory provisions leading to MFIs depending on PE funds, emphasis on efficiency and cutting down costs that led to compromise in processes and training of human resources, and the non-alighment of value system with the processes.
- The moneylending lobby also played a key role in bringing the ordinance. However, the direct role was played by bureaucrats and politicians who found that the MFI model had taken over the SHG model, which was the state's pet project and it was also a leverage point for vote banks.
- Demonetisation was a crisis imposed upon by external forces, it was not specific to microfinance industry. Microfinance industry was hit hard because it depended upon cash transactions. It is estimated that the sector wrote off about ₹ 50 billion to ₹ 70 billion because of this crisis.

Exercises

A. Multiple-choice Questions

1. The three Ks of microfinance crisis are
   (a) Karnataka, Kerala and Kolkata
   (b) Krisha, Koshy and Kiran
   (c) Krishna, Kanpur and Kolar
   (d) None of the above
2. AP crisis was driven by the issue of
   (a) Ordinance in Andhra Pradesh
   (b) RBI guidelines
   (c) Microfinance Bill in Parliament
   (d) None of the above
3. AP crisis was caused by
   (a) Reckless expansion of MFIs.
   (b) Regulatory void in microfinance
   (c) Lobby of moneylenders and bureaucrats
   (d) All of the above
4. Demonetisation led to ________________ of MFIs.
   (a) Increase in portfolio at risk
   (b) Decrease in portfolio at risk
   (c) No impact on portfolio at risk
   (d) Varied impact on portfolio at risk from place to place
5. Which of the following clause of the AP ordinance stopped the operations of MFIs?
   (a) Requirement of registration at district level
   (b) Stoppage of all lending and recovery before registration
   (c) Both (a) and (b)
   (d) None of the above
6. In the aftermath of the AP crisis, the RBI appointed the ________________ committee.
   (a) Khan
   (b) Malegam
   (c) Narasimhan
   (d) None of the above
7. Which of the following clause in RBI guidelines on NBFC-MFIs was especially from the learning of AP crisis experience?
   (a) Capital adequacy ratio
   (b) Geographical diversity
   (c) Interest rate
   (d) None of the above

8. The increase in PE funds in microfinance led to
   (a) Increase in efficiency
   (b) Emphasis on profitability
   (c) Fast growth
   (d) All of the above
9. Which of the following allegations were highlighted in the AP ordinance?
   (a) Coercive recovery and usury
   (b) Client poaching and usury
   (c) Loan waiver and coercive recovery
   (d) None of the above
10. The ICICI bank and MFI's partnership model for microfinance sector was banned because of
   (a) Client poaching
   (b) KYC norms
   (c) High interest rates
   (d) All of the above

B. Review Questions

1. What were the warnings that the microfinance sector ignored before the AP Crisis?
2. What were the provisions of the ordinance promulgated by the Government of AP that caused a crisis in the microfinance sector?
3. Which clauses/provisions of the ordinance led to the crisis in the microfinance sector?
4. Although the ordinance was issued in only one state, the effects were seen nation-wide. Why?
5. Was such a draconian regulation required to tame the microfinance sector? Justify your arguments.
6. The AP crisis was a result of regulatory failure. Comment.
7. Due to Andhra Pradesh crisis, the microfinance industry faced a huge problem of non-repayment, but in long run, it helped in improving the regulatory aspects. Comment.
8. Did commercialisation kill microfinance in Andhra Pradesh? Comment.
9. How did demonetisation affect the microfinance sector?

C. Application-based Questions

Suppose you are the head of one of the AP based MFIs in Andhra Pradesh. You have substantial exposure in the state. You are not one of the companies who has been accused of exploiting the customers. However, you know that your company is also going to be affected equally during the next few months, may be even longer.

- What would be your immediate strategy for saving your organisation from the crisis?
- What will be your long-term strategy so that you can withstand such shocks in the future?

Further Readings

- Papers by Shylendra (2006) and Sriram (2012) as referred to above are detailed accounts on the AP crisis. These may be referred to for further details.
- Mahajan (2012) and Kanitkar (2012)'s analysis of case of Sriram (2012) published in *Vikalpa* is also a further detail about the AP Crisis.
- Datta et al (2011) and Mahajan and Navin (2013) are some other useful reading.
- An unpublished paper by Shylendra (2011) 'The Microfinance Crisis: A Political Economy Perspective' also provides a critical analysis of the issue.
- A chapter titled 'Demonetization Trauma' in Roy (2018) book as referred here provides details of the impact of the crisis on Ujjvan.

CHAPTER

13 Governance Issues in Microfinance

Chapter Outline

Learning Objectives

After reading this chapter, you will be able to:

- discuss the importance of governance in microfinance sector.
- describe the regulatory provisions that direct the governance of MFIs.
- understand the experience of MFIs in terms of their governance.

13.1 What it Meant by Governance of Microfinance?

Governance is not the same as the functions of government. It means the decision-making systems and processes in the larger institutional space, in which there are interdependent actors (Kooiman, 1993; Rhoades, 1993). It also includes the ability to formulate and enforce rules (Fukyyama, 2013). A lot of discussion is available in literature, in which focus is on the governance structure in the market that dealt with contractual relations (Williamson, 1979). In a network form of market transactions, governance is embedded in the social mechanism (Jones et al, 1997). According to Mishra and Dey (2018), governance includes coordination among actors, control over the decision-making system and safeguarding of interests of actors.

In the context of microfinance, governance can be looked into at two levels:

- At the macro level, it would include formulation of rules and regulation, enforcement, the larger institutional space of Microfinance Institutions (MFIs), regulators, people, and others; the way participants coordinate, influences in decision making, and the safeguarding of interest of stakeholders, in general and people, in particular.
- At micro-level, it would require the corporate governance issues at the level of MFIs and Self Help Group Promoting Instutions (SHPI).

The role of board is an important issue in corporate governance. Conflict of interest is another issue widely discussed. When the decision maker (say Director) gains from any particular transaction, she/he should not be a part of the decision-making process. And such kinds of conflict of interest must be disclosed. In the listed companies, the disclosure norms are kept very high. However, in unlisted companies, such requirements are low. In private limited companies (it may be noted here that there are many private limited MFIs), they still have to meet less disclosure norms. The rating and SPM reports generally seek such information, but they cannot be disclosed to the public unless the company wants to. In any case, the rating and social performance management (SPM) reports do not provide raw data, they are summarised versions of the observations of the evaluators.

Another issue in corporate governance is the autonomy of independent directors. Many companies want full autonomy to the managers, which means that the Board has to act like a rubber stamp. The other extreme is an activist board, where the Board of Directors question each and every action of the managers. Rubber stamp boards are very common. Such boards ordinarily fail in foreseeing the difficulties. These often consist of people who are not professionally qualified.

13.2 Larger Governance Issues in Microfinance Sector

The larger governance system in microfinance sector has been more or less discussed in the previous chapters.

- **Institutions** The important institutions in the microfinance sector include the NBFC-MFIs, Banks, SFBs, SHPIs like NRLM implementing state level societies (such as Bihar Rural Development Society, Odisha Livelihoods Mission, and Rajeevika), NGOs (MYRADA, PRADAN, etc), industry associations (MFIN, Sa-Dhan), consulting organisations, credit bureaus, technology solution providers, auditors, rating agencies, political parties, moneylenders, and others.
- **Regulators** Reserve Bank of India (RBI), NABARD, state governments, central government
- **People** This category includes the people who are to be served by the sector

Ordinarily, a system of governance is called effective if there is a balance in safeguarding the interests of all stakeholders (for detailed discussion, see Mishra and Dey, 2018). In this criterion, where does the microfinance sector stand? We can observe that the sector still lacks a legislation for regulating. The RBI guidelines, which are nothing but an executive order, still hold the key to the regulatory aspects. Twice there had been efforts to bring in a bill in Parliament, and both times it failed. This also means that the issues of the microfinance sector are not in priority of our political class.

For the bankers, microfinance is still a fringe activity. Earlier, they were not interested in it. They found some positive aspects only when it was included under the priority sector lending (PSL). Banks ordinarily had difficulty in attaining the PSL targets, and this became an opportunity for them.

In general, state governments are not very proactive to the needs of microfinance. Andhra Pradesh was the only state that took a keen interest on this issue. And we know that it did not do much for long-term growth for the sector. Rather its initiatives (2010 ordinance and subsequent legislation) almost put the commercial MFIs to the ground. The interesting outcome of the whole AP crisis was that while the alleged violators have revived their businesses in the medium term, some genuine companies, who operated at a smaller scale, had to shelve their business.

The role of RBI has also been questioned from time to time. How come the microfinance sector grew vibrantly in Bangladesh, but in India, there were so many crises? While it is easier to blame the MFIs, the RBI cannot shy away from its responsibilities. In a way, for the RBI, microfinance is too small a segment to look into. As a regulator, it was its duty to prescribe prudential norms, but it also drove the MFIs into a larger game controlled by crony capitalists. As a result, the development-oriented MFIs quickly (and allegedly) converted into market-led loan sharks. The regulatory vacuum, probably, also led the AP government to aggressively go for an ordinance.

Could this process of transformation of the sector have been a little smoother? It would be a hypothetical question at this point of time, however, there is nothing wrong in presuming. Microfinance industry operated in a unique kind of market, which should have been looked into by the RBI. A larger consultation at the crucial moment of potential growth could have resulted in some checks and balances, which would have humbled the throttle of growth, but could have resulted in a more responsible and trustworthy market.

A question can be raised here, why should the RBI look into the concerns of an industry that is miniscule in proportion of the size of the financial market that the regulator addresses? It should be noted that microfinance sector is small in size, but it has huge implications! Its role in financial inclusion is immense. It has been able to develop banking habits in masses (particularly among women) that the banking industry would never have been able to do. In summary, the microfinance business contributed something for establishing a robust banking habits in the future. The next generation of bankers would probably reap the benefits of what microfinance did today. Looking at this aspect, it becomes the duty of the RBI to be concerned about this sector.

13.3 RBI Guidelines on Corporate Governance of NBFCs

Before looking into the corporate governance issues in Non-banking Financial Instutions (NBFC)-MFIs, let us see what corporate governance means and what the regulatory provisions are in this respect. The fundamental concept of corporate governance is more or less drawn from the way governance is defined. However, as corporate governance is about specific orgnisational contexts, it is analysed in much more detail than the way governance is understood. Corporate governance essentially refers to the role of Board of Directors, the way important decisions are made, alignment of such decisions with the larger organisational purposes, ensuring compliance with regulatory norms, having accountability and having a transparent system in which important disclosures are made. It also has to be seen that the conflict of interest issues are sorted out appropriately.

Regarding corporate governance, the NBFC-MFIs are governed by the Non-Banking Financial Companies – Corporate Governance (Reserve Bank) Directions, 2015[1] issued on 3 June 2015. This RBI order has the following provisions:

- There must be three committees – Audit Committee, Nomination Committee and Risk Management Committee. It may be noted that the Companies Act 2013 prescribes the framework for Audit Committee and Nomination Committee.
- There must be a risk management policy, in conformity with corporate governance standards. Further disclosure related to registration, ratings, penalties, overseas operations, joint ventures and asset-liability profile should be made in the annual financial reporting statements.
- Every three years, rotation of partners of audit firm should be done.
- Internal guidelines for corporate governance should be framed and approved by the Board of the Directors.
- In appointing the directors, the company should determine the suitability of the person for appointment/ continuing to hold appointment as a director on the Board, based upon qualification, expertise, track record, integrity and other 'fit and proper' criteria. It should be undertaken during appointment and renewal.
- For large companies having an asset of size ₹5 billion (500 crore) or more, supplementary information on capital, investments, risks and exposure in derivatives, off-balance assets like securitisation, NPAs, exposure to real estate sector, unsecured advances, related party transactions and remunerations of directors should be made. Management discussion and analysis on various issues ranging from industry structure, opportunities, threats, internal controls, HR aspects, prior period items and consolidated financial statement should be provided.
- Other disclosures, such as provisions for loan losses, drawing from reserves and disclosure of complaints should be made.

13.4 Risk Management in MFIs

Financial institutions like MFIs face several kinds of risks like market risk like credit risk, operational risk, liquidity risk, concentration risk, etc. MFIs are generally subject to all kinds of risks, however, the two most important of them are related to operational, credit and concentration risks.

1. https://www.rbi.org.in/Scripts/BS_NBFCNotificationView.aspx?Id=9659, retrieved on 9 April 2019

Credit risk arises from the very nature of financial decisions and transactions taking place in MFIs. The main product of MFI is to deliver loans and when the person taking loan repays it, the loan account is closed These kinds of borrowers, who take loan and pay back, are called safe borrowers. Others are risky borrowers There has been some discussion in this regard in Chapter 2.

Why does risk occur in credit transactions? There are two aspects to this, one is that the non-repayment is because of moral hazard, and two, because of the uncertainty which arises out of many factors, such as recession, adverse economic and environmental factors and so on. Moral hazard occurs under two circumstances, in the first circumstance, the borrower is not careful in making business decisions (assuming that the loan is for business purpose), and hence does not make profit. Thus, the loan remains unpaid. There can also be a situation when the borrower is not willing to pay. In both cases, there is a default in repayment However, such defaults can generate out of genuine reasons as well. If the borrower has made decisions in good faith, but it just did not succeed and he/she lost money, in that case, he/she would not be able to repay

The second important risk in microfinance is related to operational aspects. Microfinance being a cash-intensive business, there are inherent fears of the cash being stolen, the concerned officer being assaulted and cash taken away, and there are also chances of frauds. These days, MFIs have shifted to a cashless mode while disbursing the loans, however, the clients still prefer to pay in cash.

Concentration risk refers to geographical concentration and it can be driven by political agenda. We have already discussed in Chapter 12 on how due to political interventions in AP, MFIs having exposure to that state were negatively affected.

Such risks can occur due to various factors, such as inappropriate products, poor screening of clients, poor appraisal processes, poor MIS, no regular follow-up, natural disasters like flood and drought, corruption, and demotivated employees (IIBF, 2009). Ujjivan's experience was that, *frauds rose during a period of rapid expansion* (Roy, 2018:160). Fortunately, risk management has been an established practice and it is considered a function of corporate governance. As can be seen, the RBI guidelines mandate that NBFCs must have a risk management committee.

It is the role of the Board of Directors to ensure that there is a risk management system in place. It happens that smaller MFIs are often not careful with establishing a robust process and this leads to many of the risks. The author had observed an MFI in Odisha (name withheld), during 2010-11, there were a number of instances of the loan collection officer running away. Unfortunately, these officers would also take away all the records and the organisation did not have a backup of data. Such instances are not rare in microfinance. In high growth phase, some of the critical procedures are compromised. This is obviously a lapse of governance.

What should the Board do in order to assure that such risks are managed properly? The first and foremost action needed here is to have strong criteria for screening of loan applications and loan approval. Secondly, the identification of the client must be beyond doubt. Once these two criteria are fulfilled, the chances of lapses in loan repayment due to internal factors would be considerably less. The third factor that drives a good risk management process is to ensure that an appropriate employee remuneration system is there. Companies that pay commission based on loan distributed may face more risky borrowers because the loan officer then would be more concerned in increasing the loans. The companies that who have full-time loan officers are found to make better choices in selecting clients. Further, a robust monitoring system also helps. When there is an instance of non-repayment, it must be followed up and the reason behind the default should be inquired. Based on the findings, appropriate actions may be taken.

13.5 MFI Governance: International Examples

Banco Compartamos, an MFI from Mexico, was originally a not-for-profit organisation and became a regulated finance company in the year 2000. In 2007, the company went for IPO, the response to which was overwhelming. A concern arose here that grant money was used for the gainful activities of promoters. The original investors had paid USD 6 million during 1998-2000. By 2000, the book value of this investment went up to USD 126 million. For 30 per cent of shares, the MFI received USD 450 million (Rosenberg, 2007). This was a kind of surprise for the financial market. The global mainstream business media also could not stop noticing it (Armendariz and Morduch, 2010). However, many felt uncomfortable. First of all, grant money was used for this windfall gain and second, the company charged about 99 per cent interest rate per annum from its customers, (86% plus value added tax of 15% over it), who were from the low-income group (Rosenberg, 2007).

Another example from international microfinance is that of the Banco Solidario (BancoSol) from Bolivia. It was promoted in 1992 by an NGO, know as PRODEM, which had established the basic processes, systems, and clients at grassroot level earlier. It transferred its assets and clients to the newly formed bank. The bank, however, grew rapidly and attracted commercial funds also which built pressures on it to be more productive. In this process, there was criticism of mission drift, as a result of which people from PRODEM were unhappy, and slowly the latter made exit from the company (Gonzalez-Vega et al, 1996).

From pure market point of view, there was nothing wrong with the above two examples. In the case of Banco Compartamos, the promoters offloaded only 30 per cent of the shares, which anyway could be used for development purposes. There still remained the question of gains made by private investors (Rosenberg, 2007; Sriram, 2010). Similarly, in the BancoSol case, the apprehension of mission drift was there, but to a large extent, the changes were due to the unprecedented scaling up of the operations (Gonzalez-Vega et al, 1996).

What is wrong with making profits in microfinance? Why are people not comfortable when somebody makes windfall gains in this sector? There have been many more instances of profiteering of much larger scale in financial markets. Why do MFIs come into limelight? This is exactly a case of governance. First of all, microfinance sector has grown significantly with the subsidised funds. Further, the target group of the companies are the poor people. These two things bring in a certain kind of expectations, which do not match with the kind of profit these agencies received. According to Rock, Otero, and Saltzman (1998), a major issue with governing MFIs is that they have to balance the social and financial objectives, which is contradictory under various circumstances.

13.6 Indian Examples of Problems in MFI Governance

Sriram (2010) discussed examples of four MFIs, the summary of which is given here. All of them were based in Andhra Pradesh, and the paper was written a few months before the onset of the microfinance crisis.

- SHARE Microfinance was formed out of the savings collected from people in a mutually aided cooperative society. The cooperative lent to SHARE Microfinance. Initially, there were 4000 equity holders and in 2003, only two per cent of the equity was with the promoters and relatives. In 2006, the shareholder number came down to less than 3000, while 13 per cent of equity was with promoters and relatives. By 2007, the number of shareholders was 68, and 57 per cent of equity was with promoters and relatives and 40 per cent with an investment company owned by the family. Community members who were originally the promoters had exited from the board. After 2007, when venture capital companies bought shares at premium, promoter family still held 30 per cent, while other individuals had only one per cent of the equity holding. The remuneration of MD was also disproportionate (15% of personnel cost).
- Asmitha Microfiance was promoted by the family members of SHARE Microfinance. In 2003-04, the equity (₹20 million+) was held by five family members and in 2007-08, it became 324 shareholders (300 of them held only ₹3 million of equity). Next year (2008-09), 270 of them made an exist transferring their share to two shareholders. Only 2.91 per cent of shares were held outside the family. All the director positions remained with the family members. In 2008-09, the remuneration of MD including sweat equity was ₹35.2 million (11% of personnel cost). The second in line (Joint MD), who was hired from outside received a salary of ₹0.54 million!

- Spandana Sphoorty was formed in 2003-05 by 20,000 members with ₹1000 each contributing to a mutual benefit trust (MBT), which met the needed capital of ₹20 million. Next year, the holding of MBT went down to ₹17.2 million, while promoter family held ₹24.6 million. In 2005-07, MBT held ₹3.80 million worth equity, while the promoter family held ₹74 million. By 2007-08, the MBT had offloaded all its shares. Venture capitals also invested. In 2008-09, promoters held 59 per cent of the capital of ₹133.9 million. Shares were sold in premium, phase-by-phase. Remuneration was not disproportionate.
- The fourth case was that of SKS Microfinance, which was formed by five MBTs that received funds donated by SKS society. It was run by professionals and used support of renowned consulting firms. The company took no offence in paying highest salary to its employees, including CEO. It had a high profile and well-rewarded Board. Initially, in 2005, the promoter founder had an equity contribution of ₹5000; but in 2007, he was allotted ₹16 million of shares at par (all other employees got ₹8.18 million under ESPS). On the same day, investors paid ₹49.77 per share. Coincidentally, on the same day, the company had lent the founder an interest free loan of ₹16 million. After about 18 months, he sold the shares at ₹103.91 per unit, thus receiving ₹150 million in return. Employee stock option related returns were exercised in February, 2010 at a price of ₹636 per share, realising a profit of ₹550 million. It was not illegal, but it was true that senior management cashed upon the pre-IPO (initial public offer) hype very well. Also, allotments of shares to independent directors were done in a questionable price.

A resounding fact was that there was nothing illegal in the whole process, but when the objective is to make inclusive finance for the poor, such kind of profits are not accepted by the society. The key issue highlighted in the above cases (Sriram, 2010) was that it was not just commercialisation, but was like a chase for increasing personal wealth. This was not what the stakeholders expected from the company. This is where there was a flaw in governance of MFIs.

What exactly is the role of the Board of Directors? Fundamental to good governance is the ability of individual directors to work in partnership to accomplish an effective balance between strategic and operational responsibilities. Effective governance occurs when a board is able to provide guidance to management in strategic issues and is effective in overseeing management carry out the agreed upon strategic plan (Rock et al. 1998:1). Obviously, in the above cases, there was a diversion from the charted strategy. Though the objective was to make money while serving the poor, the latter was neglected over a period of time.

13.7 The Way Ahead

Fortunately, a lot of changes have taken place since the problems discussed in the previous sections. We not only have the guidelines in place, but also several MFIs who have gone public as a result, disclosure standards have been maintained. Further, the upcoming of Small Finance Banks (SFBs) also had some influence in the market, as it decreased the need for aggressive hunt for foreign funds. Now that the SFBs can accept deposits, the cost of funds would come down.

Post 2008, several prudential and disclosure norms have been followed globally. With the BASEL III norms getting implemented, the lending banks also have to be much more careful. Hopefully, this will usher in a new era. Internally also, in India, some developments have brought new hopes. Demonetisation, despite its downsides, has led to a cashless microfinance operation. Also, the goods and services tax has resulted in a transparent process of financial transactions and here regulatory control can be stronger. Under such circumstances, corporate governance is expected to improve.

Case Study 13.1 BFK Finserve Ltd's Ownership Dilemma

You have recently taken over the position of Managing Director of Bharat Festive Krishna Finserve Ltd.(BFK), which is an NBFC-MFI that operates in several states of the country. Originally, the company was known as Bharat Finance Ltd (promoted by a not-for-profit Trust), later it took over another MFI called Festive Microfinance. Last year, it took over a fintech company called Krishna Fintech, as it believed that this would provide it with a technological advantage. The company, at present, has a unique ownership structure:

- 33 per cent shares are with the original promoters of Bharat Financials (A)
- 16 per cent shares are with the promoters of Festive Financials (B)
- 20 per cent shares are with the promoters of Krishna Fintech (C)
- 24 per cent shares are with a PE firm (D)
- 5 per cent shares are with the Trust that promoted the first company, Bharat Fin. (E)
- 2 per cent shares are reserved for the Managing Director, who by mandate of the articles of association of the company, must be a professional (CA, CS, ICWA, MBA or equivalent), and must not be a relative of any of the other shareholders.

Thus, other than you, the promoters can be divided into five parts A, B, C, D, E.

Over the years, BFK has done exceedingly well. It has grown at a compound annual growth late (CAGR) of 21 per cent in the last 10 years, since it became a for-profit agency. In these years, it had two MDs (you are the third one), each having a tenure of five years. Rules of the company mandate that the tenure of five years is non-renewable and the person cannot be a shareholder of the company too. He/she has to divest his holding of two per cent which is then passed on to the new MD.

Ordinarily, the board do not intervene in the day-to-day affairs of the company. A, B and C invariably had the same voice and D also generally sided with them. E, sometimes, kept on raising issues like mission drift, the company not focussing on developmental issues, and so on. At this juncture, however, the situation is slightly different, the death of C's owner. Now the shares are owned by that person's heir, who believes that the company should be run differently. He agreed with E and for some reason, D agreed as well. It is heard that the PE is under severe pressure from government to show the former should invest in socially responsible projects.

In the last Board meeting, an important proposal was tabled for discussion. As the company had added advantage of technology enabled microfinance services, it was decided to go for expansion in a big way. This required hiring thrice the people as it had now, over the next one year and opening twice the number of new branches as it had currently. Initially, it was agreed that the required funds would be raised by issue of IPO. Unexpectedly, C, D and E opposed the idea. They were of the view that the company should not go for IPO, it was already in the eye of politicians for its high growth. The decision was not held for vote because everybody felt that more time is required the discuss the issue. Here was the discussion:

E: You cannot operate like a crony capitalist. See what people are saying about us! Have we turned into heartless moneylenders?

A: See, we are not taking grants. It is our money, we invest, we follow the code of conduct, and of course we earn a decent profit. Our rate of interest is also moderate.

E: But the donors who supported you initially are not happy.

A: But they have already exited from the company. They sold their shares and took away the profit. Why are they worried now?

E: It was my duty to point it out. I am going to put a dissent note against your IPO advice.

D: I also think we should go slow with the IPO idea. It is not the right time.

B: I agree with A.

C: I do not know, but I also feel that a bit more discussion is required.

The company had already hired investment banks and other advisors regarding the IPO issue. There was a positive rating, and the investment bankers said that it would be a successful IPO. Everything was going on well, but things came to a halt after this board meeting. You know that both the parties A, B vs. C, D, E held 49 per cent each. Your vote is going to determine the fate of IPO.

You know that A, B and C are active members of the company. D and E generally did not intervene in any of the earlier decisions. But there is a special situation now. If you support IPO (A and B), the other group, particularly the PE firm will dissent, which would not go well with the upcoming IPO issue. If you do not support the IPO, A and B will create troubles for your day-to-day operations. You spoke to a well-wisher who had thorough knowledge of the company and he that that this impasse is not going to end soon. He suggested that you should resign from the company. You know that you can easily get an equivalent job, but are concerned about what wold happen to the idea of IPO. Exit of MD at this point of time would just kill the IPO idea. Nobody would like to invest in such a company.

Discussion Questions

1. Assume that the impasse continues. What will you do?
2. Do you agree with E's criticism of the company?
3. In the next meeting, the board authorises you to cast your vote and break the impasse. They agree that your decision will be respected by everybody. What would be your decision? Prepare a 500-word note presenting your action plan after the voting is over.

Summary

- Governance is about coordination among actors, control over decision making mechanism and safeguarding the interest of stakeholders.
- Corporate governance deals with the decision making at organisational level, accountability, transparency and responsible acts.
- In microfinance, the governance space includes actors (regulators, MFIs, SHPIs, support organisations and people), their coordination and the interaction among them. The fundamental objective is to safeguard the interest of client (low-income group).
- RBI guidelines of corporate governance of NBFCs that apply to NBFC-MFIs include prescription on committees (audit committee, nomination committee and risk management committee), rotation of partners in audit firm, disclosure, internal guidelines and additional disclosures for larger NBFCs.
- In microfinance, risks like operational risks, credit risks and concentration risk prevail widely. This happens due to not having a sound risk management policy in the organisation. It is the duty of the Board of Directors to ensure this.
- Internationally, commercialisation of MFIs like Banco Compartamos and BancoSol raised eyebrows when there were observations of excessive profiteering and mission drift.
- In India, there were issues with governance of MFIs, particularly before the AP crisis. It was seen that some MFI promoters gave priority to their personal wealth gains over the organisational mission.
- Recent developments like prudential norms and licensing of SFBs are expected to make way for better corporate governance.

Exercises

A. Multiple-choice Questions

1. Governance deals with
   (a) Actions of the government
   (b) Decision-making mechanism where many organisations are involved
   (c) Actions of people
   (d) Actions of market
2. Governance includes
   (a) Regulators
   (b) People
   (c) Institutions
   (d) All of the above
3. Which of the committee is not mandatory in RBI guidelines on corporate governance?
   (a) Governance Committee
   (b) Audit Committee
   (c) Nomination Committee
   (d) Risk Management Committee
4. Disclosure is not required on which of the following?
   (a) Remuneration of directors
   (b) Related party transactions
   (c) Both (a) and (b)
   (d) None of the above

5. While selecting directors, a company must look at their
   (a) Qualification
   (b) Track record
   (c) Integrity
   (d) All of the above
6. Banco Compartamos was involved in
   (a) IPO issue
   (b) Fraud
   (c) Political influence
   (d) None of the above
7. Which of the following company was a sister concern of Asmitha Microfinance?
   (a) Spandana Spoorty
   (b) SHARE Microfinance
   (c) SKS Microfinance
   (d) None of the above
8. Which of the following was involved in IPO issue before the AP crisis 2010?
   (a) Spandana Spoorty
   (b) SHARE Microfinance
   (c) SKS Microfinance
   (d) None of the above
9. The major issue with AP organisations' governance was
   (a) Mismanagement
   (b) Wrong decisions
   (c) Loss making
   (d) Misgovernance
10. Director's role is to ensure
    (a) Alignment of strategy with mission
    (b) Alignment of profit with mission
    (c) Alignment of remuneration with mission
    (d) All of the above

B. Review Questions

1. What is corporate governance? How does it differ from the concept of governance?
2. What regulations related to corporate governance are applicable for NBFC-MFIs?
3. What are the problems with commercialisation of NGO-initiated MFIs? Describe with international experience.
4. Did commercialisation of MFIs lead to a weak governance structure in the microfinance industry? Discuss with examples.
5. 'Andhra Pradesh microfinance crisis was a result of the effort to build personal wealth of promoters of some of the MFIs'. Comment using examples.

C. Application-based Questions

1. You have promoted an organisation that operates in the field of microfinance, and you are the Chairman cum Managing Director (CMD). For the last 10 years, you have worked hard and have taken the organisation from scratch to a large and reputed firm. Your financers have pushed you to go for a professional CEO, and you agreed. Once the new CEO joined, he tried to change some board members as he believed that the existing board was not progressive. You were informed by a reliable source, however, that once the board is reconstituted, the CEO would try to displace you. You are a minority shareholder and majority of shares are held by financers. What would you do?
2. You are the HR head of an MFI. You are in the process of recruiting a few senior managers in your company (at the level of Vice President). Just before the interview of a particular candidate, you came to know, through an informal source, that one of the candidates is the daughter of a director of the company. You informed the CMD, who told that he had no idea about this matter as the concerned director never mentioned it. He told you to take the decision as per what you think is appropriate. You know that the concerned director is a powerful person in the company. What would you do?

Further Readings

- Detailed provisions of RBI guidelines on corporate governance may be analysed to gain insights into the compliance requirement of corporate governance by MFIs.
- Chapter 14 titled 'Risk Management' of the book *Ujjivan: Transforming with Technology* by Subir Roy provides the experience of the organisation in establishing a risk management system.
- Here the summary of Sriram's paper 'Commercialisation of Microfinance in India: A Discussion of the Emperor's Apparel' published in *Economic and Political Weekly* is provided.

CHAPTER

14 Technology in Microfinance

Chapter Outline

Learning Objectives

After reading this chapter, you will be able to:

- discuss the importance of technology in microfinance sector.
- describe how fintech solutions providers contribute in advancing the MFIs.
- explain the disadvantages of technology in microfinance.

14.1 Introduction

The practices in the microfinance sector have completely changed in the last five or six years, particularly after 2014, and the driver of all these changes is nothing but the use of technology. Multiple factors have transformed the sector. These factors are easy availability of smartphones, improved online payment system, automations in financial institutions and better mobile connectivity, particularly after the launch of Jio. Before 2016, it was unthinkable that the sector would have majority of its transactions in cashless mode! Some examples of technology that is used in financial services in general and applicable to microfinance are:

- Automated teller machines (ATMs)
- Point of sales machines (POS)
- Short messaging system (SMS)
- Interactive voice response (IVR)
- Internet banking
- Prepaid instruments (e-wallets, coupons, etc.)
- Debit cards and credit cards
- Kiosks

In 1998 99, when the commercial microfinance was in a nascent stage, the sector was known for self-help group (SHG) promotion activities. An organisation in South Rajasthan was well-known for its SHG-based programmes. The organisation had about 500-600 SHGs, which were driven by field level officers, known as Community Organiser. Each of such Community Organiser was responsible for 15 SHGs and about 4-5 coordinators reported to a programme officer. For managing the overall project, there was a Project Coordinator, who reported to the Director. Every day the community organiser would visit one SHG; the date used to be planned in such a way that the SHG had its meeting on that day. The model was such that every field officer visited the SHG at least twice a month. On that day, the officer would bring all the details from the SHG, like attendance, saving, collection, etc. Once in two weeks, this was reported to the head office, where the information was compiled. The reports of the current month were compiled by the first week of next month. All the data was entered in a spread sheet, and calculations on recovery rate, attendance percentage, regularity in savings, missed instalments, etc., were done.

About 8-9 years later (2008), the organisation had a different mode of reporting. While the organisational structure remained almost the same (of course, with a bit of scaling up), the reporting process had changed. By that time, mobile phones were available with everybody. The field officer then did not have to wait for the visit to head office to report the collection, attendance and other data. It was done by evening of the same day, with an SMS. If the head office did not receive any particular SHG's information, which sometimes happened because of network failure, a representative would call up the concerned person and get the information. By the next morning, all the data collected the previous day was updated. What used to take 15 days, and usually the analysis was done every month, was now available next day! The only care one has to take was to keep backup of all data, otherwise there was a risk of data loss.

In 2017-18, the field officers had smartphones and they all used a mobile phone app. All they had to do was to feed the data there. Automatically there was the updated data entry and analysis on real time basis! At the head office, there was no need for full-time data entry operators. Another advantage was that earlier, the concerned Project Coordinators and Programme Officers had to seek data from the IT Manager. Now, they can access any data or any analysis from their own computer or tab or mobile phone. The Information Technology (IT) department now is a specialised office, dealing with maintenance work only.

This is an example of a simple microfinance operation, which was further simplified by the use of IT. Now there is a smaller number of people required and the data processing and accuracy is also high. In manual, or semi-automatic systems, the chances of manual errors are always there. The organisation has gained not only in terms of reduced cost, but in terms of quality also. To add to this, enormous data can be handled by one or two persons.

14.2 Technology in Aiding Financial Inclusion

Technology is a great enabler of financial inclusion. It helps the latter in several ways:

- **Decreasing transaction cost** The major impediment to financial inclusion lies in its high cost. In microfinance, operational costs are extremely high because the transaction amounts and loan sizes are very small. There are certain administrative work that goes behind every sale of products, such as loan or insurance. This has to be done irrespective of the loan size. With larger size of loans, cost of operations decreases. But in microfinance, one has to live with the small size of loans and other products. By inducing technology into operations, the Microfinance Institution (MFI)/bank can cut down time and labour. This helps in decreasing the operating cost significantly. As a result, the organisation can have a competitive advantage in pricing.
- **Increasing speed of financial inclusion** In the absence of technological interventions, it would be impossible for MFIs/banks to connect with the customers so easily. Connecting with every customer would, otherwise, need a branch in nearby location or an executive visiting the locations. But with the onset of online and mobile transactions, connectivity with a mobile phone suffices. This brings in a tremendous amount of efficiency in the system and speeds up the achievement.
- **Avoiding bias against the poor** An allegation against the traditional bankers is that they are biased against the poor. Many times, the microfinance customers do not like visiting the banks apprehending non-response. When transactions take place through mobile phone, such personal visits are not necessary. If not bias, at least one can say that they are not comfortable working with poor. Getting posted in remote locations is not desired by majority of people. Further, a bank executive working in rural areas has to deal with tough times in many ways. His/her counterpart in the corporate finance division would easily bring in large amount of business, while working in rural areas would bring in much lower amount. This does not help the banker from the point of view of career enhancement. But with technological support, the reach of microfinance customers can be upscaled significantly, and the executive would not hesitate for this vertical. Both ways, technology helps.

14.3 Digital Financial Inclusion

The idea of digital financial inclusion is relatively new. While the need for financial inclusion has been highlighted since long, recently it has been realised that financial inclusion without the use of digital technology is near impossible. Any policy or strategy for financial inclusion must take care of digital inclusion.

Digital financial inclusion can be defined as digital access to and use of formal financial services by excluded and underserved populations. Such services should be suited to customers' needs, and delivered responsibly, at a cost both affordable to customers and sustainable for providers. There are three key components of any such digital financial services, a digital transactional platform, retail agents and the use by customers and agents of a device – most commonly a mobile phone – to transact via the platform (Lauer and Lyman, 2015).

In Bangladesh, one such electronic platform (mobile money) is called bKash. Starting in the year 2010, it already has 24 million active users as in early 2019. Initially starting as a money transfer platform, it has slowly added other services, such as airtime top up, bulk disbursement, collection services, merchant payments, etc.[1]

Thus, digital platforms are not just a way of money transfer, but they add additional financial services too. M-Pesa in Kenya, M-Shwari consumer loans by the Commercial Bank of Africa, life insurance products through Tigo mobile phone users in Ghana and WIZZIT's money transfer and additional services in South Africa are some other examples. The BHIM app in India has been a major breakthrough in democratising the use of mobile based technology in accessing financial services.

Another example from India is the BASIX Sub-K iTransactions Ltd, which has been detailed out in Box 14.1.

Box 14.1 Technology Driven Transaction: Sub-K

BASIX Sub-K iTransactions Ltd. is a subsidiary of BASIX Social Enterprise Group. It was established in 2010. Its objective is to provide technology-enabled transaction platform to the unbanked population, augment financial inclusion and bridge digital divide. It operates in both rural and urban areas.[2]

Sub-K targets remote locations of areas having less than a thousand households, within a touch point of one kilometre, offering small transactions of less than ₹ 1000 at a small cost of ₹ 10. It operates through local entrepreneurs as BC agents who serve as cash delivery points (human ATMs) and provide the end-to-end connectivity between banks and customers. This is done though the use of kiosk or mobile based technology. All kinds of banking services like cash deposit, withdrawal, remittance, fund transfer, loan repayment, credit and insurance services are provided. Government payments, Adhaar and PAN card services are also facilitated. Sub-K is a low-cost model and it leverages all possible models, such as BC and E-Mitra that allows technology-enabled transactions[3]. Its services include value added services like that of BC/CSC, facilitating G2C services through e-service delivery, business facilitation services like linking of credit, insurances and pension services, approximately 19 lakh transactions have taken place since its portal started operating.[3]

The organisation has grown steadily since its inception. By February 2018, it was operational in 23 states of India, and had a portfolio of ₹ 666 crore. It has a partnership with 14 banks with a customer base of 1.0 million. Last year, it attracted an investment of ₹ 35 crore from Accion and Nordic Microfinance Initiative which shows that its success is being recognised (Sridhar, 2018). (1 crore=10 million)

1. https://globalpaymentsummit.com/bkash-bangladesh-24-million-customers-using-mobile-money/, retrieved on 10 April 2019
2. https://subk.co.in/about.php
3. https://subk.co.in/our-work.php
4. https://subk.co.in/business-correspondence.php

The government initiative of Bharat Interface for Money (BHIM) needs a mention here. Launched in December 2016, it is a payment app developed by the National Payment System of India (NPSI) that facilitates cashless transactions. Using the Unified Payments Interface (UPI) system, the app can be used to send and receive money easily. The BHIM app was launched in the aftermath of demonetisation with the objective of making cashless transactions more inclusive.

14.4 Role of Fintech Providers

A fintech provider (fintech meaning financial technology) uses a technology platform that helps in bridging the gaps between consumer and the delivery of financial products and services. They operate with an initial high cost, but still have some advantages over the traditional financial service companies. While the banks have established protocols for appraisal, it may take some time before one gets a loan or any other product, but a fintech provider can provide it quickly because its decisions are based on algorithm-based platforms. In particular, for access of emergency funds, they have a competitive advantage over the traditional banks. As they do not keep any deposit, they do not have to go through the stringent regulatory burden that the banks face. And they anyway can become a channel for banks' services by having a partnership with the latter. Overall, they provide convenience and quick service delivery. This is one reason, why fintech providers have become popular in microfinance space (Ozili, 2018).

14.5 Models of Technological Partnership

Microfinance institutions are not technology-based organisations. Here technology is not the product, rather it is a support service that help in dealing with various services like credit, savings, insurance, remittance, etc. Hence, it is not necessary that the MFI should develop a core competence in the field of technology. A more suitable option is to take support of a technology-specialising organisation. There can be three such models of partnership:

- **Delivery Channel Model** This can be done by developing partnership with retail stores, petrol pumps, and various service outlets. Co-branding also can be done to scale up the business. This would help in going beyond the physical presence of the MFI.
- **Consortium Model** In microfinance business, the primacy of financial service cannot be denied. It is well known that financial services scale matters; which helps in sorting out issues like in risk management, liquidity and many others. There are a lot of support services that require huge investment, which can be done in consortium mode. Data consortiums are one such example.
- **Outsourced Services Model** The IT activities can be outsourced to an expert agency, which can handle the operations better and with a lower cost too. For example, call centres for customer grievances can be outsourced. Similarly, the back office functions can also be outsourced as these are primarily routine activities; it can be managed with a little monitoring and supervision. (Frederick, 2008).

14.6 Downsides of Technology in Microfinance

The main problem with the technological platforms in microfinance is that the digital platform may not be available for two flaws, the high initial investment and poor mobile phone connectivity (Ozili, 2018). Another problem is that in developing countries like India, while the payment to the clients can be made online, the repayment by customers might not be possible that way. Also, the payment practices have not improved to the extent that the day-to-day payments are made in cashless form, people are still used to cash transactions.

Low level of financial literacy and low awareness about the mechanism of digital transactions are also some of the impediments of digital finance. Further, online and mobile transactions have their own security problems. Data security can be breached easily if the customer does not make the transaction in a fully secured environment. People are also not much aware about the security features and security requirements of digital transactions (Ozili, 2018; Wyman, 2016). Agency problems may also arise due to the difference between the objectives of fintech providers and those of the people (Wyman, 2018).

In any case, as mentioned earlier in this chapter, technology is a great enabler of financial inclusion. Despite its downsides, it is an implementable activity, which is visible from the fact that after the demonetisation, the microfinance service providers swiftly shifted to cashless transactions without any hitch. With some support from the government, digital finance can make further way towards the larger goal of financial inclusion.

Case Study 14.1 eSthenos Technologies Pvt. Ltd.

Bengaluru based eSthenos Technologies Pvt. Ltd, promoted by first generation entrepreneurs Aniket Thakur and Vijayaprasad Gopurathingal, is an innovative and award-winning fintech platform with a vision to enable financial institutions in India to deliver credit to the last mile, in the most efficient manner. It is highly sophisticated and modern technological platform that delivers superior experience of originating a loan for both the financial institutions and its clients. Based on artificial intelligence and machine learning (AI/ML) based workflow, the tech platform removes many mundane and repetitive works and reduces time and cost while originating any type of retail loans, such as personal loans, MFI Loans, SME Loans, loan against property (LAP) and vehicle loans. Though eSthenos provides its platform for banks, NBFCs, home loans and LAP companies, the main focus has always been microfinance companies for which the initiative was started.

Technology is consistently cited as one of the greatest challenges faced by MFIs around the world due to lack of domain knowledge by service providers. There is also a low level of awareness on the part of MFIs to leverage the technology in comparison to the way other industries, such as e-commerce and payment companies have done in the last decade. While efficient use of modern technology can help reduce costs, improve efficiency and visibility and increase outreach, majority of MFIs still find it difficult to find a tech platform which is right for their business.

The microfinance sector in India has been vulnerable since inception due to its rural focus, which affects the population at the bottom of the pyramid. Hence, any regulatory, political or government intervention or policy change has an immediate impact on the MFIs. MFI sector was just regaining its footing from the Andhra crisis when the government announced demonetisation scheme in November 2016. Sudden announcement by the government had a devastating effect on the whole industry. With ₹ 990 billion of assets under management before demonetisation across the MFI sector, the sector had to write-off ₹ 7 billion (7,000 crore). Acute cash shortage during demonetisation led people to withhold their cash, whereas others refused to pay their instalments because of loan waiver rumours. For a cash-dependent sector like microfinance, demonetisation necessitated MFIs to invest in technology that could manage, monitor, track electronic transactions and focus on understanding customer behaviour in order to make better credit decisions.

This problem is addressed by eSthenos Technologies where its highly flexible architecture design enables user organisations in adapting and absorbing all those regulatory and unavoidable changes through its highly customisable, flexible and user-centric product platform called Gravity. Using modern AI/ML techniques, multiple internal and external microservices, Gravity reduces human interventions to improve quality of origination, reduces error and removes human bias in underwriting a customer. It drastically reduces the waiting time for a customer and improves business efficiency for users, thereby delivering positive gain for all stakeholders without compromising on the quality of the loans. It also offers business intelligence on the go where user organisations can see, analyse and evaluate its day-to-day business on real-time basis, thus giving the senior management adequate insights and inputs for faster and superior decision making.

Gravity's flexible and customisable business rule engine and more than 150 application performing interface (API) integrations give user organisations access to multiple technology products, such as CIBIL, Highmark, Perfios, SMS gateway, mail services, API banking, etc., on a single platform and thus enhancing the overall experience of loan origination. Gravity does complete risk profiling, KYC and credit bureau check in less than 10 seconds and reduces waiting time for customers. It is capable of disbursing loans to the qualified customers' account on real-time basis and is available 24x7. The platform adheres to bank grade security standards and thus is highly secured for all kinds of business transactions. All the data on the platform is encrypted with 256-bit AES encryption on the go. To make the platform user friendly, eSthenos provides the option of downloading all the legal documents in all Indian languages.

Currently, every month, eSthenos processes more than 4.5 lakh loan applications worth ₹ 800 crore and collects more than ₹ 5 billion worth of EMIs. It processes close to 25 lakh images every month coming from more than 20 states and 1000+ locations in India. Its platform has been recognised and accoladed by NASSCOM and Amazon Web Services (AWS), as the company was one of the finalists of NASSCOM's Design4India Awards (ergonomic category) and AWS AI Award under Financial Services Category.

(*Sources*: https://www.esthenos.com/, Business Standard (2019), The Week (2019) and inputs of Mr. Aniket Thakur.)

Discussion Questions

1. What are the opportunities for fintech companies in today's microfinance industry?
2. Do you think the support of eSthenos can provide competitive advantage for a microfinance institution?

Summary

- With the onset of technological applications like ATMs, POS, SMS, IVRS, internet banking, PPIs, debit and credit cards and kiosks, financial services including microfinance sector have made a breakthrough in scaling up their activities.
- Technology not just provides a platform for digital transactions, but also expands the range of services and products.
- The advantage of technology interventions in microfinance is that it helps in reducing transaction cost, speeds up the operations and neutralises the potential biases of banking and financial sector while dealing with poor.
- Digital financial inclusion refers to use of digital technology in making the financial services accessible to the low-income groups.
- There are examples like M-Pesa in Africa, b-Kash in Bangladesh and BHIM in India that help in expanding the network coverage of digital finance.
- The use of technology in microfinance can be accessed through various partnership models like delivery channel partnership, consortium and outsourcing. The fundamental factor is that technology is not the core competence of MFIs, hence partnership can be effective as well as less expensive.
- There are some problems in enabling digital finance and technological applications, such as lack of awareness among people, lack of financial literacy, poor connectivity, high initial investments and data security threats. Also, people are used to cash transactions so much that it is difficult to break this habit.
- Despite the problems, digital finance transactions have increased. In future, this can provide further boost to the cause of financial inclusion.

Exercises

A. Multiple-choice Questions

1. Which of the following is use applicable for microfinance?
   (a) Debit card
   (b) Credit card
   (c) Kiosk
   (d) Point of sales machine
2. Technology helps in which of the following aspects of microfinance?
   (a) Reducing costs
   (b) Reducing efficiency
   (c) Reducing profitability
   (d) All of the above
3. Digital finance does not relate to
   (a) Financial inclusion
   (b) Financial literacy
   (c) Prudential norms
   (d) None of the above
4. Fintech companies have advantage over the traditional banks in respect of
   (a) Size of funds
   (b) Quick service
   (c) Type of products
   (d) All of the above
5. Partnership in acquiring technology is required for MFIs because
   (a) Technology is expensive
   (b) Technology is difficult to master
   (c) Technology is not their core competence
   (d) Technology is not important in microfinance
6. Outsourced model of partnership is useful in microfinance in which activity?
   (a) Customer grievance redressal
   (b) Risk management
   (c) Monitoring of progress
   (d) Strategic planning
7. A technological platform can be used by an MFI
   (a) To expand its own business
   (b) To be agent of a bank like that of BC
   (c) To provide a greater range of services and products to customers
   (d) All of the above
8. An MFI outsources its MIS activities to a tech company. It still would have to deal with
   (a) Data analysis
   (b) Data storing and backup
   (c) Data security provisions
   (d) All of the above
9. Which of the following is not a drawback of digital finance with respect to microfinance sector?
   (a) Customers are poor
   (b) Financial literacy is low
   (c) Connectivity is poor
   (d) Threat of security breach
10. Fintech providers are not necessarily involved in
    (a) Creating link between customer and service delivery
    (b) Creating algorithms for the digital platform
    (c) Creating efficient platform
    (d) All of the above

B. Review Questions

1. What are the technology-based applications and equipments that have played key roles in transforming the microfinance related transactions?
2. Technology is not just a simple input in microfinance, it has multiplier effects. Comment.
3. What are the digital finance initiatives across the world with respect to the microfinance sector?
4. How does digital finance and technology applications help the cause of financial inclusion?
5. What are the shortcomings of digital finance?

C. Application-based Questions

1. You are a manager in a microfinance company. So far, it has worked with a manual processing of loans, but recently it has installed an automated system that replaced the earlier one. Calculate the amount of time it would save for the organisation as well as for the customer. You may use Figure 5.2 as a point of reference.
2. When technology replaces manual work, it is possible that the customer would not have any feeling towards the service provider. This goes against the principle of individual knowledge of customers that provides an advantage

to MFIs over banks. With the technology-based decisions coming up in the MFIs, identify various touch points where there is likely to have such drifting. Suggest actions that would help in building a better relationship with the MFIs' customers.

Further Readings

- Two chapters of the book *New Partnerships for Innovation in Microfinance* edited by Matthaus-Maier and Pischke, Chapter 9 'Using technology to build financial systems' by Ivatury, and Chapter 10 'Information technology innovations that extend rural microfinance outreach' by Frederick are useful reports on this issue.
- Websites of fintech companies that are involved in supporting microfinance are useful resources in advancing knowledge in this aspect.

CHAPTER

15 Transformation of Microfinance Institutions

Chapter Outline

Learning Objectives

After reading this chapter, you will be able to:

- To discuss the reasons behind transformation of organisations in microfinance
- To understand various changes that take place when organisations in microfinance
- To discuss the specific form of transformation taking place in microfinance sector and the issues faced by these changes

15.1 Introduction

The field of microfinance has undergone immense changes in the last 15-20 years. Changes have been found in all spheres of microfinance sector, such as policy, economic environment, regulations, strategies and the organisations. A unique thing found is that organisational transformation in the microfinance sector has been seen very often. Federations of informal SHGs have converted into formal organisations, not for profit SHPIs, MFIs have converted into NBFCs, private limited NBFCs have converted into listed companies, and NBFC-MFIs have converted into small finance banks or banks. During all these conversions, the organisations have to transform them not just into a new legal entity but also have to make sure that they are ready to face new challenges. Interestingly, the process of transformation is not an easy task. In this chapter, discussion on the transformational changes in this sector would be discussed.

15.2 Organisational Transformation

Organisational transformation is a well-explored area and the concept has been explained from various perspectives. The first one is in the context of change management in the case of an imposed change, and the second is a self-driven transformation based on organisations' learning.

Generally, organisations have a compulsion to change under certain circumstances. Such situations are non-routine and they appear only in long-term. One such change which makes major upheaval in the organisation is that of leadership change. With the change in leadership, the whole strategic platform changes. It is of course possible that the Board might have made changes in the leadership primarily to bring in such changes. Business strategy, product profile and reporting structure change. Similarly, new groups emerge that destabilise the existing coalitional structure. Some people would not like the new style, while some would appreciate it. However, new leadership related change is a fact of organisational life. To adjust to the new situation, the organisation goes through some changes, which often are transformational. An example of leadership driven transformation is that of IBM in the 1990s, during the tenure of Louis Gerstener, Jr.

The second kind of transformation takes place when it is driven externally, for example, when the organisation has to face the forces of merger and acquisition. During such processes, the structures and procedures of an organisation gets aligned to another. This also creates a great deal of discomfort among people. Such processes need extreme care to manage. Sometimes transformation also takes place when the regulators force an organisation to make structural changes or merge with another. In the aftermath of global financial crisis, there were several such changes. Change can also be forced by disruptive technologies.

Change also takes place if need is felt internally. These are not externally driven; rather the organisation consciously transforms itself based on its own understanding of future requirements.

Organisational transformation requires changes in several aspects of organisations. As these changes are non-routine, they affect various parts of organisation in an intricate manner. For example, any change in product line is going to change the marketing strategy, will have an impact on the topline, and customer base might also change. Further, it may also affect the production facilities, which have far-reaching implications. In financial service sector, changes often affect the workforce and information system.

The classic work of Leavitt (1965) suggests a four-dimensional framework; structure, technology, people and task for explaining organisational change. It says that change in organisations happens through interactions among these four forces. Each of these forces, by the way, is a major driver of organisational transformation. An example of complex transformational processes is the practice of business process re-engineering.

According to Balogun and Hailey (2008), there are four types of changes determined by the nature and the extent of change. The nature of change can be incremental or big bang, while the extent of change can be realignment or transformation. When the nature of change is incremental and the extent of change is realignment, it requires only an adaptation of the new changes. If the nature of change is big bang and the extent of change is realignment, it requires a turnaround or reconstruction. On the other hand, the nature of change is incremental, and the extent of change is transformational, it requires only an evolutionary approach to organisational change. Finally, if the nature of change is big bang and the extent of change is transformational, it requires revolutionary interventions.

15.3 Transformational Change in Microfinance

Ordinarily, two types of transformational changes take place in microfinance, one due to the change in legal form and two, due to externally imposed crisis. The standard organisational changes due to M&A (merger and aquisition) have been found only to some extent.

The first type of change in legal form is that of transformation from an informal body to formal organisation. This primarily takes place in the case of SHGs and their federations, who generally start as an unregistered body. Being informal and small sized bodies, they do not need to maintain records that a formal organisation requires. For example, they do not need to have practices like double entry booking, nor they require to file income tax return. Also, there is no employee who is paid regularly, everything is done by volunteers and leaders elected by the members. The situation changes when they transform to a formal federation which might be registered as a society or company or cooperative. Such a body has to meet the statutory requirement of the concerned legislation under which it is registered. It also needs to have a formal Board of Directors or Board of Governors that is accountable not just to the members, but also is liable to answer the regulatory authorities. In such processes:

- Flexible norms are replaced with rigid rules.
- Volunteers find it difficult to cope with the new changes.
- Some records need to be maintained for which there was no need earlier; for example, attendance register and audited financial statement.
- Routine activities increase.
- Signs of hierarchy are displayed slowly.

Change in legal form is an organisational design issue. As majority of MFIs started their operations as NGOs, they had a different organisational design inculcated in their DNA. The moment they adopt the NBFC form, they need a complete transformation. Otherwise, they would not be able to cope with the ongoing changes. There are several reasons behind the need of such transformation:

- **Nature of organisation** NGOs are not-for-profit organisations. They ordinarily operate out of grant funds. It does not mean that they cannot make profit, but if they have a profit, it cannot be distributed to its members. A for-profit body (such as a company), on the other hand, distributes dividends to its shareholders. Thus, for an investor, there is no motivation in investing in an NGO that would not provide him any return.
- **Nature of outcome** For-profit organisations have some immediate outcomes. At the end of the financial year, they earn a profit, which is used for re-investment, dividend distribution, and sometimes bonus to employees are also provided. However, in NGOs, the outcomes are not clearly known. In most cases, the interventions do not actually lead to any direct result.
- **Customers** Customers in for-profit bodies are known. The person who takes loan, pays the interest. The grant funds, which are the primary sources of NGOs' funds, do not come from the customers. Funds are provided by the government or some funding agency. But the NGO has to work for the development of people. Under such circumstances, the accountability of the NGO ordinarily would lie with the funding agency, not the target group. Thus, there is a difference between what the NGO is working for and to whom it is answerable. In for-profit bodies, there is no such confusion. The customer pays and buys the products or services from the company, if he/she does not get the value for money, he/she stops buying it. A grant project's beneficiary does not have that kind of choice.
- **Culture** When the basic values are based on not making profits, the working culture would be very different from a profit-making organisation. Ordinarily NGOs provide space for discussion and debates. As mentioned earlier, the outcomes are not clear in development interventions. As the (developmental) policy outcomes cannot be foreseen, these agencies rather focus on the procedural aspects (Ripley and Franklin, 1982 cited in Goggin, 1986). Hence, adhering to procedures becomes more important than attaining outcomes. In for-profit organisations, the primary goal is to earn profit and hence there is a clarity on what is to be achieved at least in the short term. Hence the work culture is very different here.
- **Structure** Some structural issues also come up during transformation. When the organisation goes into for-profit mode, the scale of operations generally increases, and hence specialisations start taking place. Multiple roles are common in small organisations, as found in NGOs. Companies with a certain size must have positions like company secretaries.
- **Compliances** An NGO is ordinarily registered as a society where the compliance requirements are smaller as compared to companies. They are also eligible for some tax waivers. NGOs registered as not-for-profit companies have lesser compliances to make. If the company is a listed one, the compliances and disclosure requirements are further higher.

In the process of change from an NGO to NBFC, there are several apprehensions commonly observed. Earlier, such observations were recorded in the case of BancoSol too (Chapter 13). In times of change, people find two different work cultures meeting at a point and there is some level of unacceptance (Box 15.1). However, such indications must be taken cautiously so that there is no real mission drift.

When an NBFC-MFI converts into an SFB, there is no change in the legal form of the organisation. However, there are still issues that have to be sorted out. The first and foremost change required is that as an SFB, the company can now accept deposits, which earlier it was not able to do as an NBFC-MFI. This single change in itself is a major one and it changes the character of the whole organisation. With the licence to accept deposits, it also assumes several responsibilities that include keeping the deposits in safety. Also, as a deposit taking bank, it has to maintain the CRR and SLR requirements.

Box 15.1 BWDA: An NGO Transformed to NBFC

A case in point was the way an NGO, Bullockcart Workers Development Association (BWDA) transformed itself into an MFI. The need for the transformation was there due to the drying up funds from the government and commercial funds were seen as a potential for scaling up. An existing NBFC was acquired and renamed as BWDA Finance Ltd. The operation was scaled up successfully, however, there were some interesting observations. The efficiency of the organisation increased, but some of the older staff members felt that in this process, the organisation did not follow rigorous processes for SHG management. Similarly, there was apprehension of mission drift also (Yeswanth, 2004).

In terms of physical space, its branches now would require sophisticated facilities for securing cash. Also, it needs proper counter (front office) where the teller can receive and disburse cash to the customers. These kind of activities are new for the SFB, and hence it would require a lot of training and orientation for the employees. New employees also have to be recruited. The loan officers who earlier were used to disbursing loans and collecting loans, now have to be more careful while dealing with the clients because these clients are now potential savings customers. In a way, these savings are nothing but another name for low cost funds for the SFB. Hence, the nature of product that the employees would have to market would be different now.

During the transformation of an NBFC-MFI to SFB, some specific issues crop up, such as the limits in ownership structure (Box 15.2). This happens because of the FDI ceiling given in the regulatory norms.

Box 15.2 Ujjivan's Transformation to SFB

When Ujjivan transformed from an NBFC-MFI to an SFB, the biggest challenge was to establish the so-far-inexistent vertical of deposits, which in the long run was expected to be 'bigger than almost the entire existing business' (Roy, 2018:173). This was a challenging task because the organisation so far had targeted people who did not have much of savings. Further, 25 per cent of an SFB's branches have to be located in the unbanked habitations having less than 10,000 population without a bank branch (Roy, 2018:173).

Another challenge was to meet the regulatory criteria related to FDI, which could not be more than 49 per cent. At that time, Ujjivan's FDI holding was 91 per cent of its equity! (Roy, 2018:172). This was attained by issuing IPO. This could have been done through private placement also, but it was not an easy option. In any case, pre-IPO placement of ₹ 2.92 billion was achieved at an issue price of ₹ 205 (Roy, 2018:176). It was done at a time when the market was not in a good condition. The organisation hired the expertise of well-known investment bankers for managing the process of IPO. Finally, the IPO was closed on 2 May 2016, raising ₹ 8.82 billion, priced at ₹ 210. It attracted 0.675 million domestic investors and was subscribed by 41 times (Roy, 2018:181).

Another operational but transformational change would be in terms of using a new MIS. With savings added to its product portfolio, the company has to now use core banking solutions (CBS) which are networked across all branches and with other banks too. This would require a high level of investments in hardware and software applications.

There are two models of implementing CBS, capital expenditure model (CAPEX) and outsourcing model through build, operate and transfer (BOT). The former has been widely implemented, while organisations like the Bank of India and Cooperative Banks (sponsored by NABARD) have implemented the BOT model (Bandopadhyay, 2016). The implementation of CBS is a complicated process as illustrated in the case of Bandhan (Box 15.3).

Conversion of an NBFC-MFI to a universal bank is also a possible option, which would be similar to an SFB. However, once an MFI becomes a universal bank, it not only goes beyond the obligations and restrictions of an NBFC-MFI, but also does not have the limitations and restrictions of an SFB. In a way, it is free to operate in a market from which it was located distantly. This kind of unprecedented freedom

Box 15.3 Bandhan's Tryst with CBS

When Bandhan was transformed into a bank, the first task was to find out a CBS that would replace its existing system called MFSol. To get an appropriate solution, it hired the services of Deloitte that prepared the request for proposal. A former NABARD officer, who had the experience of implementing CBS in cooperative banks, was hired for this specific job. Bandhan went for the outsourcing model of CBS, for which there were initial presentations by Accenture, FIS, HP-India, TCS and Wipro. Finally, four bids from FIS, HP, Polaris, and Wipro were received. All these bids recognised that there was a need to synchronise the data from micro-credit operations with the central database. At this stage, the Bandhan team visited the sites (of the bidding companies), and finally FIS was selected because it had an advantage of being a pure system integrator.

This was followed by negotiations on terms of contract. This included discussions on proposal like treatment of post-user acceptance test and commencement of banking as a new assignment (vendor preferred it as it was a source of revenue); and finally, a seven-year contract was signed without any additional cost to the bank. The terms of the contract included activities like integrating the 12,000 hand-held devices operating at field level, resuming services within two hours in a disaster recovery situation and capacity building of people to meet the regulatory requirement.

The implementation phase was no easy ride. There were six failed attempts while migrating the data from the MFSol to the new CBS.

There were some other issues as well in implementing the transformation from MFI to bank. One was the issue of how to treat the priority sector lending of other banks done through Bandhan when it was an MFI. Bandhan had obtained about `80 billion from 30 odd banks. This could not be double counted. It was considered as the lender banks' priority sector assets. There were several other routine and non-routine problems which had to be solved before the CBS became operational. It took everybody in the bank to be on a war footing to make this happen!

(*Source*: Bandopadhyay, 2016)

brings in several issues. First of all, the size of operations of a bank is enormously big and this is beyond the imagination of a microfinance operator. This could actually be a shock for many. Given the new task, the new avatar of the organisation must bring in experts from hardcore banking sector, who might not find it easy to acquaint with an MFI-like bank. The existing employees of the organisation may also find it difficult to deal with the newly hired people from a new cultural background.[1]

15.4 Uniqueness of Transformation in Microfinance

Does the organisational transformation in microfinance sector significantly differs from any other organisations? At a theoretical level, there does not seem to be much of a difference. Frameworks as mentioned in section 15.2 (task-structure technology people; or adaptation, evolution, turnaround, revolution) can still explain. However, there still lies a specific difference.

Organisations working in the space of microfinance have a fundamental mission of working for the upliftment of poor and ensuring financial inclusion. In pursuing this goal, they have their own strategy. Strategies, i.e. the long-term approaches, are reflected through the standard operating procedures. People in the organisation operate through these procedures. In times of organisational changes, as seen above, some of these procedures change to a great extent. The new procedures do not necessarily match with the existing value system and ethos that was earlier consistent with the original objectives. The new targets might be dictated by influences like call for more efficiency; this is where there is danger of mission drift.

In times of changes, the organisations must take utmost care to ensure that such drifts do not take place. As seen earlier in Chapter 13, organisations do become captive to the new market driven mechanism. The management has to ensure that the alignment with the fundamental goal of the organisation is not displaced.

1 This case has been heavily drawn from a chapter 'Building the Backbone' (Bandopadhyay, 2016: 174-199).

Case Study 15.1 Transforming the PAF Microfinance

The Poverty Alleviation Foundation (PAF) had a microfinance programme since 1998 and it used to run an SHG-Bank Linkage Programme. After running the grant-based programme, supported by NABARD and several funding agencies, for about 15 years, the organisation thought of exiting from the SHG interventions. In 2013, it already had 2500 SHGs in 10 districts of the state. During the exit, 40-60 SHGs were clustered together to make a cluster level federation, which were unregistered bodies formed at block level. In all, there were 55 cluster level federations, which formed a registered body (state level federations) called PAF Microfinance Foundation. The on-lending activities were totally managed by the state level federation. Slowly the cluster level federations became relatively inactive, however, state level federations grew strong. In 2018, the cluster level federations were dismantled and SHGs became direct members of PAF Microfinance Foundation.

The operations of PAF had spread to a few more districts. Growth was a little slow for the organisation. During the reorganisation of 2018, the organisation received membership fee of ₹1000 from each SHG, which made the contribution of ₹3 million (from 3000 SHGs existing then). Further, while exiting from the SHG operation, PAF (the NGO) had transferred an amount of ₹2 million. All these contributions are in the form of fixed deposit in banks, whose value is about ₹7.5 million at present. The senior management of the federation, presently headed by a professional, believed that it was time for expanding the operations. There was an action plan prepared and presented in the last board meeting, which was promptly approved. But they asked the source of funds for the new operations. A representative from PAF was also there in the meeting, who suggested that he should think of raising the additional funds from the market. Realising that additional funds cannot be raised under the not-for-profit mode, an NBFC was formed. The 3000 SHGs' deposits were taken as equity investment, and the new organisation, namely PAF Microfinance Pvt Ltd (PML) was registered and sought a licence for NBFC-MFI.

Very soon the CEO, who had good contacts with his peers, was able to raise some funds for PML and the expansions were also started. Within six months, by December 2018, operations had been expanded to all neighbouring 15 districts including those of the neighbouring state. With expansion, some of the existing structure were changed. The cluster offices, which were earlier dismantled, were converted into branch offices, and these branches were allowed to lend to non-SHG members also. It was, however, decided that individual lending would not be done, only Joint Liability Groups (JLGs) would be allowed. In the meantime, the savings accounts of SHGs, which the federation kept earlier, were transferred to nearby banks and the NBFC-MFI was not allowed to keep deposits.

In January 2019, the Board appointed an external expert to look into the expansion issues. The expert visited some of the areas and reported the following:

- Cluster offices were earlier managed by elected SHG members. One cluster manager (an employee) used to be there for each cluster. Now with increasing amount of work, the elected members find it difficult to contribute. They expect that some commission or salary should be provided in lieu of the additional work they were doing.
- Earlier, the records of cluster were managed manually by the cluster manager. Now that the cluster manager has been upgraded to branch manager, she/he has to manage a lot of additional records. At branch level, there is a need of additional support staff like accountant cum data entry operator. Also, a computer at each branch is needed. A financial software is also required to meet the need of managing the increasing size of data.
- Some SHG members have complained that the behaviour of the cluster manager has changed. Earlier, she/he spent more time with the SHGs. Now, she/he hardly visits the SHGs. And if the SHG members come to the branch, the manager hardly has any time to discuss their issues.

There was a suggestion that at branch/cluster level another official, other than the accountant and branch manager, should be there to look into the issues of SHGs. However, to what extent it can be done by the new avatar of the organisation was a question. The CEO said that it is time that PAF should come into the picture here.

Discussion Questions

1. What are the core issues of PML with regard to transition from federation to NBFC?
2. What can be done to improve relationships with SHGs?
3. What would be the problems if the existing way of expansion goes on?

Summary

- Organisational transformation in microfinance has been a part of its growth story. Initially, informal SHG federations became formal bodies, NGOs became NBFC-MFIs and later, NBFC-MFIs became small finance banks and universal banks.
- Transformation of organisations is a complex subject that deals with various issues, such as task, structure, people and technology. Depending on the nature and extent of organisational change, the latter can be categorised into adaptation, evolution, turnaround and revolution.
- Change from an informal body to a formal organisation brings in several issues like formation of rules, increase in maintenance of records, increase in hierarchy and volunteers being replaced by employees.
- Change from NGO to NBFC-MFI brings in enhanced scale, change in legal form, change in work culture and change in compliances. Organisation structure may also change.
- Change from NBFC-MFI to SFB and universal bank requires establishment of new physical space for collection of savings, employee orientation on how to attract and deal with deposit making clients, ensuring safety of deposits, and meeting new norms of SLR and CRR which they did not have to face as MFI. As a universal bank, the scale of operations is enormous and the restrictions are small. Here, the MFI may find such freedom very difficult to digest. Incoming lateral recruits also may bring in disruptive culture to the organisation.
- In times of change, organisations fall prey to market-driven forces, which may drift them away from their original mission. Hence, the management must be careful enough to prevent any such occurrences.

Exercises

A. Multiple-choice Questions

1. Which of the following organisations does not go through transformation in microfinance sector?
   (a) Informal SHGs/Federations
   (b) NGOs
   (c) Universal banks
   (d) NBFC-MFIs
2. Organisational transformation takes place, when there is
   (a) Change in leadership
   (b) M&A
   (c) Disruption by technological and environmental forces
   (d) All of the above
3. Major changes in organisations due to external forces do not include
   (a) Change in leadership
   (b) M&A
   (c) Disruption by technology
   (d) Environmental and policy disruptions
4. When the nature of change is incremental, but the extent of change is transformational, what kind of approach should be followed for organisational change?
   (a) Adaptation (b) Evolution
   (c) Turnaround (d) Revolution
5. In organisational change circumstances, according to Leavitt (1965), which of the following dimension is affected?
   (a) People
   (b) Structure
   (c) Technology
   (d) All of the above
6. During transformation of informal to formal bodies, which of the dimension need not be changed?
   (a) Rules (b) Records
   (c) Members (d) Procedures
7. An NGO transforming into MFI necessarily sees changes in which of the following?
   (a) Culture
   (b) Leadership
   (c) Products
   (d) All of the above
8. Which of the following kind of changes requires the organisation to have a change in its legal form?
   (a) NGO to NBFC-MFI
   (b) NBFC-MFI to Small Finance Bank
   (c) Small Finance Bank to Universal Bank
   (d) All of the above

9. Which of the following is not observed during the transformation of NBFC-MFI into an SFB?
   (a) Front office is established
   (b) Core banking solution implemented
   (c) Employees are oriented
   (d) Volunteers become employees

10. If an NBFC-MFI transforms into SFB or Universal bank, which of the following compliance is not a new addition?
   (a) CRR
   (b) SLR
   (c) Priority sector lending
   (d) None of the above

B. Review Questions

1. What are the generic issues in transformation of organisations? How are such changes in microfinance sector different from other industries?
2. Point out three problems associated with transformation of informal SHG federations to formal bodies. How can the concerned agency cope with this situation?
3. What are the problems associated with transformation of NGOs into commercial MFIs?
4. An MFI transforming into an SFB and a universal bank brings in very different challenges. Do you agree with the statement? Elaborate.
5. Transformation of organisations in microfinance is not possible without compromising their values. Comment.

C. Application-based Questions

1. Go through the case study given in Case Study VI (Ujjivan). How did the organisation deal with the transformational issues?
2. Many MFIs have issued IPO in the last 8-9 years. What kinds of transformation issues did they face for being a listed company?

Further Readings

- The three boxes 15.1, 15.2, and 15.3 are summaries of detailed account given in Yeswanth (2004), Chapter 15 'MFI to SFB via IPO' in Roy (2018), and Chapter 'Building the Backbone', Bandopadhyay (2016), respectively. These cases/chapters would provide further insights into the issues of transformation.
- For a general understanding of the issues of organisational change, please go through the readings related to organisational change or transformation which are available in textbooks of strategic management (for example Johnson et al. *Exploring Strategy,* Chapter 14 'Leading Strategic Change').

CHAPTER

16

Funding Issues in Microfinance

Chapter Outline

Learning Objectives

After reading this chapter, you will be able to:

- describe the different kinds of funding and financers who have funded to microfinance sector.
- describe the various instruments of funding like grant, equity and debt.
- discuss the role of structured funding like securitisation in microfinance.

Since microfinance was led by market, the issue of funding has become an important one. Earlier, it was done on grant basis, hence there was not much complexity. The primary objective was development; governments and funding agencies had a duty to finance microfinance projects. However, since early 2000s, commercial organisations have grown immensely. In this context, the whole funding environment has changed. Today, it looks more like a financial market than a policy-driven programme.

However, with the incoming of private funding, the complexity has increased. It was discussed earlier in Chapter 13 that due to the private investors' influence, there were situations of mission drift. The original mission of microfinance was compromised. Under such circumstances, it is important to understand the nuances of funding in the sector.

16.1 Types of Funding in Microfinance

Broadly, there are two kinds of funding that can be found in the microfinance sector, public funding and private funding. It can be in both forms, grant and investment. Public funding includes government grants, interest subsidies, bilateral and multilateral funds, etc. Private funding includes individual donors and donor agencies, private funds (PE firms, hedge funds, large individual investors, etc.) and investments by public in bonds or equity through stock exchange. Figure 16.1. provides a diagrammatic view of the type of funding.

Grant-based funds are generally provided for specific activities. Further, grants are often provided not purely as grant instruments, rather are blended with loan products. For example, in the District Poverty Initiatives Project (DPIP) in Rajasthan, the cost of common interest group promotion was provided in the form of grant to implementing agencies. However, for the livelihood activities, the groups have to take a loan with subsidies depending on the type of community (for SC/ST, the subsidy was higher). Similarly, there are also interest subvention programmes, where the groups have to pay a subsidised interest rate.

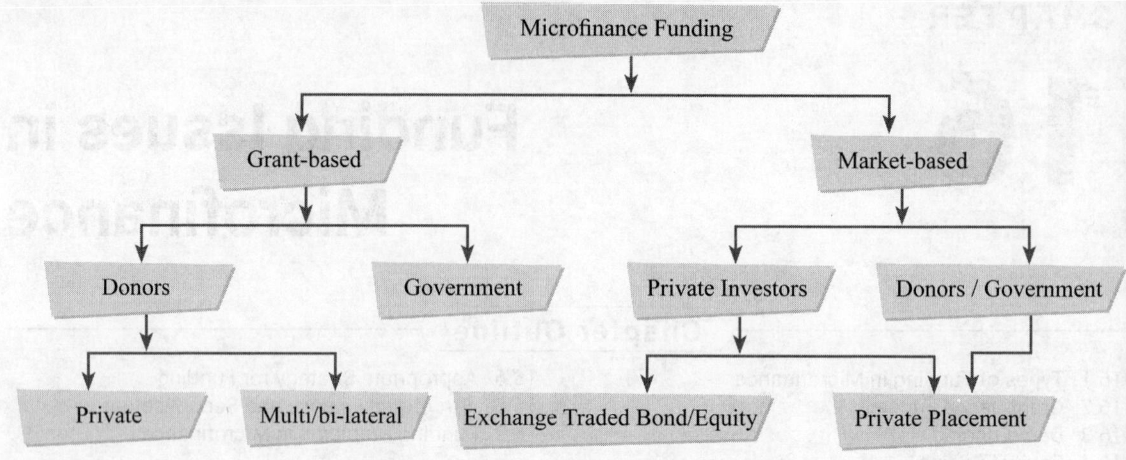

Fig. 16.1 Funding Types in Microfinance

Market-based funds are provided in the form of debt or equity instruments. It can also be provided in the form of deposits if the concerned agency is allowed to receive it. Examples of different kinds of funding are given in Table 16.1.

Foundations have contributed in various ways to microfinance. Generally, they are open to grants too. However, under some circumstances, they also provide debt/equity investments. In any case, such investments/grants are ordinarily directed at some larger social goals that match with the objectives of the foundation. Grants, technically, are directed towards not-for-profit activities. However, sometimes it is channelled to for-profit agencies too. In microfinance, activities like capacity building and R&D usually have no investors. For such activities, grants may be sought. It may also be provided by the funding agencies as an initial encouragement to undertake something innovative and if found successful, in future, debt/equity instruments may be used.

Table 16.1 Different Kinds of Funding

Type of funder	Example	Type of funding
Public funders	Corporate/Private foundations (Ford Foundation, Bill and Melinda Gates Foundation, Tata Trusts, etc.)	Grants Debts/Equity
	Multilateral Agencies (The World Bank, Asian Development Bank, etc.)	Grants Debts, Equity, Guarantee
	Bilateral Agencies (DFID, SIDA, USAID)	Grants Debts, Equity, Guarantee
	Government Agencies (SIDBI, NABARD)	Grants Debts/Equity
	DFIs (Kfw, AECID, FMO, etc.)	Grants Debts, Equity, Guarantee
Individual investor	Small Investor	Deposit, Bond (debt), Equity
	HNI	Debt, Equity
Private institutional investor	Banks	Debt, Equity
	Private Equity Firm	Debt, Equity
	Pension Funds /Mutual Funds	Debt, Equity
	NGOs (Accion, FINCA, etc.)	Debt, Equity
	Microfinance Investment Vehicles (MIVs) (Oikocredit)	Grants Debts, Equity, Guarantee

Source: Adapted from *Earne and Sherk* (2014)

NGOs like Accion and FINCA have also invested in microfinance organisations. These agencies, being involved in microfinance activities themselves, have a sound understanding of the sector, and hence they make their judgement based on these insights.

Development Financial Institutions (DFIs) have a dual goal, development and market-based growth. However, they invest in business activities, hence their primary targets are debt instruments. Under certain specific situations, they may go for equity or grants. Sometimes, they go for blended instruments, such as part debt and part grant.

Banks generally go for debt funding. In India, loans to microfinance sector are considered as priority sector lending. Hence, the banks have an interest in extending such loans. Private equity firms generally look for equity investments, and sometimes debt instruments are also acceptable for them. These organisations ordinarily look forward to high rate of return, hence they also want some say in Board or other influential positions. Pension funds and mutual funds are generally conservative investors. They have to have a large proportion of funds to be invested in safe avenues. Hence, they generally prefer debt instruments.

Individual investors ordinarily go for initial public offer (IPO) or secondary market deals. High net worth individuals (HNIs) may go for a private placement also. Conservative investors would generally invest in debt instruments while those having risk bearing capacity prefer equity instruments.

Multilateral and bilateral agencies have larger goals tied up with their funds. Hence, they can go for any kind of instrument. Further, these agencies have a large group of investor countries, and hence influences of such countries are also reflected while making investment decisions

16.2 Grant-based Funding

Grants are funds provided to an Microfinance Instution (MFI)/Self Help Group Promotions Institution (SHPI) for various purposes which are not directly linked with profit making. This fund is retained by the recipient without any consideration. Grants are provided either for a specific purpose, or it could be an untied grant; the former is seen more often. If a certain investment can have profit-orientation, then there is no need of making a grant. Ordinarily, grants are supposed to cater to projects which are purely welfare-oriented. For example, a school building in a remote location, health camp in an area, water conservation in a village, etc. Grants are also appropriate in disaster-affected situations, where immediate relief is required. However, sometimes it is seen that profit-oriented activities like microfinance needs a kick-start before it can deliver. Suppose, financial literacy campaign in an unbanked area is very poor, and without capital, nothing could take off. Similarly, development of a specific technology that would help easing the transactions may be a profitable activity once it is rolled out. But, to begin it, no investor would like to take the risk. It would thus require a critical funding, which can be done in the form of grant. Generally, grant funds are not provided directly to Non-banking Financial Companies (NBFCs), as there are tax implications for the donor. Hence, it is provided to not-for-profit organisations. For example, grants to BASIX were provided to Indian Grameen Services (IGS), its developmental wing.

16.3 Debt Funding

Debt is a multidimensional instrument. It can be provided in various forms, senior term loans, syndicated loans, subordinated debts and bonds (Earne and Sherk, 2014).

Bonds are simple debt instruments but unlike ordinary loans, they are tradeable. They can be coupon-bearing, or zero-coupon bond. Coupon bearing bonds keep on paying periodic (say annual) interest rates. Zero-coupon bonds do not pay regular interest and are issued at maturity value but at a deep discount. For example, an MFI issues a 10-year bond of ₹100,000 at 12 per cent coupon rate. This means, every year the investor would receive ₹1200 and at the end of maturity period, will receive the principal amount back. It is possible that the bond is issued at discount or premium depending on the market conditions, but the interest is paid on its face value only. This is an illustration of a 12%-coupon bearing bond. Suppose it had been a zero-coupon bond and someone invests in it. The issuing company will issue it at a deep discount. Suppose the issue price is ₹40,000. In that case, the bond yield will be around 9.6 per cent. In order to get a return of 12 per cent, the bond should be purchased at ₹32,198.

Senior term loan and syndicated loans are technically the same. The former is issued by a specific financer while syndicated loans are provided by a group of lenders. Syndicated loans are generally preferred for large investments, where a single agency may not be able to provide such huge loan. Senior term loans have priority over all other loans, and they are paid after the depositors. Such loans have a number of conditions so that the borrower does get space for making risky decisions (Earne and Sherk,2014).

Subordinated debts, also known as junior security, have higher risks and they are paid before all other debts, except equity. Subordinated debts are eligible as Tier-2 capital, subject to some conditions like it should have a maturity period of five years. Further, Tier-2 capital cannot be more than Tier-I capital. Subordinated debt can also be offered as convertible debt, which means there is an option to convert it into equity.

16.4 Equity Funding

Equity refers to shareholding of a company. Suppose a company owns five million (50 lakh) shares, each priced at ₹10, owned equally by five investors. Assuming all the shares have been paid up, the company has now shareholders' equity of ₹50 million (5 crore). Each investor owns one crore rupees of share. Suppose another investor is invited who agrees to invest an additional amount of ₹25 million. Now, the new shareholding pattern will be, such as five investors, ₹10 million each, and sixth investor, ₹25 million. Suppose, for a new ambitious project, the company needs not ₹25 million, but ₹125 million, and the new investor says that it would invest only in the form of equity. In that case, the new investor would retain ₹125 million of equity, while the original promoters would have a total equity of ₹50 million. This also means that the control over the company would be shifted to the new investor. In order to avoid such situations, the promoters may bargain that it should be invested in the form of part equity and part debt. It is also possible that the promoters would demand a premium over the book value (say ₹50 per share). In that case, the new investor would own only 2.5 million shares. The existing promoters retain the control.

During 2007-08 to first quarter of 2010, large MFIs in India had a deal of about USD 500 million from various overseas private equity firms in equity and debt (Srinivasan, 2010). Many of the NBFC-MFIs have been promoted by people who did not have their own funds. Vijay Mahajan had to raise equity in order to meet the required capital for registering BSFL, the NBFC wing of BASIX. Samit Ghosh of Ujjivan had to raise funds from outside. Examples given in Chapter 13 in the case of Spandana, SHARE and SKS also showed that the promoters, originally, had a small contribution in the original ownership structure.

Equity funding is a double-edged sword. Technically, the equity investors own the share, and this in turn makes the investor an owner of a part of the company. Such ownership is useful in controlling company only when the investor owns majority shares or gains support of majority shareholders. Once an investor has the control, he/she can appoint the Board of Directors, and in turn control the management of the company. As in the microfinance business, the promoters are generally minority shareholders, this is a little tricky. There can be issues of hostile takeover, or there can be situations like SKS Microfinance, when the board made the founder exit. For the investor also, it is not an easy walk. Unlike debt, when somebody invests in equity, he/she cannot expect an assured return. The company can declare dividend only when there is enough surplus. The option lies with the management, not with the investor. If they want regular return, they may go for preference share, who would get a fixed return and would have priority over the equity shareholders during liquidation. But preference shareholders do not have voting rights over the decisions of the company, unless such decisions are related to the specific class of preference shareholders.

For listed companies, equity funding can be raised from the public. SKS Microfinance was the first Indian MFI to issue IPO, which took place in 2010. Later Equitas, Ujjivan and some others also went for this instrument. Initial public offer is a complex process and requires several disclosures, but this is domestic investment, which is beneficial for meeting regulatory norms. A small investor who invests in a company through stock exchange does not pose any threat of controlling the company. And such retail investors also do not always look at the dividend return, rather they look at the potential of appreciation of the stock value. When the price rises, they can sell it off and book profit.

16.5 Appropriate Strategy for Funding

Thus, we see that there are three different ways of funding an NBFC, and for a deposit-keeping company, there is another way of funding, i.e. deposits. However, deposits are non-capital liabilities, and hence in order to meet the minimum criteria of net owned funds or capital, one needs equity and debt investments. Grants are not easy to get and these days, there is a little grant available for microfinance related activities.

It is important to attract investments, but more important is to have a proper pricing for that investment. If the company has an upper hand in the negotiation process, for example, having a very good rating, it can bargain for a high price or premium. On the other hand, if the investor knows that the company does not have a good rating, or it is desperate to get funds, the situation would be reverse and the company would have to issue the debt or equity at a discount or at a lower premium.

It must be noted here that the market for private equity and debt has become very complex these days. In the aftermath of global financial crisis, a number of regulatory changes have taken place. For financial services institutions, there have been stringent prudential norms mandated as a part of BASEL III. Thus, the investor community also knows that they cannot expect super normal rate of return any more. With this knowledge, they are very cautious on where to put their money.

Earlier, such decisions ordinarily went to companies and instruments with good rating. However, with the kind of doubts raised over ratings, they are now going one step further and having their own due diligence process also. Some investors would have their private rating, while some would ask for multiple ratings.

What should be the mix of equity and debt? As discussed earlier, both have their own pros and cons. In equity investment, there is no need of a fixed return, which is good for the company, but then ownership would be diluted. On the other hand, debt instruments demand a fixed return and financiers also demand some say in decisions. They can also nominate some directors as per the norms. Ideally, debt and equity should be as per the optimal level of leverage. Higher the leverage there is, higher are the risks. Lower the leverage, lower the return would be.

Illustration 16.1 A company has ₹100 million of equity and ₹400 million of debt. Thus, every single rupee of equity has leveraged four rupees of debt. If the company raises another ₹200 million of debt, with the same equity, the leverage ratio (debt equity ratio) would be higher. This is good for the company. However, if the leverage is higher, the owner has less risk in proportion to the total amount invested (debt + equity) in the business. Manager can take bolder decisions and this would pose a risk for the investor. On the other hand, suppose with the same equity, debt is only ₹250 million, the proportion of money invested by the shareholder out of the total investment would be high. Thus, the shareholder would pressurise the manager to make safe investment. The risk is lower for the investor here as the leverage is low. But in such a case, return is also low because the managers would not take risks.

It may be noted here that there are theories of capital structure in finance literature that explain the issue of the right blend of debt of equity. Modigliani and Miller (M&M)'s theory is that value of a firm is independent of its capital structure (debt/equity mix). On the other hand, static theory of capital structure says that firms see if the tax benefit from the extra borrowing equals to the risk from the additional debt (Ross, Westerfield and Jordan, 2008). Similarly, the Traditional Approach of Capital Structure and the Net Income Approach say that value of the firm can be increased through an appropriate mix of debt and equity. Equity investors keep on increasing the return on equity until it offsets the benefit from cheaper debts (Van Horne and Wachowicz Jr, 2001). It is clear that debt increases return on equity, but it also brings in its own risk. Hence, generally companies prefer and regulators also suggest a suitable mix of debt and equity.

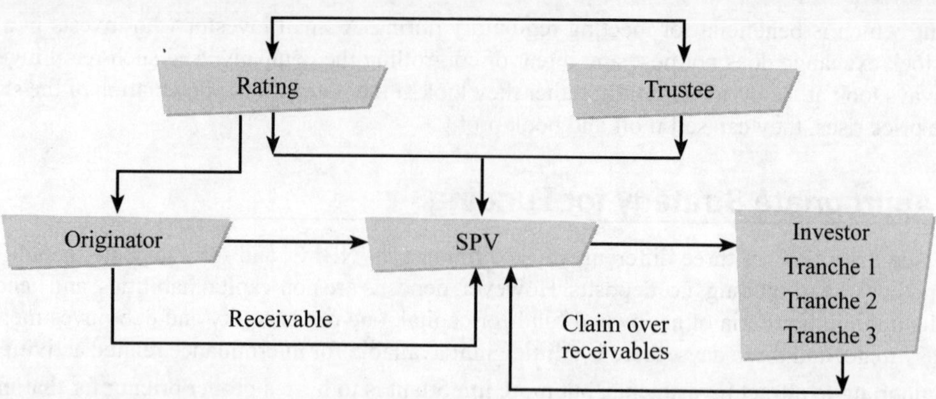

Fig. 16.2 Process of Securitisation (adapted from Hattenrauch and Schneider, 2009)

16.6 Structured Finance and Securitisation

While debt and equity are simple instruments, in the recent past, a large number of specialised financial instrument have been brought out. This includes collateralised debt obligations (CDO), collateralised bond obligations (CBO), collateralised mortgage obligations (CMO), credit default swap (CDS), and hybrid securities which have features of both debt and equity. Collateralised instruments, such as CDO, CBO and CMO are based on the underlying assets of loans and are converted into securities which are tradeable. An example of hybrid security is convertible bond, which has characteristics of both debt and equity. Credit default swap or CDS is like an insurance policy in which one keeps on paying a premium to offset the possibility of default.

Another related financial instrument is securitisation, which has been used very often in microfinance business. Securitisation is nothing but converting the future cash flows from receivables to securities. As a part of this, the originator of the security transfers the assets to a third party, a special purpose vehicle (SPV), which is generally formed as a trust. All the assets are then classified into different tranches and each tranche is then rated by rating agencies. Investors buy these securities depending on their risk appetites (Figure 16.2). This makes the illiquid assets liquid, quarantines the investor from the risk of bankruptcy of the originator company and keeps the asset away from the company's balance sheet, thus freeing up the need for meeting capital to risk asset ratio (CRAR) requirement.

Illustration 16.2 Suppose an MFI has a receivable of ₹3000 million, which is to be paid back with 18 per cent interest in the next five years. The amount would be paid back in EMIs. Every month the company would receive ₹50 million. The present value of the receivable is about ₹1970 million (say ₹2000 million for simplicity) (calculated using annuity formula). Out of these receivables, suppose 50 per cent of advances are very good quality assets, and there is only one per cent chance of default. Another 30 per cent of assets are of average quality and there is a probability of 5 per cent of default, and the remaining assets are risky, they have 20 per cent probability of default. These three categories of assets will be converted into three tranches of securities, and accordingly they would be sold to investors, as given in Table 16.2.

Table 16.2 Example of Different Tranches in Securitisation

Tranche	Default risk	Receivable in ₹ million	Present value in ₹ million	Traded value (hypothetical) in ₹ million
1	1%	1500	1000	1200
2	5%	900	600	650
3	20%	600	400	350

Thus, the third investor is taking a lot of risk, and hence he/she bargains for a very low price, while the first tranche picks up the safest security paying the premium.

What did the originator company gain? First of all, there is an immediate cash flow (in the above example, ₹2200 million, which is higher than the present value of securities, i.e. 2000 million). The greatest benefit here is that the illiquid asset was converted into a liquid asset. Now this receipt will be available for reinvestment in the business, such as expansion of area of operations. Second, the asset earlier was a part of the receivable, hence it required meeting the CRAR norms. Risk weighted assets of ₹2000 million would require an equivalent capital of ₹300 million for an NBFC-MFI (15% CRAR). Now this becomes an off-balance sheet asset. Another thing is that the rating of the MFI becomes separated from the rating of the assets (different tranches).

There are some positive features that help the investor also. Now the investor knows that the assets are of different classes. Hence, he/she would invest in the relevant class of asset. A high-growth oriented investor would invest in tranche 3, while a safe investor would invest in tranche 1. Also, the investor is shielded from the bankruptcy of the company because the assets have been transferred to an SPV. The trustee of the SPV has to take utmost care that the receivables are kept in proper order. Box 16.1 shows that securitisation has been a popular instrument for MFIs in India.

Box 16.1 Securitisation in Microfinance

There have been several instances of securitisation in microfinance. ICICI Bank in India undertook securitisation of assets of several MFIs, starting in 2003. BlueOrchard Microfinance Securities based in Delaware had a deal with MFIs of several countries (Hattenrauch and Schneider, 2009). During 2009-10, MFIs in India raised ₹ 867 crore through various securitisation deals (Sreenivasan, 2010).

16.7 Funding Problems in Microfinance

Microfinance sector's funding problems have cropped up consistently because of the dynamic nature of the business and the regulatory environment. Situations ranging from an almost no-regulation to increasingly regulated situation have been there. In the aftermath of AP crisis, the RBI issued new guidelines in 2011. Further, in 2015, there was licensing of small finance bank (SFB) and Payments Bank (PB) which brought in further regulations. The institutional set up also has changed significantly in the last 10 years. A new category of NBFC-MFI was formed, and now we have the SFBs. All these have their own ownership structure, which requires different kinds of financing mechanism.

However, the positive part is that all the MFIs have strengthened themselves. Several of them have gone for IPO. It is expected that many other financial innovations will take place for financing their operations.

Case Study 16.1 Funding Options of Sarvonnati Microfinance

"You cannot have the cake and eat it too...", said Ms. Rajani Talukdar, Chairperson of Sarvonnati Microfinance. It was a discussion of senior management of the organisation on funding possibilities for the planned expansion.

Sarvonnati Microfinance is an MFI headquartered in Kolkata and operates in some districts of Jharkhand. The organisation started its microfinance operations in 2005 as a small programme of Sarvonnati, an NGO based in Bankura (West Bengal). In 2014, it was converted into an NBFC (Sarvonnati Microfinacne Pvt. Ltd)., and soon it obtained the NBFC-MFI licence. At that time, it had a portfolio of ₹ 750 million. As of now, in March 2019, its portfolio has grown to ₹ 2000 million. Initially, the organisation operated in Bankura and nearby areas. Slowly, it has expanded to a few districts of Jharkhand also. Seeing its growth being smooth in the last four and half years, the management got ideas of expansion. It wants to cover all the districts of Jharkhand and West Bengal, and also expand to other neighbouring states like Bihar, Chhatisgarh and Odisha. For this expansion, it needs about ₹ 500 million. At present, it has an equity base of ₹ 235 million (paid up equity for 23.5 million shares) and has another ₹ 150 million in its reserve.

"See, we have close to ₹ 400 million as paid up equity and reserves. Our valuation says that each of our share is worth ₹ 42. We can provide only 11.9 million shares in lieu of that. You will own about 33 per cent of shares in the new ownership structure", said the CFO.

"Then, guarantee that a fixed return of 12 per cent is payable every year".

"You cannot have the cake and eat it too", said Ms. Talukdar. "With equity investment, we cannot guarantee a fixed return. As of now, we are not in a position to issue preference shares. Why do not we settle for a debt investment?"

The discussion continued. Investors were not ready to take the shares with a huge premium. After a lot of discussion, it was agreed that they would pay maximum `38.50 towards a share. However, they still wanted a substantial influence, if not complete control. Ms. Talukdar suggested that the investor should increase the amount of investment, and the company was ready to issue a part debt and part equity kind of structure.

Discussion Questions

1. Suppose the investor agrees to settle for a 49 per cent holding and debt investment of `100 million. How much would they have to invest?
2. What are the implications if the company gives majority stake to the PE firms?
3. What is the optimal ownership structure for this company, if the promoters do not want to forego the control?

Summary

- Microfinance funding is of two types, grant-based and market based. The market-based funding can be either debt or equity.
- Grants are generally intended for not-for-profit purpose. Under some circumstances, it is also provided for for-profit agencies, but is routed through the not-for-profit wings of the MFI.
- Debt instruments can be senior debts, subordinated debts, syndicated debt and bonds.
- Equity instruments can be in the form of private placement or through IPO.
- There is a need for an appropriate mix of debt and equity in any MFI.
- Structured finance and securitisation are also some of the instruments that can be used in MFIs.

Exercises

A. Multiple-choice Questions

1. What is/are the following kind of instrument (s) used in microfinance?
   (a) Grantb (b) Debt
   (c) Equity (d) All of the above
2. Grant is ordinarily provided to
   (a) NGOs (b) MFIs
   (c) Bank (d) All of the above
3. Debt instruments do not include
   (a) Debentures (b) Equity
   (c) Senior loan (d) Bonds
4. Which of the following is true for equity holders?
   (a) They have the first right over residual during liquidation
   (b) They get a fixed return
   (c) They can participate in ratifying major decisions
   (d) None of the above
5. If a company leverages its equity higher and higher over the years,
   (a) Its risk profile improves
   (b) Its risk profile deteriorates
   (c) Risk profile is not affected
   (d) Cannot be determined
6. Which of the following does not come under structured finance?
   (a) CDO
   (b) CMO
   (c) CBO
   (d) None of the above

7. Credit default swap has some similarity with a /an __________ product.
   (a) Debt
   (b) Equity
   (c) Insurance
   (d) Savings
8. Securitisation helps in
   (a) Converting illiquid assets to liquid assets
   (b) Converting debt into equity
   (c) Converting assets into liability
   (d) None of the above
9. Which of the following is not true about securitisation?
   (a) Creates off-balance assets
   (b) Creates surplus funds for reinvestment
   (c) Shields investors from bankruptcy of the originator company
   (d) None of the above
10. The investor gains from securitisation by
    (a) Assured return of fixed rate of interest
    (b) Assured return from the assets, even if the originator's rating goes down
    (c) Assurance of microfinance business to continue for ever
    (d) None of the above

B. Review Questions

1. What are the different instruments available for financing microfinance business?
2. How is grant different from equity and debt? What purpose does it serve?
3. Describe the process of securitisation.
4. What does the investor gain from securitisation?
5. For an MFI, which one is better, debt or equity investment?

C. Application-based Questions

Suppose an MFI has total ₹ 500 million in hand, out of which, half is equity and half is debt. You are a part of an investment company, which the MFI has approached for investment. You can invest up to ₹ 400 million. What kind of instrument will you like, debt or equity? Assume that you want a return of around 12-15 per cent. You also know that debt instrument provides a return of 10–14 per cent, while equity investment provides a return of 12–18 per cent.

Further Readings

- Jayadev and Rao's paper in *IIMB Management Review,* 'Financial resources of the microfinance sector: Securitisation deals Issues and challenges Interview with the MFIs Grameen Koota and Equitas' is a useful reading for understanding the financing environment in MFIs.
- *Guide to Structured Finance* by Vinod Kothari is a useful reading for understanding the issue of securitisation.
- Srinivsan's Microfinance India: State of the Sector Report 2010 has a useful chapter titled 'Investment climate—getting better'. The Microfinance India: State of the Sector Report 2011 (by Srinivasan and Tankha) has a similar chapter, 'Investment climate—Fairweather Partners'. Both will provide a proper idea of investment climate of microfinance.
- Van Horne and Wachowicz Jr (2001) and Ross, Westerfield and Jordan (2008) for capital structure theories.

CHAPTER

17 Future of Microfinance

Chapter Outline

Learning Objectives

After reading this chapter, you will be able to:

- discuss some important issues that may shape the future of microfinance.
- present a set of scenarios for future of microfinance.

17.1 The Future of SHG-Bank Linkage Programmes

There are more than eight million self-help groups (SHGs) and the flagship programme of National Rural Livelihood Mission (NRLM) is based on these institutions. Several states have their own programmes and some Microfinance Institutions (MFIs) lend through SHGs. However, it has been seen that the alternative channels like Joint Liability Groups (JLGs) and individual lending have also increased simultaneously. Initially, JLGs were thought as a fast-track arrangement and with the governmental action in Andhra Pradesh, some believed that non-SHG channels of microfinance would not survive, or at least will get a second seat. This did not occur and more and more MFIs and banks today are going for such channels.

The eight million-odd SHGs covers about 105 million of households, which is more or less the same as the number of poor households in India. This means that the SHGs have saturated in the country. The only change now would be delimiting the SHGs, adding new members as a result of children attaining majority, and replacing the older members who die. These kind of changes are going to be incremental in nature and in all probability, no revolutionary change is expected in the SHG landscape in the future.

Further, the SHGs are of different qualities and not all of them have gone through the rigorous process of institutionalisation. This would discourage the banks and MFIs to focus on lending to SHGs; nobody likes a weak SHG to take its products forward.

Another disturbing trend has started in many states; SHGs have become the channel of pushing political agenda. Distribution of mobile phones, announcement of subsidies and interest-free loans in the election year are some of the things done by ruling parties of some states. Further, in some places SHGs have been engaged as service providers in many government schemes, such as mid-day meal for primary schools. There is nothing wrong in SHGs providing such services, but such thing being enforced through state is not a good sign. This will cater to anything but the fundamental cause of financial inclusion.

Since the beginning, there had been a lot of grants in building SHG institutions. Now that the SHGs have been saturated, there is a question on whether such grants would be available for building the capacities of these institutions. If the regulators want the SHGs to play an important role in financial inclusion, they must make efforts so that SHGs are hand held to become stronger institutions rather than becoming delivery channels for government schemes or vote bank for political parties. It is true that the future institution building efforts would be of very different nature. These efforts might focus more on building governance capabilities, improving formal records and helping them to make market linkages and enterprise building.

There have already been some precedents in this regard. Many NGOs and government programmes have propounded something called Microfinance Plus, which includes livelihood promotion, enterprise development and some other activities. The idea was that SHGs are base level institutions and must move forward to the next level (i.e. enterprise-based livelihoods). This is where some support is expected to come up. However, what would happen to the weak SHGs is still not clear. The strong SHGs would take advantage of such initiative. The weak SHGs would require further capacity building support. If not received, it is possible that the benefits are cornered by a few, which wold defeat the ultimate goal of the programme.

17.2 Technology Influences the Future

According to Graham Wright, the Founder and Group Managing Director of Microsave, fintech holds the future of microfinance. He mentioned that majority of transactions had already been automated. He added that by digitising the payment system and delivering the product in electronic channels like mobile phones, and hand held equipment, the financial inclusion services will reach to everybody and in turn will democratise the credit services (Millitzer, 2017).

There is no second thought regarding what Wright said about the influence of technology in microfinance. Technology holds the future. But one must be aware of the meaning of this statement and it must be interpreted in its context. It does not mean that technology holds everything in future microfinance. Technology enables the financial services, but technology is not the same as financial services; otherwise every technical expert would be a finance expert. The point here is that technology is important in furthering the cause of microfinance. It can help in reducing the cost of operations, in speeding up service delivery and in supporting the making of effective appraisal. Without the support of technology, an MFI just cannot operate effectively.

The implication of use of advanced technology in microfinance is enormous and all such implications are practically applicable to MFIs. First of all, the delivery of future microfinance operations would be very different from the way they are delivered now. Loan applications can be done online, this implies that the loan officer does not have to go village to village to collect loan application. The moment customer information for this loan application is sought, the credit officer would get the complete credit history through its own organisational experience, credit bureau report and other feedback channel. Credit appraisal system would become very easy, disbursal will be done through mobile payment or NEFT, collection would be done by electronic clearing and identity based information like Aadhar will help further, (although now Aadhar linking has become non-mandatory). Thus, human intervention would come down substantially. This has already started to a great extent. In near future, this is going to the standard practice.

What is not going to change are the specific characteristics of microfinance. Small loans having high transaction cost, bankers ignoring the low-income group and policy-driven disruptions are going to stay here. Hence, microfinance managers have to play with their specialised skills which are related to understanding the specific needs of low-income group customers. With increased automation, the banks might lose out the aspect of knowing their customers personally. The microfinance officials must not leave this aspect. Their individual attention to customers, even if the transactions are automated, is very much required and that is where they should focus. This will also be a differentiating factor that would determine the competitiveness of microfinance institutions in this market.

Information technology can help in this regard. So far, the focus has been on issues like customer identification, credit appraisal and payment system. One thing that has been left out is the issue of knowledge management in microfinance. The access to information has to be institutionalised. Customer database and their details have to go beyond the transactions. More research has to be done on their need. Knowledge transfer in the event of a field officer or any important person leaving has to be institutionalised. This may hold an important component in enhancing the role of technology in microfinance.

17.3 Bank Licence – the End of MFIs?

Barring a few exceptions, the promoters of microfinance institutions always dreamed of converting the MFI into a bank. Some of them became Non-banking Financial Company (NBFC)-MFI because they did not get the bank licence. Bank licence requires a high level of investment, and the licensing criteria is not in the reach of everybody. Hence, NBFC-MFI is the easiest way if one wants to operate in microfinance sector. Recently, the government has become open to such ideas. The licensing of differentiated banks, particularly the SFBs, is a progressive stance in this regard.

Being a bank has several advantages. As of now, the NBFC-MFIs cannot accept deposits. They have to depend on hard-to-come equity; the other option is to go for debt, mainly bank loans. This increases the cost of funds immensely. Deposits are easy way out. In India, even today, the credit deposit ratios of less developed districts are lower in comparison to cities and developed areas. Thus, having deposit would bring down the pressure on raising high cost funds. Further, being an NBFC-MFI restricts the business. The qualifying assets norms, interest rate cap and multiple lending norms are not applicable to banks. A bank licence opens the door of various avenues that are not available to NBFC-MFIs.

In the recent years, one of the NBFC-MFIs, Bandhan, became a universal bank. Several MFIs became small finance banks (SFBs). One large MFI (BFIL) has been taken over by a private bank, in all probability, the former would operate like the microfinance wing of the bank, while also being a channel for delivering the banking services. Thus, the space for pure NBFC-MFIs has been decreasing. Does it mean that the days of MFIs are over? What if all the MFIs are consolidated and integrated with banking sector?

In near future, it does not seem to be possible. The microfinance industry has its own advantages, it could grow because there was a space in the market where the banks could not fulfil the needs of people. This space grew not because the bankers were not interested or were not capable, but some structural limitations also stopped the banks from going into the microfinance sector. High transaction cost and the high break-even point of banks are some of the entry barriers, that is why even if a bank wants to open a branch in remote area, it cannot go forward. The way the form of a bank or its branch is conceptualised, it is very difficult to operate with a low-cost model. Further, banks by nature are a conservative group of institutions. The regulatory regime ensures them to stay conservative.

It is possible that the MFIs which have become banks, slowly, would downplay their microfinance business. Universal banks anyway do not require to cater to this sector, except for meeting the branch expansion norms and priority sector lending norms. Small finance banks have to meet some requirements, but some of them, in the future, would qualify to be a full-fledged bank. Then they would not be under any obligation to serve the sector.

Thus, the niche for microfinance sector is going to stay here. Many not-for-profit organisations in the microfinance sector have been converting to the form of NBFC-MFIs. The latter has an advantage of being independent from the grant-based funds. So far, in India, MFIs have shown that they have been profitable (in fact they are criticised for their profiteering!), and hence, this category of business would continue in the long run.

17.4 Damage by Loan Waivers

Microfinance sector has been invariably affected by political interventions. There have been direct attacks on the sector by way of bringing in laws against the MFIs, as happened during the AP crisis. With increasing regulatory provisions such things may not happen in the future, although one cannot rule out such possibilities. There are some indirect ways which are not indented to influence the sector, but some interventions like demonetisation also brought in the crisis.

There is one specific kind of political intervention that needs a mention here, i.e. the loan waiver programmes of government. Ordinarily the loan waiver schemes have been for the farm sector and the loans from public sector banks are waived-off. In all probability, the loans of MFIs may not be targeted by the political parties. But the problem is that whenever there is such an announcement, the expectations of customers, that the MFI loans would be waived-off, are likely to rise. There is no dearth of examples when politicians have openly said, even if it is not part of their formal party policy, that MFI loans need not be repaid.

This kind of act damages the microfinance sector in two ways, first, the political instigation not to repay loan directly hampers the recovery loans, second, it indirectly pollutes the banking habits. The second implication is dangerous because when the client takes a loan, he/she expects that there is no need to repay. Going back to discussion in Chapter 2, it can be easily deduced that the proportion of safe borrowers would come down, which ultimately would be made up by increase the price of credit, i.e. interest rate. Thus, the customers are back to a high-interest regime.

Loan waivers are not specific to the microfinance sector. This is a larger political agenda. However, a good governance regime should ideally make a level playing field, which provides equal opportunity to lender as well as borrower. Any loan waiver should be left to specific and local situations, rather than making it a generic policy.

17.5 Will Information Asymmetry Decrease?

One problem associated with microfinance is that the lenders do not have proper information about the client. There are issues with KYC, but with the Aadhar being issued to everybody in the country, this problem has slightly come down. Further, there are small MFIs that are not NBFCs. Hence, they do not come under the RBI guidelines that mandate the qualifying assets and multiple lending norms. These are, however, aberrations and to a large extent, can be controlled in future.

There are two issues that need understanding regarding information asymmetry in microfinance. One, the efficacy of credit bureau in dealing with small loans is questionable. The past data are not available for a large number of borrowers. There was no KYC document that could integrate all the records genuinely. Voter card used to be the only document with people, and this was not the best document to provide a unique identity. Earlier, voter cards did not mention the date of birth. The income tax PAN card was more reliable, but low-income group never required it. Many MFIs took initiative to prepare PAN card of borrowers. Aadhar, in that sense, is the most authentic and reliable document. When Aadhar was mandatory, it was a boon for the credit bureaus; now the mandate has been diluted, but things still can be in place as many transactions are now Aadhar linked. Another problem was that, initially the credit bureau just did not get the cooperation of MFIs till the blow of regulatory whip.

The second problem with credit bureau is an intricate one. Microfinance sector by its design lends to groups. In SHGs, the lending is not done to the member, rather it is done to the group. In a group, the lender has no information on which particular member took the loan. Further, although there are provisions in the RBI guidelines that a member cannot be part of two groups, there is no mechanism to verify this.

With these kinds of problem in hand, information asymmetry has affected the credit bureau. Now, the regulatory provisions and the Aadhar links have improved the situation, but there still lies some problem. It is expected that with a technology-enabled regime of microfinance, the information asymmetry would get a proper attention.

17.6 Regulated Regime for Microfinance

Till 2010, the microfinance sector was almost in an unregulated regime. Then came the AP ordinance and later, the RBI guidelines were issued. Further, the SROs have also increased membership. Many NGOs that ran microfinance operations are tuning up for NBFC licences because the grants for microfinance have dried up. This has one clear result, there is less space for unregulated microfinance.

Coverage of regulators has now increased. More and more organisations are now under regulatory purview. Further, the depth of regulation has also got a boost. In the last five years, one MFI became bank and several MFIs became small finance banks. Banks, being deposit accepting bodies, have to meet stringent regulatory norms. With all the banks now having core banking solutions, monitoring and supervision has become relatively easier. The Reserve Bank of India can find out the violation of rules and norms with much less difficulty.

To increase the access to capital, some of the MFIs have already gone for initial public offer (IPO). Listing a company is not just a question of raising capital from the market. It needs a high level of disclosure, which was not there earlier. It also requires meeting additional regulations, such as quarterly audit. The Securities and Exchange Board of India (SEBI) becomes an additional regulator. Now that the microfinance service providers are offering various other products, such as insurance, the relevant regulators of such sectors like Insurance Regulatory and Development Authority (IRDA) also have an indirect regulatory coverage on the MFIs.

The state governments have their own mechanism to regulate the microfinance sector, as was done by Andhra Pradesh. The government also has its control over the issue of money laundering which requires compliances by all financial services providing agencies, including the MFIs. Thus, over a period of time, the reach of regulations and the depth of regulations have increased immensely over the microfinance providers. There are, however, some areas of gaps. The not-for-profit organisations who provide microfinance services are still out of the RBI or any other regulators. Similarly, the SHPIs that are involved in on-lending and SHG management and are facilitating the process of microfinance as part of a government programme are technically not under any regulator (although being a part of the government programme itself is under several rules and norms). But, being a part of the government scheme does not assure that they are under a proper regulatory regime. Ultimately, the programme implementation structure (such as National Rural Livelihood Mission (NRLM)) is not expected to regulate microfinance. Can a bank be left unregulated if it is owned and operated by government? That said, it is not easy to regulate the SHG-based lending programmes. It would require a high level of documentation and integration with other systems.

While regulating, the regulators have to be careful that the industry operates in smooth way. There have been instances, like that in increasing the capital adequacy norms and the AP ordinance, when the idea was to put a clutch on the unsavoury elements, however, the implications were much larger. Regulatory gaps have led to an unprecedented level of growth in the microfinance industry, which led to imprudent practices. However, too much restrictions would kill the industry. The cost of not having microfinance is higher than the high cost of microfinance business.

In a nutshell, it can be said that the space of regulated microfinance is expanding in terms of width as well as depth. The space for unregulated ones has been narrowing. However, there is still a substantial range of organisations that are not a part of the existing regulatory regime. This creates a problem for the whole sector. It is expected that these unregulated parts, over a period of time, are integrated to the regulatory regime. This will also create a more efficient system of financial markets for microfinance business.

Summary

- SHGs have saturated over all parts of India. There can only be incremental changes in the SHGs compositions.
- SHGs are of different qualities. No bank or MFI would deal with weak institutions, they would rather prefer JLGs and individuals.
- SHGs have also been used as service providers and sometimes also as delivery channel for freebies for vote bank. This does not help the cause of financial inclusion.
- Regulators must assure that investment on institution building of SHGs continue.
- Technology has already influenced the microfinance sector by enabling the process of customer identification, credit appraisal and payment system. An MFI must be equipped with advances in technology, otherwise it will not be able to compete.

- However, the specific knowledge about customers would still be held by MFI officials. This will be a differentiating factor for enhancing competitiveness of MFIs. Technology in knowledge management can aid this area further.
- NBFC-MFI promoters would prefer to become a bank because the latter decreases the cost of funds and enhances autonomy. One of the MFIs has already become a bank and some others have become SFBs.
- However, the niche of microfinance is still going to stay because the structure of banks and some regulatory requirement does not allow them to operate at very small scale.
- Loan waivers have influenced the microfinance sector in two ways. Politicians have directly encouraged the borrowers not to repay and indirectly, the loan waivers pollute the banking habits of people.
- Credit bureaus have not been effective in microfinance because of lack of past information and the lack of clarity of who took the loan in an SHG.
- The space for regulated microfinance has increased over a period of time, however, there are still a substantial number of unregulated microfinance organisations.

Exercises

A. Multiple-choice Questions

1. Which of the following true about SHGs?
   (a) SHGs are a well-regulated set of organisations
   (b) There is a saturation of SHGs in India
   (c) Weak SHGs are preferred by banks
   (d) All of the above
2. SHGs are vulnerable to
   (a) Loan sharks
   (b) High rate of interest by banks
   (c) Political interventions
   (d) None of the above
3. Which of the following does not apply to technology in microfinance?
   (a) MFIs must use technological advancement to grow
   (b) Technology helps in fast processing of data
   (c) Technology helps in democratising microfinance
   (d) Technology comes before financial services in microfinance
4. Which of the following is not yet focussed by microfinance with regard to application of technology?
   (a) Knowledge management
   (b) Customer identification
   (c) Credit appraisal
   (d) Credit disbursal
5. MFIs want bank licence because
   (a) It provides higher profit
   (b) It decreases regulatory compliances
   (c) It increases access to deposits
   (d) All of the above
6. Which of the following is not correct in relation to influence of banks on MFIs?
   (a) Banks provide cheaper loans to clients
   (b) MFIs can deliver banking services through business correspondent (BC) model
   (c) MFIs will not survive when banks flourish
   (d) None of the above
7. Loan waivers affect microfinance by
   (a) Polluting banking habits of people
   (b) Rising expectation of further loan waivers
   (c) Political campaign not to repay loans
   (d) All of the above
8. Which of the following microfinance organisation is not under the RBI regulations?
   (a) NGO-MFIs
   (b) NBFC-MFIs
   (c) Small finance banks
   (d) All of the above
9. Credit bureaus in India, in relation to microfinance, face which of the following problem?
   (a) Difficulty in identification of customers
   (b) Not having access to member-level data in SHGs
   (c) Non-cooperation of NBFC-MFIs
   (d) None of the above
10. Which of the following is true about regulation of microfinance?

(a) More and more microfinance organisations have been under regulatory control

(b) There is only one regulator in microfinance, i.e. RBI

(c) IRDA has nothing to do with MFIs

(d) All of the above

B. Review Questions

1. SHG management is not an endless process, it is going to decline in near future. Do you agree with this statement? Justify.
2. What are the areas of microfinance in which technology has not yet played an important role? What are the opportunities for technology in such areas?
3. Once an NBFC-MFI becomes a bank, it would have no incentive in operating in microfinance sector! Comment.
4. The easiest way to kill microfinance is to go ahead with loan waivers. Comment.
5. Discuss the pros and cons of credit bureaus in microfinance.
6. Regulatory space for microfinance is ever increasing. Comment.

C. Application-based Questions

1. Prepare a scenario based on the assumption that SHGs have saturated and there would be no changes in the number of SHGs. Based on this scenario, suggest changes to NRLM guidelines and strategy.
2. Compile the major regulations for the microfinance sector and find out the lapses. Suppose tomorrow, a legislation on microfinance has been introduced. How should that legislation address these shortcomings?

Case Studies

I Institutions or Livelihoods: Priority in PAGA

Mr. R. K. Anand, Commissioner-cum-Chief Administrator of the programme named as Poverty Alleviation through Group based Approach (PAGA), was in deep thought about what to do. He was reprimanded by the Hon'ble Chief Minister of the state on the slow progress of the PAGA project. A few days ago, he was the undisputed leader of the ambitious long-term project. Even today, his ability and expertise on microfinance-based livelihood promotion is not in question. The problem is that results would not be visible so soon.

PAGA was launched by the Government of Poorva Pradesh in 2015, and four years have already been over since then. The long-term project was supposed to be completed in 10 years. Having a budget of ₹105 billion, the project targeted eight million people to be brought out of the clutches of poverty. After four years, the project has spent only ₹4.5 billion against a budget of ₹32.50 billion. This was the bone of contention. Generally, under such circumstances the concerned official is replaced with one who can perform better. But Mr. Anand, a very senior bureaucrat, was handpicked by the Chief Minister himself. Even the concerned minister of Rural Development Department, under whom the PAGA project is established, was not in a position to do anything. Hence, the matter was referred to the Chief Minister.

The state of Poorva Pradesh, having a population of about 100 million, has about 40 per cent of people below the poverty line, which means these people at times find it hard to get two square meals. The predominantly agriculture-dependent state had long ago implemented an agricultural development programme, which helped the medium and large farmers to flourish. Its programme on small farmers' development could only benefit 14-15 per cent of the target group. Two decades ago, a subsidy-based entrepreneurship development programme was implemented, which was infamous for its corruption, resulted in loan default to the extent of 80 per cent of borrowers. Based on all these learning, the PAGA programme was designed. One of the major strategy of PAGA was that it would be implemented through self-help groups (SHGs) (informal institution having 10-20 members each).

The programme was really ambitious; not just because it targeted complete elimination of poverty, but also because of its unconventional strategy of implementing through SHGs. The idea was that if SHGs could be strengthened, then peer pressure would result in prompt repayment. The SHGs would be the foundation of all interventions.

An SHG was supposed to continue savings for three months; followed by 3-4 months of internal lending which was necessary before grading of SHG. If the SHG reaches a certain grade, then it would be provided bank loans. In 18 months, the SHG could take a full-scale entrepreneurial loan up to ₹500,000 of which 25 to 50 per cent could be provided as subsidy (50% for ST/SC, and 25% for others). For formation and strengthening of one SHG, an amount of ₹25,000 was provided.

The idea of the project was mooted by the Chief Minister whose party had come to power promising a better future for the poor people of the state. He handpicked Mr. Anand, who had an impeccable record of efficiency and honesty, as a young district collector he had done exemplary work in a tribal district and later, had successfully completed many other government initiatives. Mr. Anand visited a few other states and countries to study livelihood promotion programmes and concluded that a community-based microfinance programme would best serve the need of poverty alleviation. Accordingly, the project was designed and the government agreed to provide the support.

Mr. Anand was convinced that SHGs were the building blocks of PAGA. His first push was to promote SHGs. Unfortunately, there were not many trained people who could undertake such activities. It took about two years to recruit and train such a base of human resources. For the last two years, these functionaries have been engaged day in and day out in formation and strengthening of SHGs. By now, about 300,000 SHGs have been formed (against a target of 600,000 SHGs).

But the Chief Minister was unhappy because he wanted some significant results before he goes for the next election which would be due in another six months. "Mr. Anand, what would I say to my people?", he asked. "I provided you all the funds your asked for and a free hand. You could not hardly spend 10 per cent of allocated funds. Any other officer would have done better". The Chief Secretary who was also present in the meeting pointed out, "PAGA is a poverty alleviation programme. In the four years, you have not touched the income generation part; what is the priority – SHGs or people's livelihoods?"

"SHG formation and strengthening is a slow process. It requires intensive efforts on the part of concerned functionaries. Unless these SHG become strong enough we cannot provide them subsidy and large loans. Otherwise it would go down to drain", replied Mr. Anand. He further added that the sometimes institution building process is hampered by conflicts among people, without resolving that progress could not be made. The Chief Minister was not convinced. However, he had faith in the officer. He asked to present a roadmap before him in a week's time. The message, of course, was clear. The bureaucrat fraternity was not happy. If the government changes, his exit would be imminent.

Discussion Questions

1. Is it worth to spend a number of years in institution building before the livelihood interventions?
2. Suppose you replace Mr. Anand to take the programme ahead; what would you do?
3. Do you think the CM was expecting too much from the PAGA project?

II Scaling up the SHG Programme

ABC Foundation (ABCF) is an NGO working in the Maitripur district of an Eastern Indian State. It has been operating in the area for the last two decades and is well-known for its successful SHG programme. It has about 600 SHGs which are running quite well. Ms. Krishna Prabha, the Director of ABC foundation, is familiar with the district. She is also well-known in the civil society circle of the state. The district administration takes her advice on various matters related to rural development.

The district of Maitripur is quite backwards in terms of human development. A few programmes have been implemented in the district in the past; however, poverty headcount is still quite high (around 60% of people are still under poverty line). A recently launched programme of livelihood promotion is planned to be implemented in the district. The new programme titled 'Maitripur District Livelihood Programme' (MDLP) plans to cover three lakh households and has a target to eradicate poverty completely from the district. The programme will be implemented through SHGs and for each SHG there is a budget of ₹10,000 (₹200 million in total). The amount will be released in five equal instalments to the district in five years. Banks will lend to the SHGs for their enterprise projects and the government has also agreed to provide subsidies towards this.

The district administration earlier had sought expression of interest from NGOs, ABCF was considered to be the most suitable one. The criteria put by the government to select able NGOs for implementation were quite strict. Using the criteria, the District Collector (DC), who is the chairperson of the MDLP Implementation Committee, found that only ABC Foundation was meeting all the requirements.

Ms. Prabha were called for a meeting afterwards in which she was asked to prepare a detailed proposal for formation and management of 20,000 SHGs in the next five years and facilitate the members to come out of poverty.

The DC told Ms. Prabha, "This is going to be a great opportunity for you. So far, your annual budget was around ₹10 million every year; this programme will provide you ₹40 million every year". This was good news for Ms. Prabha; but, prima facie, she felt a bit of discomfort. She had expressed interest to implement the programme but had no idea that ABCF would be allocated the task of managing 20,000 SHGs, a huge number as compared to the 600 SHGs they managed. Further, ABCF had come to the figure of 600 SHGs over eight years, while MDLP would be implemented in only five years. She told she would take some time as she needed to discuss this with her colleagues. The DC insisted that she looks forward to the involvement of ABCF. "There are vultures ready to take a slice of the cake. I do not want such thing to happen in this district. The committee decided to allocate it to ABCF because you have been here for long and you have a good track record. You will be accountable", he added.

Next day, there was a meeting of all the senior officials of ABCF on this issue. One of the two SHG Coordinators, Mr. Sagar, a senior person having long experience in SHG management, believed that this programme was just impossible to implement. He said, "Prabha Ji, you must read the fine prints before taking any decision. Earlier, we implemented a donor funded programme on SHG, which gave us free hand. The MDLP is quite rigid in terms of fund release (see Exhibit II.(a)). The previous donor committed funds for a certain period and provided the salary and administrative costs for the employees and the organisation for the complete period. We were free to spend the money as per our own requirement. But here, it is tied up with a number of SHGs and their stages. In MDLP, you get only 10 per cent of money as advance, and the rest in six equal instalments each on completion of certain tasks. We are not acquainted with this type of output-based work".

Exhibit II.(a) Fund release pattern under MDLP

Instalment	Proportion of fund	Tasks to be completed before fund release	Cumulative time period (maximum)
1	10%	Signing of agreement	0 day (beginning of the programme)
2	15%	Formation of SHGs; Opening of bank account; Savings started	3 months
3	15%	Internal lending for 6 months	9 months
4	15%	Completion of training and exposures	12 months
5	15%	Bank linkage (getting loan from bank)	18 months
6	15%	Forming SHG federations, Initiation of income generation activities	24 months
7	15%	Completion of livelihood project	36 months

The other SHG coordinator, Ms. Rashmi, a rural management graduate, who has been working in ABCF for last one year pointed out a few other details:

- The ₹40 million of funds to be released to the district in a year must be utilised in the same year. Otherwise, it will lapse (no spill over for the next year).
- The livelihood activities are slotted for the last 18 months of an SHG cycle, this is not sufficient to enhance incomes significantly.
- In the structure of ABCF, it costs much higher to strengthen an SHG even if we limit interventions to a three-year cycle (see Exhibit II.(b)).

Exhibit II.(b) Structure of SHG Programme in ABCF

Designation	Responsible for	Salary per month in ₹
Community Organiser	15 SHGs	4,000
Project Officer	4 Community Organisers	12,500
SHG Coordinator	5 Project Officers	25,000

Note: In addition, 10 per cent of salary is provided for travel of staff; additional 10 per cent of all these costs are spent on administrative activities.

- At present, there are only two SHG coordinators, hence the overall coordination is managed by the Director (Ms. Prabha) at no additional cost. However, running 20,000 SHGs means it will have about 67 SHG coordinators, which will require a few other managers for coordination, who are likely to charge a salary of about ₹30,000 to ₹50,000 per month. A full-time accountant will also be required, whose salary would be around ₹15000-₹20000 per month.
- While the funds designated for each SHGs are fixed, the salary and administrative costs are likely to increase (at least 10% per year).

Ms. Rashmi added that SHG operations are already standardised. After 18 months of an SHG management cycle, when the federations are formed, the intervention can be less intensive and the SHGs can maintain themselves. However, each federation which includes 300 SHGs, has to be provided a support of ₹300,000 that includes preparation of livelihood projects, bank linkage, skill building, and supporting in implementation of livelihoods. She also told that the existing process of loan appraisal, which was done by the organisation as it was part of the donor funded project, is very lengthy and takes about four to six weeks. It could be completed in one week. She told that banks take very little time to do such things.

Ms. Prabha asked the two SHG coordinators to work out the detailed calculations in two days. Ms. Rashmi was of the view that if the structure was changed (30 SHGs – one Community Organiser), then the cost could probably be covered from MDLP funds. Mr. Sagar told that it would seriously compromise the process, which in turn will hamper the quality of SHGs.

Ms. Prabha heard from informal sources that the DC positively expected her to take up the programme. She also believed that the DC, operating with the government guidelines, would not be able to make any changes in the funding pattern. However, non-financial relaxations could be requested. The DC was ready to consider the existing 600 SHGs as part of the project, she was told.

There were other concerns as well. The MDLP programme would, in a way, be a saviour for ABCF, which was drying out of funds, particularly for the SHG programme, and had committed funds for employees' salary for only a year. Gone are the days when funding agencies provided grants for SHG management. On the other hand, Ms. Prabha, did not want to do a low-quality work and dilute the reputation of the organisation. She was in a dilemma whether to take up the programme or not. She also had to take into account the fact the district administration had been constant source of support for ABCF, about one-third of funds came from government projects. Saying no to the programme might also hamper the relationship with the government, as the DC is relying solely on the organisation.

Discussion Questions

1. Should ABCF go for the project?
2. What are the pros and cons if ABCF implements the project?
3. Develop a year-wise plan for implementing the project.
4. What relaxations should Ms. Prabha ask for if she decides to implement the project?

III Annapurna Finance Private Limited

Annapurna Finance Pvt. Ltd. (formerly known as Annapurna Microfinance Pvt. Ltd, AMPL) is an MFI headquartered in Bhubaneswar. This organisation was promoted by People's Forum, a social development organisation, which has been continuing its microfinance activity since the 1990s. In 2005, its microfinance operations were scaled up and became a separate programme named as Mission Annapurna. In 2009, the promoter acquired an NBFC and transferred the microfinance operations to the for-profit agency, which was later known as AMPL (Klus, 2013).

The vision of AMPL can be read as 'establishment of a self-sustainable and economically empowered rural, tribal and sub-urban society' (AMPL, 2017:4). The organisation had set a goal of empowering ten lakh poor women and households and create opportunities for 2.5 lakh entrepreneurs (AMPL, 2017:4-5).

The operations of AMPL are mainly spread in two states, Odisha and Chhatishgarh. By the end of Financial year 2016-17, it had a gross loan portfolio of ₹12.38 billion and a revenue of ₹2.31 billion, and about 0.9 million customers. It recorded a profit after tax of ₹189.1 million, which is substantial in the sense that it was also the year of demonetisation.

Products and Services

- Group loans through SHG and JLG Models
- Individual loans
- Safe water and sanitation loan products (new toilet loans, hand borewell loan, water connection loan, water purifier loans)
- Microenterprise loans
- Home improvement loans
- Dairy development loans
- Solar light loans

Other than offering these products, the organisation acts as business correspondent (BC) for DCB Bank and IDBI Bank. It also has provided insurance products to its clients in collaboration with various insurance providers.

Human Resource Management

The organisation had about 2300 employees, as of March 2017, recruited from various sources like direct recruitment, lateral recruitment, campus placement, etc. The new employees are inducted through rigorous training programmes covering various issues of vision, mission, SHG management, RBI guidelines, code of conduct, etc. The organisation makes efforts to provide an all-round career building avenue for employees and keeps on innovating to maintain a high level of employee engagement.

Internal Control Mechanism

Its branches are regularly audited and findings are shared. Field visits are undertaken regularly to ensure that the systems and procedures are followed. The findings are shared with the audit team at the head office, which in turn keeps an eye on the compliances. The findings are later shared with the Board of Directors. The organisation also has a robust internal audit mechanism. It has implemented an audit scoring tool, which helped in standardising its practices and reducing errors.

Risk Management

Microfinance has a lot of risks that include the risks of default by customers, risks associated with handling cash and the risks regarding geographical concentration. The organisation has developed a three-tier risk management structure, Board Committee, Management Risk Committee and Risk Management Unit. Using multiple levels of data and regular monitoring of same, the company makes a risk analysis and takes decision to manage these risks (AMPL, 2017:48). It has also fixed threshold norms for geographical concentration norms. In order to prevent theft and frauds related to cash, it has been encouraging cashless transactions. (AMPL, 2017:49)

Technology

The organisation keeps pace with the changing technological advancements in the financial services sector. It has android-based modules for Field Credit Officers, Branch Manager and Appraisal Officer. The modules are applicable both for SHG as well as JLG model of service delivery. The data structure and the information on bank details of customers have been updated, which would help in making cashless transactions (AMPL, 2017: 44). Apps have also been developed for recovery and tracking of loans. In partnership with Artoo (through its Intelligent Digital Loan Origination System), it has experimented with the use of tablets for loan processing (AMPL, 2017: 45). For better monitoring and control, the organisation has also been using geo-spatial information system. Online loan approval system has also been started through the use of e-FIMO (AMPL, 2017:45). It has a plan to have an integrated framework including cyber security, IS audit, outsourcing of IT services and IT policy and governance (AMPL, 2017:62).

Corporate Governance

The organisation has a Board of Directors including executive and non-executive directors. Three of the 11 directors are independent directors and five are nominee directors. Complying with the company laws, the organisation has appointed various committees, such as Audit Committee, CSR and SPM Committee, Nomination and Remuneration Committee and Risk Management Committee. The Nomination and Remuneration Committee has reviewed the performance of the boards and committees.

Discussion Questions

1. Calculate the important financial ratios for AMPL. What do you get from this analysis about the financial health of the organisation?
2. How do you asses the performance of AMPL in terms of governance of the organisation?
3. Operationally, do you think AMPL has a robust system of management?
4. Can you prepare a social performance report of the organisation based on the information given in the case? What more information is required for this purpose?

Table III.(a) Balance Sheet as at 31 March 2018 (figures in ₹ million)

I. Equities and Liabilities	31 March 2018	31 March 2017
Shareholders' fund		
Share capital	460.21	403.49
Reserves and surplus	1,966.27	1,310.19
	2,426.49	1,713.68
Non-current liabilities		
Long-term borrowings	8,399.59	8,293.38
Long-term provisions	283.52	26.47
	8,683.11	8,319.85
Current liabilities		
Short-term borrowings	780.00	130.00
Other current liabilities	8,311.92	5,010.28
Short-term provisions	34.77	137.46
	9,126.69	5,277.74
Total	20,236.28	15,311.28

II. Assets		
Non-Current Assets		
Fixed Assets		
Tangible assets	51.97	39.43
Intangible assets	13.55	9.09
Deferred tax assets (net)	109.03	54.49
Long-term loans and advances	4,735.25	2,702.30
Other non-current assets	885.91	579.74
	5,795.72	3,385.05
Current Assets		
Current investments		
Cash and bank balances	3,045.13	4,057.32
Short-term loans and advances	11,112.99	7,615.00
Other current assets	282.45	253.91
	14,440.57	11,926.23
Total	20,236.28	15,311.28

Note: Amounts have been rounded off to two decimals, hence there may be minor differences from the actual figures.
Source: *AMPL*, 2018

Table III.(b) Statement of Profit and Loss for the Year ended on 31 March 2018 (figures in ₹ million)

I. Income	2017-18	2016-17
Revenue from operations	3,236.36	2,310.97
Other income	173.66	163.76
Total income	3,410.03	2,474.73
II. Expenses		
Employee benefit expenses	768.66	533.59
Depreciation expense	31.88	24.21
Finance costs	1,734.39	1,380.34
Provision for standard and non-standard assets	491.33	92.35
Other expenses	246.25	154.74
Total expenses	3,272.51	2,185.22
Profit before tax	137.52	209.51
Tax expense		
Current tax	96.60	157.19
Deferred tax	(54.54)	(56.74)
Total tax expenses	42.06	100.44
Profit for the year	95.46	189.07
Earning per equity share - annualised		
Basic (₹)	2.30	5.25
Diluted (₹)	2.07	4.70
Nominal value per share (₹)	10.00	10.00

Note: Amounts have been rounded off to two decimals, hence there may be minor differences from the actual figures.
Source: *AMPL*, 2018

Table III.(c) Cash Flow Statement for the Year ended 31 March 2018 (figures in ₹ million)

A. Cash Flow from Operating Activities	**31 March 2018**	**31 March 2017**
Profit before tax	137.52	289.51
Adjustment to reconcile profit before tax to net cash flows	-	-
Depreciation and amortisation expense	31.88	24.21
Provision and write-offs	491.33	92.35
Profit on sale of current investments	(91.00)	(98.58)
Management stock option compensation	12.38	-
Operating profit before working capital changes	582.11	307.49
Movements in working capital	-	-
Increase in other current and non-current assets	(24.54)	(110.84)
Increase in loans and advances	(5,718.45)	(2,936.40)
Increase / decrease in other long-term liabilities, current liabilities, and provisions	184.98	(18.60)
Cash used from operations	(4,975.89)	(2,758.35)
Direct taxes paid	(118.86)	(196.67)
Net cash used in operating activities	(5,094.76)	(2,955.02)
B. Cash Flow from Investing Activities		
Purchase of fixed assets	(48.88)	(34.00)
Proceeds from sale of fixed assets	-	1.05
Increase in fixed deposits (net)	(458.26)	(192.16)
Profit on sale of current investments	91.00	98.58
Net Cash used in investing activities	(416.14)	(126.54)
C. Cash Flow from Financing Activities		
Proceeds from issuance of equity share capital	605.80	329.08
Proceeds from long-term and short-term borrowings	9,350.33	8,107.90
Repayment of long-term and short-term borrowings	(5,568.07)	(3,563.44)
Dividend paid on preference shares (incl. divided dist. tax)	(2.08)	(2.11)
Net cash from financing activities	4,385.98	4,871.43
Net increase in cash and cash equivalents (A+B+C)	(1,124.91)	1,789.87
Cash and cash equivalents in the beginning of the year	3,827.70	2,037.83
Cash and cash equivalents at the end of the year	2,702.79	3,827.70
Components of cash and cash equivalents	-	-
Balance with banks	-	-
On current accounts	2,518.45	2,673.82
Deposit with original maturity of less than 3 months	180.00	1,150.00
Cash on hand	4.34	3.88
Total cash and cash equivalents	2,702.79	3,827.70

Note: Amounts have been rounded off to two decimals, hence there may be minor differences from the actual figures.

Source: AMPL, 2018

IV BASIX

BASIX was found by Vijay Mahajan in the year 1996. It was the first commercial MFI of India. In fact it has many firsts to its credit, such as it was the first MFI to secure an external commercial borrowing, first MFI to receive a bank loan, first MFI to raise equity, first MFI to get a CRISIL rating and first to offer microinsurance (Bandopadhyay, 2016).

It should be clear to the reader that BASIX does not refer to any single organisation, rather it is a congregation of various agencies as a part of the BASIX Social Enterprise Group. The holding company is known as Bhartiya Samruddhi Social Investment Servies (BASICS Ltd). It comprises the following entities:[1]

- **Bharatiya Samruddhi Finance Limited (BSFL)** It used to be the flagship organisation of the group. This offered microfinance services. At some point of time, until the AP crisis, it used be the source of about 90 per cent of revenue of the group.
- **Indian Grameen Services (IGS)** It was the developmental wing of the organisation. It existed before the establishment of BASIX, but later became a part of the group.
- **BASIX Consulting** Drawing experiences of BASIX, it provides consulting support to other organistions.
- **BASIX Academy for Building Livelong Employability (BA-LAB)** This is a skill development initiative of the organisation.
- **BASIX-Krishi** It helps in the agriculture and business development services of BASIX as a part of which its main activity is developing supply chains for agricultural commodities.
- **BASIX Sub-K** It provides cashless financial services to people using the BC Model. In the recent past, this company has grown significantly.
- BASIX Municipality Waste Ventures Ltd, works on solid waste management.
- **C-TRAN Consulting** This is an organisation working on the issues of environmental, energy and climate change related matters. It was originally established as an independent company, later BASIX group acquired majority stake.
- The Livelihood School, renamed later as Institute of Livelihood Research and Training (ILRT), is responsible for imparting livelihood education / training and conducting research.
- Krishna Bhima Samruddhi Local Area Bank (KBS-LAB) was originally established by BASIX; now it has been divested and is no longer owned by the group.

Motivation

To understand BASIX organisations, one must know the motivation behind it. Vijay Mahajan was a graduate of IIT Delhi and IIM Ahmedabad. He was also a mid-career fellow in Woodrow Wilson School of Public and International Affairs. Having experience in the industry, he along with some others, such as Deep Joshi, an MIT graduate, founded Professional Assistance for Development Action (PRADAN) in 1982. While working in PRADAN, Vijay and some of his colleagues observed that there was a dire need of credit at the grassroot level. Poor people used to get credit from local moneylenders at an exorbitant rate of interest (5 to 10 per cent per month). But banks did not consider the poor as creditworthy and did not lend them. Here was an opportunity for business, which would contribute positively to the society. Financing the poor, even with a profit, would help them and add to their livelihoods. Grant money would not be sufficient for such initiatives. There was already the proven experience of microfinance by organisations like SEWA and Grameen Bank. Hence, the idea of a commercial MFI came up and BASIX was established.

Products and Strategy

Initially, credit was the primary product of the organisation. After five years of experience, in 2001, it conducted an impact assessment which said that about half of the customers became better off, about a quarter

1. http://www.basixindia.com/index.php?option=com_content&task=view&id=37&Itemid=51. Retrieved on 13 April 2019.

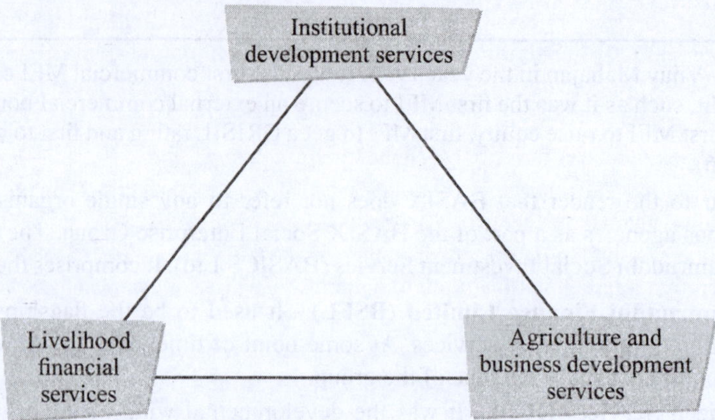

Fig. IV.(a) Livelihood Triad

remained at the same level, while the other quarter of borrowers became poorer. This was an eye opener for the organisation, and it started various other products. A new approach known as 'Triad' (Figure IV.(a)) was conceived which had three components, financial services, institution building services and agriculture and business development services.

Growth

BASIX was not the number one MFI in Indian microfinance industry. Although it was the first to start such operations, the followers quickly overtook it. By 2009, within Andhra Pradesh, it was a distant fifth in terms of number of clients served (Sriram, 2012). By March, 2010, it had a total loan outstanding of USD 712 million, covering 11.76 lakh of active borrowers in about 30,000 villages (Harper et al, 2011).

What was Different?

BASIX put substantial effort on developing its human resources. Being the first mover in the industry, it did not have the luxury of having a trained cadre of people. In a way, it not just prepared people for its own firm, rather it trained them for an industry. Many people who later joined other MFIs received initial orientation with BASIX. It is the thorough orientation at BASIX which made people conservative in terms of expanding business.

The organisation had a quarterly review meeting, in which people from all spheres were invited to participate. It was an example of how an organisation can be transparent in its operations.

While working for the expansion of business, BASIX also made efforts in policy advocacy. It made regular contacts with state and central governments and other regulatory bodies and communicated the need for promoting microfinance industry. It played a crucial role in promoting the industry association, MFIN.

Internationally also the organisation made a presence. Vijay Mahajan was elected as the member of executive committee of CGAP in 2006. In 2010, he became the chair of the executive committee of CGAP.

As an individual as well as the person representing BASIX, Vijay made a series of efforts before the microfinance crisis and in its aftermath, to bring in a proper working environment.

The Downfall

After the AP Crisis in 2010, recovery of loan was hit adversely. This led to financial problems in BASIX. Coincidentally, the organisation had recently started massive expansion.

Present Scenario

Even today, the microfinance operations of the organisation have not been revived effectively. However, initiatives like Sub-K have succeeded and the latter is doing extremely well.

Discussion Questions

1. How is BASIX as an organisation different from others?
2. What are the strategic mistakes done by BASIX?
3. Prepare a strategy for revival of microfinance operation of the organisation?

V Bharat Financial Inclusion Limited (BFIL)

The Bharat Financial Inclusion Limited (BFIL), formerly known as SKS Microfinance Ltd, is the largest microfinance company in India, as on March 2018, having a gross loan portfolio of `125.94 billion. It has 1567 branches all over the country and has more than seven million borrowers. Its interest rate is also one of the lowest (19.75% per annum) in comparison to other NBFC-MFIs). The company has shown exceedingly good performance having a 44.3 per cent compound annual growth rate (CAGR) in its assets under management (BFIL, 2018).

Mission

To provide financial services to the economically weaker sections. (BFIL, 2018)

Vision

To serve 50 million households across India and other parts of the world and also create a commercial microfinance model that delivers high value to our customers. (BFIL, 2018)

Origin

BFIL is the renamed version of the company called SKS Microfinance Limited. The roots of the company go back to 1997, with the establishment of Swayam Krishi Sangam (SKS Society) as a not-for-profit entity. Considering the limitations of running a not-for-profit, in 2003, the organisation transformed into a private limited company and expanded microfinance operations. Initially, the company was held by five mutual benefit trusts and later, private equity funds were also invested. It was registered as an NBFC in 2005, and was converted into a public limited company in 2009 (SKS, 2010). In 2016, the company was renamed as Bharat Financial Inclusion Limited.

The founder of SKS was Dr. Vikram Akula, a graduate of Tufts and Yale and a Ph.D. from University of Chicago. Under his leadership, SKS grew fast and by 2009, it was already the largest MFI in India. The issue of initial public offer (IPO)was addressed during his tenure in 2010.

The Business

The main business of BFIL is lending to poor. These loans are of small amount, which is why it comes under the purview of microfinance, and such loans are invariably unsecured in nature. The market for such finances traditionally were characterised by high interest rate. BFIL attempted to fulfil this gap by providing cheaper loans. Other than extending loans, the organisation also has other financial and non-financial products. The company has a tie up with several organisations for selling their products for which BFIL provides loans. This includes tie up with TNS Mobile India for mobile phones, Usha International Ltd and Singer India Ltd for sewing machines, Hero Cycles Ltd and TI Cycles Ltd for bicycles, Eureka Forbes Ltd for water purifiers, Hero MotoCorp Ltd for two-wheelers, TTK Prestige Pvt Ltd for pressure cookers, and Godrej & Boyce Mfg Co Ltd and Samsung India Electronics Pvt Ltd for refrigerators. The organisation has also started home improvement loans.

The company lends primarily through the group lending model that uses peer pressure and this helps in making the borrowers make prudent decisions. This furthers the financial discipline in the borrowers, and hence helps in decreasing the moral hazard.

Operations

BFIL operates in 342 districts of India through its 1567 branches. It has expanded to almost all parts of India including 16 states and about half of the districts of the country. A highlight of the organisation is that 80 per cent of its operations are located in rural areas, this is significant in the context of increasing share of urban microfinance.

Financials

In the last financial year (2017-18), BFIL recorded a revenue of ₹ 21.02 billion and profit after tax of ₹ 4.55 billion (details in Table V.a). It has grown consistently in the last five years and has been able to maintain a steady financial health.

The company has maintained capital adequacy ration of 33.2 per cent, which is way higher than the statutory requirement of 15 per cent.

Human Resources

At present, the organisation has 16,021 employees. To facilitate the field based employees who generally keep on moving place to place, BFIL uses the biometric attendance system. Also, it has a sound training system in place for induction of new employees. A human resource information system is followed to facilitate fast processing of HR related services like approvals. Recruitment at manager level is generally done through lateral hiring from banking and financial sector. The Great Place to Work Institute of India has categorised BFIL as one of the 15 best workplaces of 2018 (BFIL, 2018).

Corporate Governance

The Board of Directors of the company has qualified and experienced people, including bankers, investors, industry experts and professionals. Six of the eight directors are independent directors (BFIL, 2018).

In the aftermath of the IPO and the AP microfinance crisis, the company was highly criticised for its questionable corporate governance practices, such as providing extraordinary benefits to its promoters (Sriram, 2010). Later, the founder Dr. Vikram Akula, left unceremoniously. In the recent years, however, there have been positive reports in this regard.

Technology

BFIL has been using state-of-the-art information technology for managing its business. Its operations are technology driven and now the mobile technology is being used for enhancing its effectiveness. This helps in making the last mile delivery easier, this is particularly important because its area of operations includes remote villages. As the functionaries are based in field to help them in providing reliable data, it has enabled them with a GPS-based platform. Even the HR compliance has been automated. As a result of its effort, the company has transformed the purely cash based transactions into cashless mode (BFIL, 2018).

Risk Management

Based on its experience of AP Microfinance, BFIL avoids geographical concentration to avoid any political fallout. It has a portfolio mix of different states and has put a limit that any state's gross loan portfolio would not exceed 15 to 17.5 per cent of the total gross loan portfolio. Other than this, it has an integrated cash management system, a strong product and process design, and an internal audit mechanism certified with ISO 9001:2015. The company also has been a member of all credit bureaus that helps making customer data available for decision making (BFIL, 2018).

Good Practices

The company has taken several steps to assure client protection. This includes maintaining confidentiality of client data, transparent mechanism and responsible way of pricing of interest rates, redressal of client grievances and assuring that the employees follow proper recovery practices. Strict KYC norms are followed and records of credit bureaus are verified which helps in avoiding over-indebtedness of the clients.

Merger with IndusInd Bank

BFIL is in the process of merger with IndusInd Bank. The process of merger is at an advanced stage and upon the merger, BFIL will be a subsidiary of the bank. The merger is going to provide several advantages to BFIL. It will have low cost funds because of the savings and deposit products and as a result, it can bring down the interest rate further. Being part of a bank, it would have a more robust risk management framework and it would be less prone to the political and other risks, such as the AP microfinance crisis and demonetisation.

Discussion Questions

1. How is the financial health of BFIL? Has it been growing satisfactorily?
2. What are the good practices followed by BFIL?
3. What challenges will it face in the event of merger with IndusInd Bank.

Table V.(a) Performance of BFIL

Operation Performance					
Operational Highlights	**Mar-14**	**Mar-15**	**Mar-16**	**Mar-17**	**Mar-18**
No. of branches	1,255	1,268	1,324	1,399	1,567
No. of districts	294	314	323	322	342
No. of employees	8,932	9,698	11,991	14,755	16,021
No. of members (in million)	5.78	6.40	6.97	6.70	7.27
Disbursements for the year (₹ in billion)	47.87	6,8.90	120.87	146.66	184.72
Gross loan portfolio (₹ in billion)*	31.12	41.84	76.88	91.49	125.94
Financial Highlights	**Mar-14**	**Mar-15**	**Mar-16**	**Mar-17**	**Mar-18**
Incremental borrowings* (₹ in billion)	37.03	55.61	83.09	80.22	124.01
Total revenue (₹ in billion)	5.44	8.03	13.20	17.27	21.02
Profit after tax (₹ in billion)	0.69	1.87	3.03	2.89	4.55
Total assets (₹ in billion)	24.97	46.98	71.53	104.17	115.30
Return on average asset	2.30%	4.30%	4.20%	0.8%	2.8%
Return on average equity	16.70%	21.60%	25.10%	3.9%	14.3%
Comparison of FY18 and 17	**FY18**		**FY17**		
Particulars	**(₹ in billion)**	**% to Revenue**	**(₹ in billion)**	**% to Revenue**	**Increase/ Decrease**
Income from operations	19.17	91.20%	15.53	89.90%	23.40%
Other income	1.84	8.80%	1.74	10.10%	5.70%
Gross revenue	21.02	100%	17.27	100%	21.70%
Employee benefit expenses	5.26	25%	4.06	23.50%	29.60%
Finance costs	7.10	33.80%	6.22	36%	14.10%
Other expenses	1.62	7.70%	1.34	7.80%	20.70%
Depreciation and amortisation	0.13	0.60%	0.12	0.70%	3.70%
Provisions and write-offs	2.35	11.20%	3.59	20.80%	(34.6)%
Total expenditure	16.47	78.40%	15.35	88.80%	7.30%
Profit before tax	4.54	21.60%	1.92	11.20%	135.80%
Tax expense	(0.007)	0%	(0.96)	(5.6)%	(99.3)%
Profit after tax	4.55	21.70%	2.89	16.80%	57.20%

ource: *BFIL*, 2018)- rounding done for figures

VI Ujjivan Small Finance Bank (USFB)

Introduction

Ujjivan was founded by Mr. Samit Ghosh in the year 2004, initially, as a private limited company. In 2005, it received the NBFC licence. The organisation has an exemplary model of microfinance business that sustained through many crises.

The idea of Ujjivan came to Mr. Ghosh when he already was an astute banker. He was an MBA from Wharton and had international exposure of working in leadership positions of banks having global stature. Thus, he knew the ins and outs of the banking sector. What intrigued him was the potential of banking with poor. There were already some established models, such as the Grameen Bank of Bangladesh. The first thing Mr. Ghosh did was to visit various microfinance models and during this process, he met people like Vijay Mahajan of BASIX, Muhammad Yunus of Grameen Foundation and Al. Fernandes of MYRADA. These visits and interactions convinced him to establish a new microfinance organisation.

An interesting fact that distinguishes Ujjivan is that it operates primarily in the urban areas although traditionally microfinance was considered appropriate for rural areas only.

With a humble beginning as an organisation, Ujjivan started at a time when microfinance industry was already in the growth stage. It did not have the first mover advantage and it had to play in a field where there already were some known players. The journey of Ujivan is interesting.

Growth

The growth of Ujjivan can be categorised into various phases. The first two years (2005-07) are termed as the pilot phase. During this period, the company had expanded to three cities, Bengaluru, Kolkata and Delhi and already had 17 branches with a staff strength of 285. It had acquired 24,000 customers and had disbursed ₹135 million as loan (Roy, 2018: 97). This phase helped the organisation in understanding its customers.

It was followed by a high growth phase for about three and half years (2007-10) till the AP crisis emerged. By the end of 2010-11, the organisation had 351 branches, staff strength of about 4000, disbursement of ₹20.73 billion, and already had about a million customers (0.992 million).

This phase of growth was dented by the AP Crisis, which was visible in the financial result of 2011-12. During 2012-16, the organisation revived and again recorded a high rate of growth. By the end of financial year 2015-16, it had a gross loan portfolio of ₹53.89 billion, customer numbering 3.3 millon, revenue of ₹10.28 billion and net profit of ₹1.77 billion. In September 2015, Ujjivan also received the in-principle approval for being a small finance bank (SFB). In May 2016, the organisation successfully issued IPO and raised 8.82 billion, oversubscribed 41 times!

Before it could transform itself into SFB, Ujjivan had to tackle another crisis, this time, it was not exactly targeted at microfinance, rather it was on the whole country. In November 2016, the unexpected demonetisation was announced and it hurt the microfinance industry. Ujjivan had a tough time sailing through this. Despite this problem, Ujjivan continued its plan to commence the business of SFB.

The robust mechanism and achievements of Ujjivan have led it to have a good rating as given in Table VI.a.

Fund Raising

The initial capital came from Mr. Samit Ghosh himself and Ramamoorthy (₹1.1 lakh each), in January 2005 Some friends contributed further, but only in August that year, they were able to acquire a substantial fund from Bellweather Microfinance Trust (₹24 million). All this took the organisation to have a capital base of 28 milion (Roy, 2018:89). This helped the organisation to apply for NBFC licence. Later, the pilot phase of the programme was capitalised by two significant FDIs, Unitus and Michael and Susan Dell Foundation (MSDF) who together contributed ₹35 million.

Table VI.(a) Ratings Provided to Ujjivan

Credit Ratings		
Rating Agency	**Instrument**	**Rating**
CARE	Long-term Bank Loan Rating	CARE A+
CARE	Long-term Debt Rating (Non-convertible Debenture)	CARE A+
CRISIL	Short-term Rating	CRISIL A1+
ICRA	Long-term Rating (Non-convertible Debenture)	ICRA A+
ICRA	Short-term Rating	ICRA A1+
Credit Gradings		
CRISIL	MFI Grading	mfR1

Source: https://www.ujjivan.com/html/credit_ratings.php. Retrieved on 23 March 2019

Operations

Ujjivan operates across the country, its area of operations includes 24 states /union territories of India. By the end of 2015, it had operations in 209 districts of India and had a network of 470 branches. It has operations in all regions of India and about two-third of its customers were from rural and semi-urban areas, which are generally treated as underserved and unserved areas in terms of banking operations (Ujjivan, 2016.129). The organisation offered group as well as individual loan products as follows:

- **Group Loan Products** business loans, family loans for education, home improvements, repayment of existing debts, etc., agricultural loan, emergency loan that is disbursed in 24 hours, education loan, top-up loans and Viswas loans (for loyal customers). The amount of loan generally ranges from ₹5000 to 50,000 (different loans have different kinds of limits) (Ujjivan, 2016).
- **Individual Loan Products** agricultural loans, higher education loan, home improvement loan (both secured and unsecured), business loan, livestock loan, Pragati loan and secured business loan (Ujjivan, 2016).

Before any loan is processed, initial information like credit bureau data is analysed and it is seen if the customer meets the eligibility criteria. Loan appraisal is done based on various information, such as repayment capacity and then the file is processed. Personal discussion and credit check is done further before sanctioning of loans. Upon loan disbursement, regular monitoring of loan utilisation is done (Ujjivan, 2016).

Human Resources

The organisation has a very experienced team of senior management. Mr Samit Ghosh, the CEO and MD already had three decades of global banking experiences in banks like Citibank, Standard Charted, Bank of Muskat India, and HDFC Bank (Ujjivan, 2016). Ujjivan has more than 11,000 employees. The organisation has a sound HR policy which led it to be consistently ranked by the Great Place to Work® Institute. It has an employee stock option plan as well (Ujjivan, 2018).

Welfare Activities

Through its corporate social responsibility (CSR) wing namely Parinaam foundation, the organisation has undertaken several initiatives of community development. These initiatives include repair of water pump and tanks in schools, upgrading government hospitals, rain water harvesting, building bus stands, building and repairing toilets in schools, etc. It has also contributed to the cause of Swach Bharat Mission. An important initiative of the organisation includes a financial literacy programme named as Diksha (Ujjivan, 2016).

Financials

In the fiscal year 2023–24, Ujjivan Small Finance Bank (USFB) demonstrated robust financial performance. The bank reported a net profit of ₹1,281 crore, marking a 17% year-on-year increase. Net Interest Income (NII) rose by 26% to ₹3,409 crore, supported by a Net Interest Margin (NIM) of 9.3%. The Gross Loan Book expanded by 24% to ₹29,780 crore, with disbursements reaching ₹23,389 crore. Total deposits grew by 23% to ₹31,462 crore, and the Current Account Savings Account (CASA) ratio stood at 26.5%. The bank's balance sheet size increased by 21% to ₹40,422 crore, and Earnings Per Share (EPS) improved to ₹6.65. These figures reflect USFB's strong growth trajectory and operational efficiency.

Technology

Small Finance Banks need to be technology savvy. This would help them in maintaining competitiveness, particularly when they have to compete with established large banks. The loan officers of Ujjivan use tablets to access information of customers, credit bureau reports, and other details The organisation uses BR.Net as its core banking solution and it has been integrated with its front end operations. It uses open source softwares for its email and complaint portals. Ujjivan uses IBM's private cloud resilience services which helps it in running a secure business operation (Ujjivan, 2016).

Risk Management

Risk management includes a number of dimensions. The first one is the need of fulfiling the prudential norms like capital adequacy as per the Basel II norms. For meeting operations risk, the organisation takes a number of measures, such as granting individual loans to people only if they have a good track record of repayment, mandating co-borrowers, requiring guaranteers if the amount of loan is more than one lakh rupees and making a higher provisioning for the individual loans than group lending products (Ujjivan, 2016). Further, microfinance business deals with cash transactions, hence there is always a chance of fraud. In some instances, people with questionable integrity were removed. A vigilance vertical was also set up (Roy, 2018: 160). Branch credit policies were formulated and branch profiling was done based on the various risk parameters (Roy, 2018: 164).

Crisis Management

When the AP crisis occurred in 2010, the immediate need was to maintain liquidity. This was done through funds from SIDBI, IDBI Bank and some developed world markets. Other than this, debt servicing, operating expenses, meeting the requirement of good customers was required. In some states like Tamil Nadu and West Bengal, there was a possibility of spread of the non-repayment. Another problem was to clarify the confusion of staff members. Staff salaries had to be paid regularly. Finally, community contacts had to be strengthened, particularly using the Parinam Foundation networks (Roy, 2018: 119).

As the banks suspended their lines of credits, Ujjivan used instruments like non-convertible debentures and securitisation for acquiring funds. It also raised equity capital to the tune of ₹128 crores, which was a significant achievement as it happened during the difficult times. This could be done due to the existing investors' references (Roy, 2018: 124).

Internalising the learning from the crisis, the organisation signed an agreement with various credit bureaus to avoid this kind of problem. Internal processes and documentation quality were also strengthened (Roy, 2018: 124). It also had a brand communication strategy in place that helped it communicate with the outer world effectively. Social media was also used to reach out to communicate its point of views (Roy, 2018: 125).

When the demonetisation took place in 2016, the immediate task was to communicate to own staff members who were spread out in field. As a matter of principle, it strictly did not receive any payment in the specified bank notes (invalid ones), and initially halted the collection for three days, which was later extended to one week. Customers were also told that these delays would not make any impact on their credit profile. Payment terms were also relaxed.

The overall theme was to pay whatever you can, but keep paying something so that the relationship is kept alive and on completion of one loan repayment, the customer would be considered for another. The cardinal concern conveyed to the field staff was, do not pressurise the customers as that will make him/her hostile and go to local leaders (Roy, 2018:197).

Events were also organised for Ujjivan staff members who felt stressed because of hostility by customers and in these family events, staff was engaged in communication and reassurance.

Transformation

Transforming the organisation from an NBFC-MFI to an SFB is an arduous task. The organisation had a three-phase plan for this, prepare, transform and grow. In the preparation phase, it planned to meet the changed regulatory norms, redesign products, improve technologies to meet the new system and train its people to meet the new challenges. In the transforming phase, it would consolidate its existing operations in the new organisation structure and regulatory framework. This phase would not include adding to the branch network, but new products would be added. This was required because as an SFB, it would have savings products which earlier, it was not allowed to offer. In the growth phase, it would go for geographic expansions as well as cover new segments of customers (Ujjivan, 2016: 130).

Present Situation

Strategically, USFB completed a reverse merger with its holding company, Ujjivan Financial Services Limited, consolidating into a single listed entity. This move enhanced shareholder value and streamlined corporate governance. The bank expanded its branch network by adding 123 new branches, totalling 752 across 26 states and union territories. The customer base grew to approximately 9.1 million, with 9.1 lakh new customers added during the year. USFB also increased its focus on secured lending, with the share of secured products in the loan portfolio rising to 30.2%, driven by growth in affordable housing and MSME segments. Additionally, the bank declared a final dividend of ₹1.5 per equity share for FY 2023–24, reflecting its commitment to delivering shareholder returns.

Discussion Questions

1. Analyse the financial situation of Ujjivan. Does it have a sound financial status?
2. How robust are the systems and processes that Ujjivan has in place?
3. How did Ujjivan survive through crises like AP microfinance crisis of 2010 and the demonetisation in 2016?
4. How did it cope with the challenges in transforming the organisation from an MFI to an SFB?

Table VI.(b) Balance sheet as on 31 March 2024 (in thousand rupees)

Capital and Liabilities	As on 31.3.24	As on 31.3.23
Capital	19,314,285	21,547,066
Employees Stock Options and Purchase Outstanding	723,238	512,205
Reserves and Surplus	36,097,398	20,031,799
Deposits	314,621,598	255,376,822
Borrowings	21,708,153	26,414,640
Other Liabilities and Provisions	11,757,490	9,286,243
Total	**404,222,162**	**333,168,775**

Assets		
Cash and Balances with Reserve Bank of India	25,183,148	23,052,710
Balances with Banks and Money at Call and Short Notice	184,768	1,783,218
Investments	97,660,182	85,103,075
Advances	268,829,191	212,896,611
Fixed Assets	4,266,643	2,828,799
Other Assets	8,098,230	7,504,362
Total	**404,222,162**	**333,168,775**
Contingent Liabilities	1,449,074	950,034
Bill for collection	–	–

Table VI.(c) Profit and Loss Statement for the Financial Year 2023–24

Particulars	2023–24	2022–23
I. Income		
Interest Earned	56,771,541	41,649,947
Other Income	7,867,519	5,891,909
Total	**64,639,060**	**47,541,856**
II. Expenditure		
Interest Expended	22,677,039	14,670,926
Operating Expenses	22,790,991	18,020,597
Provisions and Contingencies	6,356,123	3,851,116
Total	**51,824,153**	**36,542,639**
III. Profit		
Net profit for the year	12,814,907	10,999,217
Profit brought forward	5,068,695	(723,518)
Total	**17,883,602**	**10,275,699**
IV. Appropriations		
Transfer to		
(a) Statutory Reserves	3,203,727	2,749,804
(b) Investment Reserve Account	–	3,404
(c) Capital Reserve	–	–
(d) Preference Dividend	–	220,000
(e) Equity dividend*	683,410	1,465,944
Basic (₹) (Refer Schedule 18 (25))	6.65	5.82
Diluted (₹) (Refer Schedule 18 (25))	6.54	5.81

Table VI.(d) Cash Flow Statement for the Financial Year 2023–24 (in thousand rupees)

Particulars	For the year ended March 31, 2024	For the year ended March 31, 2023
A. Cash Flow from Operating Activities		
Net profit/(loss) after taxation	12,814,907	10,999,217
Tax adjustment	4,206,748	3,673,159
Net Profit/(Loss) before taxation	**17,021,655**	**14,672,376**
Adjustments for:		
Depreciation on Bank's Property	982,896	902,785
Loss on sale of Land, Building & Other assets (net)	14,722	6,701
Expense on employee stock option	116,216	90,247
Provision for Non Performing Assets	1,885,324	498,068
Provision for Standard Assets	264,125	(322,365)
Provision for depreciation on investment	–	(3,404)
Interest earned on fixed deposits	103,785	(108,631)
Profit on sale of available for sale (AFS) securities	117063	–
Amortisation of premium on HTM investments	241,464	255,662
Preference dividend to eUFSL adjusted pursuant to the scheme of amalgamation	110000	–
Operating Profit/(Loss) before Working Capital changes	**20,415,554**	**15,991,439**
Adjustments for :		
(Increase) /Decrease in Advances	(57,817,904)	(50,362,965)
(Increase)/Decrease in Investments in other than HTM securities	(4,900,637)	(25,577,285)
(Increase)/Decrease in Other Assets	(4,396,509)	(1,065,153)
Increase/ (Decrease) in Deposits	60,958,136	72,454,654
Increase/ (Decrease) in Other Liabilities	2,058,921	1,960,894
Cash generated from/(used in) Opeartions	**16,317,561**	**13,401,584**
Direct Taxes paid (net of funds)	(492,930)	(2,803,717)
B. Cash Flow from Operating Activities		
Proceeds from sale of Fixed Assets	21,612	9,202
Investment In HTM securities (Net)	(7,780,871)	(18,248,700)
Deposits (created)/encashed with Banks and financial institutions (Net)	1,674,472	(1,464,056)
Purchase of Fixed Assets including WIP	(2,456,818)	(1,253,562)
Net Cash Flow used in Investing Activities (B)	**(8,541,605)**	**(20,957,116)**
C. Cash Flow from Financing Activities		
Proceeds from issue of equity shares (net of issue expenses)	202,634	4,661,212
Increase/(Decrease) in Borrowings (Net)	4,706,487	8,779,023
Preference dividend including interim dividend paid during the year	–	(110,000)
Equity dividend paid during the year	683,409	(1,465,944)
Net Cash Flow generated from Financing Activities (C)	5,187,262	11,864,291

Net Increase/(Decrease) in Cash and Cash Equivalents (A+B+C)	2,095,764	1,505,042
Cash and Cash Equivalents at the beginning of the year	23,136,947	21,631,905
Cash and Cash Equivalents acquired pursuant to scheme of amalgamation (refer note 18(41))	6,911.00	
Cash and Cash Equivalents at the end of the year	25,239,622	23,136,947
Notes to Cash Flow Statement:		
Cash and Cash equivalents includes the following:		
Cash and Bank Balances with Reserve Bank (Schedule 6)	25,183,148	23,052,710
Balance with Bank and Money at Call & Short Notice (Schedule 7)	184,768	1,783,218
	25,367,916	24,835,928
Balances not considered as part of Cash and Cash equivalents		
Less: Bank Deposits with original maturity more than 3 months or Bank Deposits under lien	128,294	(1,698,981)
Cash and Cash Equivalents at the end of the year	25,239,622	23,136,947

References

Accion (n.d.) About Accion: Our History. URL: https://www.accion.org/about-accion/history/ retrieved on 8 April 2025.

Akhtar, F. (2024). 'Financial Inclusion Worldwide' in Anon. *Impact Finance Barometer 2024*, by Convergences Zero Carbon Poverty. pp. 5. URL: https://www.convergences.org/wp-content/uploads/2024/09/BFI-2024_VFINAL_EN_compressed.pdf retrieved on 8 April 2024.

Alexander, G. (2001). "An empirical analysis of microfinance: Who are the clients?" P aper presented at 2001 Northeastern Universities Development Consortium Conference.

AMPL. (2017). "Annual Report 2017". Bhubneswar: AMPL.

AMPL. (2018). "Audited Financial Statement of Annapurna Finance Private Ltd". Bhubaneswar: AMPL.

Anon. (2017). "Key Figures in Financial Inclusion – World". *Microfinance Barometer 2018*. Paris: Convergences. http://www.convergences.org/wp-content/uploads/2018/09/BMF_2018_EN_VFINALE.pdf. Retrieved on 17 April 2019

Akerlof, George A. (1970). The Market for 'Lemons': Quality Uncertainty and the Market Mechanism. *Quarterly Journal of Economics*. The MIT Press. 84 (3): 488–500.

Armendariz, B. and Morduch, J. (2010) *The Economics of Microfinance*. 2nd edition, Indian reprint. New Delhi: PHI Learning Pvt. Ltd.

BASIX. (2011). Evolution of Ag/Bds. http://www.basixindia.com/new/?paged=2: Retrieved on 5 April 2019.

Bologun, J. and Hailley, V. P. (2008). *Exploring Strategic Change.* Third edition, Prentice Hall

(18 Jan 2018). "Demonetisation-induced pain almost gone for microfinance sector: experts". *Business Line*. https://www.thehindubusinessline.com/economy/demonetisationinduced-pain-almost-gone-for-microfinance-sector-experts/article10040243.ece. Retrieved on 29 March 2019

CGAP. (2004). "The Impact of Interest Rate Ceilings on M1icrofinance", Donor Brief 18, Washington DC: CGAP

Business Standard (7 Jan 2019). "eSthenons Technologies Enables NBFCs to On-board MSME Borrowers under 30 Minutes". https://www.business-standard.com/article/printer-friendly-version?article id=1190107001561

CGAP. (2001). "Resource Guide to Microfinance Assessments". Focus Note No. 22. Washington DC: CGAP

Chambers, R. (December 2006). "What is Poverty: Concepts and Measures. Poverty in Focus" International Poverty Centre. Brazil: UNDP

Chambers, R. and Conway, G. (1992). "Sustainable Rural Livelihoods: Practical Concepts for the 21st Century". IDS Discussion Paper 296. Bringhton: IDS

Cooper, R. G., (1994). "Debunking the Myths of New Product Development". *Research Technology Management* 37: 40-50

Cooper, R. G., Easingwood, C. J., Edgett, S. J., Kleinschmidt, E. J., and Storey, C. (1994). "What Distinguishes the Top Performing New Products in Financial Services". *Journal of Product Innovation Management* 11, 281 299

Datta, S., Dutta, S, and Bhaskaran, R. P. (2011). "Crisis in Indian Microfinance. A Tale of Growth and (No) Regulation". Paper presented in 86th Annual Conference of Western Economic Association International (WEAI), 29 June-3 July 2011, San Diego.

Dash, R. N. (2019). The Last Mile: India's Experiment with Rural Finance. New Delhi and Seattle: Konark Publishers Pvt Ltd.

Datta, S. K. (2003). "Systems and Processes of Credit Operations: The Case of BASIX" in Shylendra, H. S., Sen, P. K. and Panda, S. M. *Cases in Microfinance*. Anand: IRMA, pp. 152-171.

De Mel, S., McKenzie, D., and Woodruff, C. M. (2008). "Returns to capital in microenterprises: Evidence from a field experiment". *Quarterly Journal of Economics.* 123 (4): 1329-1372

DFID. (1999). Sustainable Livelihoods Guidance Sheets. https://www.ennonline.net/attachments/871/dfid-sustainable-livelihoods-guidance-sheet-section1.pdf, retrieved on 17 April 2019

Drewnowski, J. (1977). "Poverty: Its meaning and measurement". *Development and Change.* 8: 183-208

Dror, D. M. and Piesse, D. (2014). "What is Microinsurance?". in: (Eds. Radermacher R, and Roth, K). *A Practical Guide to Impact Assessments in Microinsurance* (preliminary version), Microinsurance Network and Micro Insurance Academy, p. 23-39.

Earne, J. and Sherk, L. (2014). "Funding. In Ledgerwood et al.". *The New Microfinance Handbook: A financial market system perspective.* Washington DC: The World Bank

Economic Times. (13 March 2019). "Small finance banks start on a strong wicket: ICRA". https://m.economictimes.com/markets/stocks/news/small-finance-banks-start-on-a-strong-wicket-icra/articleshow/68394962.cms, Retrieved on 27 March 2019.

Edgett, S. J. (1996). "The New Product Development Process for Commercial Financial Services". *Industrial Marketing Management* 25: 507-515

FAO/FFM. (2010). "Agricultural Production Lending A Toolkit for Loan Officers and Loan Portfolio Managers". revised version by Food and Agriculture Organisation and Frankfurt School of Finance and Management, Frankfurt

Fernandez, A. P. (1995). "Self help groups - The Concept". Rural Management Systems Series Paper 22. Bangalore: MYRADA.

Fernandez, A. P. (2017). "Conceptual and structural differences between SHGs formed between 1984-2000 and after 2000". Rural Management Systems Series Paper – 69 (B), Bengaluru: MYRADA

Fernando, N. A. (2006). "Understanding and Dealing with High Interest Rates on Microcredit: A Note to Policy Makers in the Asia and Pacific Region", Manila: ADB

FINCA. (www). Global History. http://www.finca.co.tz/who-we-are/history/global-history/. Retrieved on 30 April 2018.

Fisher, T. and Sriram, M. S. (Eds). *Beyond Micro-Credit: Putting Development Back into Micro-Finance.* New Delhi: Vistaar Publications

Frederick, L. I. (2008). "Information technology innovations that extend rural microfinance outreach". In Matthaus-Maier and Pischke. Eds. 2008. *New Partnerships for Innovation in Microfinance*. Germany: Springer and KFW

Fukuyama, F. (2013). "What is Governance?" *Governance*, 26(3), 347–68.

Gaurav, S. and Mankar (10 October 2017). Demonetisation's blow to microfinance sector, https://www.livemint.com/Opinion/jVE367mp7AamTbHD5dG0lK/Demonetisations-blow-to-microfinance-sector.html. Retrieved on 29 Mar 2019.

George, D., Venkata N. A. and Mugwang'a, T. (2010). "Individual Lending". Optimising Performance and Efficiency Series. Lucknow: Microsave

Goggin, M. L. (1986) "The 'Too Few Cases/Too Many Variables' Problem in Implementation Research". *The Western Political Weekly,* 39 (2), 328–347.

Gonzalez-Vega, C. Schreiner, M., Meyer, R. L, Rodriguez, J. and Navajas, S. (1996). "BANCOSOL: The Challenge of Growth for Microfinance Organizations", Economics and Sociology Occasional Paper No. 2332, Ohio: The Ohio State University

Government of Andhra Pradesh (2010). Andhra Pradesh Micro Finance Institutions (Regulation of Money-Lending) Ordinance, 2010. Hyderabad: Government of Andhra Pradesh

Harper, M. (2003). "Do we really need SHG federations? (Ten Commandants)". http://www.ruralfinanceandinvestment.org/sites/default/files/Do__we__really__need__SHG__Federations_pdf.pdf, date: 18 January 2019

Harper, M., Iyer, L. and Rosser, J. (2011) *Whose Sustainability Counts?: BASIX's Long March From Microfinance to Livelihoods.* New Delhi: Sage Vistar

Harper, M. (2003). "Self-help Groups and Grameen Bank Groups: What are the differences?"

Huttenrauch and Schneider. (2008). "Securitisation: A Funding Alternative for Microfinance Institutions". In Matthaaus-Maier, I. and von Pischke, J. D. (Eds) *New Partnerships for Innovation in Microfinance.* Springer and Kfw. USA and Germany.

IFAD. (2010). "New Approaches to Social Performance Assessment and Management in Microfinance." IFAD.

Imp-Act. (2005). "Social performance management in microfinance: Guidelines Imp-Act Programme," Sussex: IDS

Jain and Bakshi. (12 April 2018). "Demonetisation effect: Microfinance NPAs remain elevated in many states." *Business Standard,* https://www.business-standard.com/article/economy-policy/demonetisation-effect-microfinance-npas-remain-elevated-in-many-states-118041200039_1.html. Retrieved on 29 March 2019.

Jones, C, Hesterly, W. S., and Borgatti, S. P. (1997). "A General Theory of Network Governance: Exchange Conditions and Social Mechanisms". *Academy of Management Review,* 22 (4): pp. 911-945

Kagan, J (reviewer). (2019). "Five Cs of credit". Updated March 22, 2019. https://www.investopedia.com/terms/f/five-c-credit.asp. Retrieved on 2 April 2019.

Kapoor, S. and Sinha, G. (2013). "Factors Influencing New Product Development in Microfinance Institutions: A Perspective from North Indian Microfinance Institutions." *Journal of Innovation Economics & Management*: 11: 83-105

Khandkar, S. R. (2005). "Microfinance and poverty: Evidence using panel data from Bangladesh". *World Bank Econopmic Review.* 19:263-286

Klus. (March 2013). "A Diagnosis of Social Performance Assessment at Annapurnal Microfinane Ltd." Klus Consulting Pvt. Ltd.

Kooiman, J. (1993). "Governance and Governability: Using Complexity, Dynamics and Diversity," in J. Kooiman (ed.), *Modern Governance: New Government Society Interactions.* London, Newbury Park, and New Delhi: Sage.

Kumar, S. (2016). "The Impact of Federations on the functioning of SHGs: an empirical study." in Jayadev, M. And Sundar, D. K. (Eds). *Changing contours of Microfinance in India,* London and New York: Rutledge

Lauer, K. and Lyman, T. (2015). "What is Digital Financial Inclusion and Why Does it Matter?," Blog, https://www.cgap.org/blog/what-digital-financial-inclusion-and-why-does-it-matter. Retrieved on 10 April 2019.

Ledgerwood, J. (1999). *Microfinance Handbook: An Institutional and Financial Perspective.* Washington DC: The World Bank

Livemint. (2 August 2018). "RBI bars Fino Payments Bank from enroling new customers". https://www.livemint.com/ Retrieved on 27 March 2018

Leavitt, H. J. (1965). "Applied Organisational Change in Industry: Structural, Technological, and Humanistic Approach". In March, J. G. (ed.) *Handbook of Organizations.* Chicago: Rand McNally & Company.

Levitt, T. (1965). "Exploit the Product Life Cycle". *Harvard Business Review*, 43: 81-94.

M2i Consulting.(2012). "Microfinance Code of Conduct and Compliance Assessment of Bandhan Financial Services Pvt. Ltd". M2i Consulting.

Mahajan, V. and Navin, T. (2013). "Microfinance in India: Lessons from the Andhra Crisis". in Kohn, D. (Ed.) *Microfinance 3.0: Reconciling Sustainability with Social Outreach and Responsible Delivery.* Springeropen, and KFW

Mbeba, (2008). "Basic Financial Management and Ratio Analysis for MFIs Toolkit". Lucknow: Microsave

M-Cril.(2009). "M-Cril Analytics 2009". Gurgaon: M-CRIL

MFIN, (2024). Micrometer data as on December 2024. Issue 52. Gurgaon: MFIN

Microfinancegateway, (www). https://www.microfinancegateway.org/what-is-microfinance, 28.11.2017

Militzer, J. (12 January 2017). "Fintech or Die: Five Ways Microfinance Can (and Must) Respond to the Digital Age". https://nextbillion.net/fintech-or-die-five-ways-microfinance-can-and-must-respond-to-the-digital-age/. Retrieved on 14 April 2019

Mishra, P. K. and Dey, K. (2018). "Governance of agricultural value chains. Coordination, control and safeguarding". *Journal of Rural Studies,* 64, pp. 135-137

Mondal, D. K. (8 November 2017). "Demonetisation: Micro-finance industry sees ₹7,000 crore write-offs". *Business Today* .https://www.businesstoday.in/current/economy politics/demonetisation-mfi-industry-note-ban-anniversary-industry-micro-finance-institutions/story/263524.html. Retrieved on 29 March 2019.

MYRADA 30B. n.d.. "Guidelines For Financing Self-Help Groups". Rural Management Systems Series Paper - 30B, Bengaluru: MYRADA, https://myrada.org/rms-paper/. Retrieved on 4 April 2019

MYRADA 30C. n.d. "Guidelines For The Evaluation Of Self-Help Groups (To decide if MYRADA's involvement can be phased out". Rural Management Systems Series Paper – 30C, Bengaluru: MYRADA, https://myrada.org/rms-paper/. Retrieved on 4 April 2019

NABARD. (2017). "Status of Microfinance in India". Mumbai: NABARD

Nayak, B. B. (2015). *The Synergy of Microfinance: Fighting Poverty by Moving beyond credit.* New Delhi: Sage.

Otero, M. (1986). "The Solidarity Group Concept: Its Characteristics and Significance for Urban Infromal Sector Activities". PACT (Private Agencies Collaborating Together) https://www.centerforfinancialinclusion.org/publications-a-resources/browse-publications/369-the-solidarity-group-concept-its-characteristics-and-significance-for-urban-informal-sector-activities. Retrieved on 30 April 2018

Ozili. P. K. (2018). "Impact of digital finance on financial inclusion and stability". *Borsa Istanbul Review.* 18 (4): 329-340

Pitt, M. and Khandkar, S. R. (1998). The impact of group-based credit programs on the poor households in Bangladesh: Does the gender of participants matter?" *Journal of Political Economy.* 106 (5): 958-996

Qazi, M. (3 January 2018). "The poor need a micro-pension scheme". *Business Line.*

Raju, S. S. and Chand, R. (2007). "Progress and Problems in Agricultural Insurance". *Economic and Political Weekly.* 42 (21). p. 1905-1908

RBI. (25 January 2006). "Financial Inclusion by Extension of Banking Services - Use of Business Facilitators and Correspondents". RBI/2005-06/288.

RBI. (2014a). "RBI releases Guidelines for Licensing of Small Finance Banks in the Private Sector". https://rbidocs.rbi.org.in/rdocs/PressRelease/PDFs/IEPR1090GLS1114.pdf. Retrieved on 28 March 2019.

RBI. (2014b). *Report of the Committee on Comprehensive Financial Services for Small Businesses and Low Income Households* (Nachiket Mor Committee). Mumbai: Reserve Bank of India.

RBI. (2016a). "Master Circular- 'Non-Banking Financial Company-Micro Finance Institutions' (NBFC-MFIs) – Directions". Updated on 20 April 2016 https://www.rbi.org.in/Scripts/BS ViewMasCirculardetails.aspx?id=9827). Retrieved on 25 March 2019.

RBI. (6 October 2016). "Operating Guidelines for Payments Banks". https://rbi.org.in/scripts/NotificationUser.aspx?Id=10635&Mode=0. Retrieved on 28 March 2019.

RBI. (3 July 2017) "Master Circular on SHG-Bank Linkage Programme". RBI/2017-18/11FIDD.FID.BC.No.\12.01.033 /2017-18, https://rbi.org.in/scripts/NotificationUser.aspx?Mode=0&Id=11032. Retrieved on 27 March 2019.

Rhodes, R. A. W. (1997). "Understanding Governance: Policy Networks, Governance, Reflexivity, and Accountability". Buckingham and Philadelphia: Open University Press.

RMK. www. Rashtriya Maila Kosh. http://rmk.nic.in/. Retrieved on 18 January 2019.

Rosenberg, R. (2007). "CGAP Reflections on the Compartamos Initial Public Offering: A Case Study on Microfinance Interest Rates and Profits". CGAP Focus Note 42. Washington DC: CGAP

Ross, S.A., Westerfield, R. W., and Jordan, B. D. (2008). *Fundamentals of Corporate Finance.* New Delih: McGraw Hill

Roy, S. (2018). *Ujjivan: Transforming with technology.* New Delhi: Oxford University Press

Rutherford, S. (2008). "Micropensions: Old Age Security for the Poor?". in Matthaaus-Maier, I. and von Pischke, J. D. (Eds) *New Partnerships for Innovation in Microfinance.* Springer and Kfw. USA and Germany.

Rutherford. S. and Arora, S. (2009). *The Poor and Their Money.* Practical Action Publishing

Saltzman, SB, and Salinger, D. (1998). The ACCION CAMEL: Technical Note. Bethesda MD: Development Alternatives Inc.

Sharma, A. K., Sengupta, S., Roy, I., and Phukan, S. 2021. Financial Inclusion Index for India. *RBI Bulletin, September* 2021.

SEEP. (2010). *Pocket Guide to the Microfinance Financial Reporting Standards Measuring Financial Performance of Microfinance Institutions.* Washington DC: SEEP

Seibel, H. D. (2005). "The Microbanking Division of Bank Rakyat Indonesia: A Flagship of Rural Microfinance in Asia". in Harper, M. and Arora, S. (eds.). *Small Customers, Big Market: Commercial Banks in Micro-Finance.* Practical Action Publishing, pp. 7-20

SEWA. (n.d.). About SEWA Bank: History. URL: https://www.sewabank.com/about/history retrieved on 8 April 2025.

SEWA. (2024). Annual Report 2024. URL: https://www.sewabank.com/annual-report retrieved on 8 April 2025.

Sen, A. (1981). *Poverty and Famines: An Essay on Entitlement and Deprivation.* Oxford: Charendon Press

Sen, A. (1999). *Development as Freedom.* Oxford University Press.

Shiller, (2012). *Finance and the Good Society.* Princeton: Princeton University Press

Shylendra, H. S. (2006). "Microfinance Institutions in Andhra Pradesh". *Economic and Political Weekly.* 41 (20). p. 1959-1963

Srinivsan, N. (2010). *Microfinance India: State of the Sector Report 2010.*New Delhi: Sage

Sridhar, G. N. (21 March 2018). "Basix Sub-K raises ₹35 cr from Accion, Nordic Finance". *Business Line,* https://www.thehindubusinessline.com/money-and-banking/basix-sub-k-raises-rs-35-cr-from-accion-nordic-microfinance/article23309722.ece. Retrieved on 8 April 2019

Sriram, M. S. (2010)."Commercialisation of Microfinance in India: A Discussion of the Emperor's Apparel". *Economic and Political Weekly*, 55 (24), pp. 65-73.

Sriram, M. S. (2012). "The AP Microfinance Crisis 2010: Discipline or Death". *Vikalpa. 37 (4). pp. 113-127*

Sriram, M. S. (2018). "Inclusive Finance India Report 2017". New Delhi: Sage

Streeten, P. (1979). "Basic Needs: Premises and Promises". *Journal of Policy Modelling.* 1: 136-146

The Week (7 January 2019). "eSthenons Technologies Enables NBFCs to On-board MSME Borrowers under 30 Minutes". https://www.theweek.in/wire-updates/business/2019/01/07/pwr1--esthenos%20technologies%20pvt%20ltd.html. Retrieved on 23 Mar 2019.

Ujjivan. (2016). "Draft Red Herring Prospectus, Ujjivan". Bengaluru: Ujjivan

Ujjivan. (2018). "Annual Report 2017-18". Bengaluru: Ujjivan

Ujjivan. (2024). Annual Report 2023-24, Bengaluru: Ujjivan

Van Horne, J. C. and Wachowicz, Jr., J. M. (2001). *Fundamentals of Financial Management.* 11th Edition. New Delhi: Prentice Hall.

Von Pischke, J. D. (1991). *Finance at the Frontiers: Debt Capacity and the Role of Credit in the Private Economy.* Washington DC: The World Bank

Voss, J. (2014). "Self-Regulation in the Financial Markets". https://blogs.cfainstitute.org/marketintegrity/2014/06/24/self-regulation-in-the-financial-markets/. Retrieved on 6 April 2019

Williamson, O. E. (1979). "Transaction-cost Economics: The governance of contractual relations". *The Journal of Law and Economics*, 22, 233-261

WOCCU. (2002). "A Technical Guide to PEARLS: A Performance Monitoring System". Madison WI: World Council for Credit Unions Inc.

World Bank. (2005). "Scaling-Up Micro Insurance: The Case of Weather Insurance for Smallholders in India". Washington: IBRD.

World Bank. (2016). *Migration and Remittances Fact Book 2016.* Third Edition, The world Bank Group. http://siteresources.worldbank.org/INTPROSPECTS/Resources/334934-1199807908806/4549025-1450455807487/Factbookpart1.pdf. Retrieved from 1 April 2019.

World Bank. 2022. *The Global Findex Database 2021: Financial Inclusion, Digital Payments, and Resilience in the Age of COVID-19*. Washington, DC: World Bank. https://www.worldbank.org/en/publication/globalfindex

Wright, G., and Sharma, M. K. (2010). "The Andhra Pradesh Crisis: Three Dress Rehearsals … and then the Full Drama". MicroSave India Focus Note 55. http://www.microsave.net/files/pdf/IFN 55 The Andhra Pradesh Crisis 3 dress rehearsals and then the Full Drama.pdf. Retrieved on 29 March 2019.

Wyman, O. (2016). "Accelerating financial inclusion in south east Asia with digital finance". Asian Development Bank. https://www.oliverwyman.com/content/dam/oliver-wyman/v2/publications/2017/jan/Accelerating-financial-inclusion-in-south-east-asia.pdf. Retrieved on 10 April 2019

Yeswanth, D. (2004). "BWDA to BFL: Transformation of an NGO to MFI". http://www.microfinancegateway.org/sites/default/files/mfg-en-case-study-bwda-to-bfl-transformation-of-an-ngo-into-an-mfi-2000.pdf. Retrieved on 12 April 2019.

Index

O

P

Q

R

S

Book Revie

Microfinance Management
by Pradeep Kumar Mishra
@2019 Cengage Learning India Pvt. L

Dr. Nabendu Paul
T.A. Pai Management Institute Bengaluru,
Manipal Academy of Higher Education

Mr. Mallikarjun Gudadinni
Indian Institute of Technology, Mandi

Professor Pradeep Kumar Mishra has beautifully brought into the limelight many issu related to the microfinance industry. The book not only provides a coherent understandi of the industry as such but also gives a different perspective of looking at finance throu the lens of development economics. The book is praiseworthy for its contextual clarity a comprehensive coverage.

Dr. Nabendu Paul (TAPMI) and Mr. Mallikarjun Gudadinni (IIT, Mandi)
Quoted in *NUJBMS*, 6 (3): 26, (July, 2023).